Language Policy for the Multilingual Classroom

BILINGUAL EDUCATION & BILINGUALISM
Series Editors: Nancy H. Hornberger, *University of Pennsylvania, USA* and Colin Baker, *Bangor University, Wales, UK*

Bilingual Education and Bilingualism is an international, multidisciplinary series publishing research on the philosophy, politics, policy, provision and practice of language planning, global English, indigenous and minority language education, multilingualism, multiculturalism, biliteracy, bilingualism and bilingual education. The series aims to mirror current debates and discussions.

Full details of all the books in this series and of all our other publications can be found on http://www.multilingual-matters.com, or by writing to Multilingual Matters, St Nicholas House, 31–34 High Street, Bristol BS1 2AW, UK.

BILINGUAL EDUCATION & BILINGUALISM
Series Editors: Nancy H. Hornberger and Colin Baker

Language Policy for the Multilingual Classroom
Pedagogy of the Possible

Edited by
Christine Hélot and Muiris Ó Laoire

MULTILINGUAL MATTERS
Bristol • Buffalo • Toronto

This book is dedicated to the memory of our beloved Australian colleague Professor Michael Clyne of the University of Melbourne/Monash whose contribution to the field of sociolinguistics has been and will ever be immense. We are honoured to publish his contribution in the present volume.

Library of Congress Cataloging in Publication Data
A catalog record for this book is available from the Library of Congress.
Language Policy for the Multilingual Classroom: Pedagogy of the Possible/Edited by Christine Hélot and Muiris Ó Laoire.
Bilingual Education & Bilingualism: 82
Includes bibliographical references and index.
1. Multicultural education. 2. Education, Bilingual. 3. Multiculturalism.
4. Literacy. I. Hélot, Christine.
II. Ó Laoire, Muiris.
LB1576.L335 2011
370.117–dc22 2011000615

British Library Cataloguing in Publication Data
A catalogue entry for this book is available from the British Library.

ISBN-13: 978-1-84769-367-9 (hbk)
ISBN-13: 978-1-84769-366-2 (pbk)

Multilingual Matters
UK: St Nicholas House, 31–34 High Street, Bristol, BS1 2AW, UK.
USA: UTP, 2250 Military Road, Tonawanda, NY 14150, USA.
Canada: UTP, 5201 Dufferin Street, North York, Ontario, M3H 5T8, Canada.

The policy of Multilingual Matters/Channel View Publications is to use papers that are natural, renewable and recyclable products, made from wood grown in sustainable forests. In the manufacturing process of our books, and to further support our policy, preference is given to printers that have FSC and PEFC Chain of Custody certification. The FSC and/or PEFC logos will appear on those books where full certification has been granted to the printer concerned.

Typeset by Techset Composition Ltd., Salisbury, UK.
Printed and bound in Great Britain by Short Run Press Ltd.

Contents

Part 2: Deconstructing the Myth of Monolingualism

Perspectives on Identities, Ideologies and Politics

Contributors

Zvi Bekerman, PhD teaches Anthropology of Education at the School of Education and The Melton Center, Hebrew University of Jerusalem. He is also a Research Fellow at the Truman Institute for the Advancement of Peace, Hebrew University. His main interests are in the study of cultural, ethnic and national identity, including identity processes and negotiation during intercultural encounters and in formal/informal learning contexts. He has published numerous papers in these fields of study and is the Editor (with Seonaigh MacPherson) of the refereed journal *Diaspora, Indigenous, and Minority Education: An International Journal*.

Adrian Blackledge is Professor of Bilingualism in the School of Education, University of Birmingham. His research interests include the politics of multilingualism, linguistic ethnography, education of linguistic minority students, negotiation of identities in multilingual contexts, and language testing, citizenship, and immigration. His publications include *Multilingualism, A Critical Perspective* (with Angela Creese, 2010), *Discourse and Power in a Multilingual World* (2005), *Negotiation of Identities in Multilingual Contexts* (with Aneta Pavlenko, 2004), *Multilingualism, Second Language Learning and Gender* (2001, with Aneta Pavlenko, Ingrid Piller and Marya Teutsch-Dwyer) and *Literacy, Power, and Social Justice* (2001).

Michael Clyne is Emeritus Professor of Linguistics at Monash University, Melbourne, and Honorary Professorial Fellow at the University of Melbourne, having held professorial appointments at both universities. His main research fields are bi-/multilingualism/language contact, sociolinguistics, inter-cultural communication, second language acquisition and language policy. These are the areas of most of his 30 books and over 300 articles. He is on the editorial board of numerous journals; among his awards are civil honours from Australia, Austria and Germany, membership of Australian and Dutch academies, an honorary doctorate from Munich and research prizes from the DAAD and the Alexander von Humboldt Foundation.

Angela Creese is Professor of Educational Linguistics. She is author of a number of books and articles on multilingualism and linguistically diverse classrooms. Her books include *Multilingualism. A Critical Perspective* (2010); *English as an Additional Language: Approaches to Teaching Linguistic Minority Students* (2010); Vol. 9: *Ecology of Language, Encyclopedia of Language and Education* (2009); *Teacher Collaboration and Talk in Multilingual Classrooms* (2005) and *Multilingual Classroom Ecologies* (2003). Her research interests are situated in educational linguistics, linguistic ethnography, teacher collaboration and multilingual pedagogies in community learning contexts.

Anne-Marie de Mejía is Associate Professor at the *Centro de Investigación y Formación en Educación* at Universidad de los Andes, Bogotá, Colombia. She holds a PhD in Linguistics in the area of Bilingual Education from Lancaster University, UK and is author of a number of books and articles in the area of bilingualism and bilingual education both in Spanish and English. Her latest publications include *Forging Multilingual Spaces* (2008) and *Empowering Teachers across Cultures*, jointly edited with Christine Hélot.

Alexander Funk is a doctoral student and Chancellor's Fellow in the Linguistics department at the CUNY Graduate Center, with a BA in music and English from Yale University. His research interests range from the applied realms of second language acquisition and pedagogy to the theoretical investigation of prepositions, particles and the syntax–semantics interface. He currently teaches in the English department at Hunter College, and in the Master's Program in TESOL at Queens College.

Christine Hélot is Professor of English and teacher educator at the University of Strasbourg, France. She holds a PhD from the University of Dublin (Trinity College) and a *Habilitation* from the University of Strasbourg. She is author of a number of books and articles in French and English on bilingualism in the family and school contexts, language educational policies in France, language awareness, intercultural education and children's literature. Her latest publications include *Forging Multilingual Spaces* (2008) co-edited with Anne-Marie de Mejía as well as the trilingual volume *Empowering Teachers across Cultures* (2010) also co-edited with Anne-Marie de Mejía.

Kate Menken holds a doctoral degree from Teachers College, Columbia University. She is an Associate Professor of Linguistics at Queens College of the City University of New York (CUNY), and a Research Fellow at the Research Institute for the Study of Language in an Urban Society at the

CUNY Graduate Center. Her position is a joint appointment between Queens College and the Graduate Center. Her research interests are in the areas of language policy, bilingual education, secondary emergent bilinguals, U.S. education reform and high-stakes testing. She is author of *English Learners Left Behind: Standardized Testing as Language Policy* (2008) and co-editor (with Ofelia García) of *Negotiating Language Policies in Schools: Educators as Policymakers* (2010).

Carola Mick holds a PhD in applied and sociolinguistics of romance languages (Spanish, French) from the University of Mannheim. After concluding her discourse analytical PhD research project with domestic workers in Peru she is now working as a research assistant in Educational Sciences within the LCMI research unit at the University of Luxembourg. Her domains of research concern plurilingual literacies and critical discourse competence in Luxembourgish primary schools. Her present research foci are on discourse theory and socio-cultural theory of education.

Tatyana Kleyn is an Assistant Professor at the City College of New York in the Bilingual Education and TESOL program. In 2007 she received an EdD from Teachers College, Columbia University in International Educational Development, with a specialization in Bilingual/Bicultural Education. She is co-author of *Teaching in Two Languages: A Guide for K-12 Bilingual Educators* with Adelman Reyes. She is currently working on a book for teenagers called *Immigration: Stories, Struggles and Debates*. She has also published about the cultural, linguistic and educational needs of the Garífuna people in Honduras.

Pierrot Ngomo taught German as Foreign Language at several colleges and high schools in Cameroon before he obtained his doctoral degree in Applied Linguistics at the University of Hamburg (2004). He is currently conducting his postdoctoral research program (titled *Language Acquisition and Communication in the Multilingual Context of Cameroon on the Basis of Family and Societal Interactions*) on the field of Research on Multilingualism at the University of Hamburg. His research areas are Early Child Language Acquisition, Language Policy and Language Planning, Discourse Analysis and Research on Individual & Societal Multilingualism and Communication.

Bernadette O'Rourke is a Lecturer in Spanish and General Linguistics at Heriot-Watt University, Edinburgh. Her areas of research broadly include sociolinguistics and the sociology of language, focusing on the role of language in the construction of social difference and social inequality, particularly in minority language contexts. She is author of *Galician and Irish in the European Context: Attitudes towards Weak and Strong Minority Languages*. She is committed to disseminating the finding of her research outside academia and is currently an Edinburgh Beltane Public Engagement Fellow.

Former President of IRAAL, Senior Lecturer at the Institute of Technology, Tralee, **Dr Muiris Ó Laoire** has recently been appointed Full Professor of Language Revitalization Studies at the new International Centre for Language Revitalization at AUT (Auckland University of Technology), NZ. He has written and lectured widely on language education policies and multilingualism and contributed to a wide range of national and international committees on language policy issues.

Ute Walker is a Senior Lecturer in Linguistics and Second Language Teaching in the School of Language Studies at Massey University in Palmerston North, New Zealand. Apart from her academic interest in aspects of bi/multilingualism Ute has supported multilingual outcomes among migrant communities through advocacy and promotion of language maintenance and family biliteracy projects. Her research interests include bi/multilingualism in relation to identity, settlement and education, as well as distance language education. Recent publications explore bilingual migrants' self-positioning in blogs and the role of community in preserving Spanish in Latin American communities in New Zealand.

Introduction: From Language Education Policy to a Pedagogy of the Possible

C. HÉLOT and M. Ó LAOIRE

While the multilingual classroom presents ample and creative openings for effective language learning and intercultural understanding, these opportunities are frequently lost. On the one hand, teachers can easily underestimate the complexities of the multilingual classroom, and on the other hand, even if they are aware of such complexities, they might not always know how to best exploit the potential of plurilingual students. There is still a lingering tendency in most classrooms to approach the teaching and learning of languages as if monolingualism were the norm, that is, education partners including teachers tend to overlook the fact that bilingual or plurilingual learners of any target language are not the same as monolingual learners. Confronted with the daily contingencies and challenges of administration, assessment and curriculum, educators may lose sight of what Creese and Martin refer to as '... a range of complex inter-relating issues around the promotion of multilingualism in educational settings' (Creese & Martin, 2003: 6). Results from research on metalinguistic awareness (e.g. Jessner, 2006; Kemp, 2007) underline the qualitative differences between bi/plurilingual and monolingual learners. Yet, teachers in the multilingual classroom may continue to underestimate the competence of plurilingual students and to silence their voices, rather than using cross-linguistic learning strategies and learners' metalinguistic awareness as learning resources across languages and even across school disciplines.

While there have been pioneering initiatives to validate learners' plurilingualism in our classrooms (Candelier, 2003; Creese & Martin, 2003; García *et al.*, 2006; Hélot, 2007; Kenner & Hickey, 2008; O'Laoire, 2006), the reality for many multilingual learners is that their languages are all too often silenced, unheard in the classroom or worse still envisaged as impeding the development of the language of schooling and of learning in general. One cannot underestimate the lingering influence of a century of history during which most schools in Europe were the main agents for the implementation of the one language/one nation ideology. Educators may still continue to see the teaching of the school language as the central mission of schools, and other languages as separate school subjects rather than potential media of learning. In other words, the 'imagined' creative potential of the multilingual classroom collides with 'reality' where educators tend to see students from linguistically diverse backgrounds bringing their home language to school as an extra burden rather than as a learning resource.

However, changing perspectives on learners' home languages from 'problem' to resource means that students' plurilingual repertoire must be acknowledged and their plurilingual competence supported in school. In other words, students from diverse language backgrounds are setting a new challenge for our traditionally monolingual school systems; they are forcing educationalists to question entrenched ideologies of language and confronting teachers in their everyday classrooms to rethink their relationships to language learning and the issue of diversity (whether linguistic, cultural, ethnic or social).

When individual teachers endeavour to support and develop holistically an inclusive approach in the classroom, including their students' various languages in their pedagogical activities, they may generally be working out an individual positioning or belief set. Sometimes, teachers are not necessarily aware that such choices are a form of engagement. For example, when confronted with young learners who do not know the school language, they have no other choice but to develop new pedagogical approaches that will help plurilingual children to make sense of their learning experiences at school (Hélot, 2010). Despite all the reflection and documents published at the European level on the importance of plurilingualism for our societies, one specific domain is still lacking sufficient attention, that is, teacher education and professional development. The profound shifts in our societies in relation to mobility and migration, to new forms of and access to knowledge, and the growing inequalities affecting poor and wealthy countries, demand that schools rethink their approach to learning, rather than *forcing* students to adapt to an education system based on a 19th-century world view.

The main actors at the heart of this change of perspective are teachers. Teacher educators, thus, have a special responsibility to make prospective teachers aware of what is at stake in any educational endeavour, of the traditional tendency of education systems to reproduce social inequalities as well as of the potential spaces for innovation for reversing traditional power relationships. We know the role language may play in the reproduction of inequalities, so that nowadays, when plurilingual students are silenced in a classroom, ignoring their language competence becomes a form of discrimination. Yet, making teachers aware of this requires that teacher education curricula take societal multilingualism seriously and put it at the centre of their professional development agenda. If more third-level institutions across the world are indeed addressing teacher education in the light of perceived new needs for the 21st century, the issue of multilingualism in education remains constrained by a monolingual habitus (Bourdieu, 1977) that is proving extremely difficult to shift.

Despite the important body of research on bilingual education and more recently on multilingual education, many models are still characterised as monoglossic (García, 2009), and intended only for the elite and dominant languages. The reality in many classrooms today is that the linguistic needs of bi/plurilingual children are not met. This is the case because education systems throughout the world have been slow to question the very essence of language education, and in Europe, for example, the main agenda of European institutions remains the acquisition of the language of schooling, the teaching of 'foreign' languages and the development of a European identity. In other words, educational language policies reflect the reluctance to acknowledge a central concern in our societies today, that is, the question of migration. After all, language contact in school, as in society, is the result of migration rather than foreign language teaching. In other words, if we acknowledge that multilingualism is already present in our schools through and in the students who speak several languages, we need to question the way we conceive of 'foreign' language learning. We need to broaden our vision of what language learning really is, and to also envision learning through the means of languages other than *the* language of schooling. In a sense, such a vision takes away from the centrality of the school language, and challenges its hegemonic role in education. This may explain the hesitation at national level to implement educational policies that would be truly multilingual. Thus, one can understand how the initiatives of individual teachers are restrained by top-down policies that pay lip service to multilingualism and also by the lack of support for bottom-up language policies at the school level. However, the interactions, interrelationships and pedagogies of multilingual classrooms are beginning to receive more attention from researchers, and emergent research in language policy is opening new perspectives.

Rethinking Language Policies for Multilingual Schools

All schools and educational institutions, whether they realise it or not, operate from and within a certain policy. While certain languages are selected to be taught, only certain standard varieties are accepted; while other languages are introduced at earlier or later points in learners' education, some remain in the margins or are expected to be taught outside of the school system. And one should not forget that curricula are mediated and examined in a predetermined and prearranged manner usually through 'the' school language only (Shohamy, 2006). Even when no explicit unequivocal policy exists in a school, teachers, administrators and learners may still operate within fixed structures and out of implicitly agreed policy paradigms. Indeed, it is quite often the case that in schools with plurilingual students, policies are not pre-planned or thought out, but they simply evolve as implicit policies. The occurrence of these 'implicit' policies is often explained by 'force of history' factors; that is, a certain policy is adhered to because such a policy has always been in place.

A school language policy, conceived as a response to a problem or an initiative at one point of time in the school's history, tends to be transmitted and perpetuated through school administration systems from academic year to academic year and often become part of a school's tradition. Policy content in many schools thus casts a long historical shadow: *'We teach French in this school because we have always taught French here' 'It's always worked for us' 'It is part of the school's tradition'*; it becomes difficult to distinguish between tradition and policy in school contexts. New policies tend to be called for when unprecedented situations arise which appear to shake the securities of staid tradition and new solutions are called for. This may often be the case when plurilingual students begin to constitute a critical or noticeable mass in classrooms. Somehow multilingualism in such classrooms will be problematised in a similar fashion as in society at large and might be seen as some kind of threat to social cohesion: and this might lead to stricter rules insisting on the exclusive use of the school language, without teachers or administrators being aware that they are in fact putting a language policy in place.

But new situations can also give rise to creative questioning, and divergent perspectives may begin to emerge. The question of appropriate mother tongue/bilingual support for immigrant learners is often raised, for example, and particularly by student teachers who feel overwhelmed at the beginning of their career by all the demands made on them. But often they ask how the linguistic needs of such learners should be met in the short term: in other words, how these plurilingual learners can become just like their monolingual peers. But in cases like this and in situations not previously experienced in schools, new policies are called for, and differing responses emerge at the state and local level. What school administrators and teachers often demand are new regulations and directives from the centre as to how the curriculum should be mediated and implemented, therein providing the motivation for what is termed centralist institutionalised policy. Thus, policies in schools that have to do with language, for example, are often dictated and governed by nationally devolved benchmarks of expectation and performance. But these emerging responses from the state can either collide with the demands from the local community, or be tacitly accepted and met with no resistance.

Moving Beyond Top-Down Approaches

Placing the multilingual classroom at the very centre of a national language policy may be of little help in legitimising the heretofore 'unheard' voices of multilingual students in our schools. As Ricento (2006: 13) reminds us, language policies as they emerged in post-colonial sociolinguistic situations have best served the interests of the former language of colonisation rather than the languages and rights of indigenous minorities. Language policy evolving as top-down directives has been shown to bolster the powerful and dominant at the expense of the local and the indigenous. Driven by critical theory and postmodern thinking, new frameworks of language policy have been emerging in recent years (e.g. Corson, 2009; Ricento, 2006) with a shift of focus from the authoritative top-down processes to implementation at the micro-level. At the heart of these post-structuralist and more post-modern approaches to language policy, one finds three crucial concepts, which help to advance our understanding, that is agency, ideology and ecology (Hornberger, 2006).

Until recently, the roles of individuals and groups in the processes of language use, attitudes and ultimately policies have been frequently overlooked. Today, language policy is being reconceptualised as a *complexity* of human interactions, negotiations and productions mediated by interrelationships in contested sites of competing ideologies, discourses and powers. This refers to the will and aspiration of people who have policy *done to them* through the different agendas of the State polity. It includes a focus on what specific language policies mean in the daily interactions and micro-interactions of people in their everyday life and working situations. It means that one can envisage policies also from the point of view of what is possible for people to do, what spaces they can find to negotiate their own engagement with language(s) and what is impossible.

When it comes to implementation of policy there has also been much rethinking. Implementation has long been perceived as an administrative process (Fischer, 2003), devoid of values (Hajer & Wagenaar, 2003), interests or emotion (Wagenaar & Cook, 2003). Ball (1997), for example, draws attention to the importance of both human agency and context in policy and implementation. He suggests that policies are '... awkward, incomplete, incoherent and unstable', that 'local conditions, resources, histories and commitments will differ and that policy realization will differ accordingly' (Ball, 1997: 265). Perhaps in some places policies have been more about 'empowering the possible with people at the centre' but in many other places it is still very much administration centred for purposes of social control and oppression. Thus, the *interpersonal dimension of language policy* has not been stressed enough and this has not been without consequences in the educational field. Indeed, such a perspective applied to language policy in schools might be the only feasible model for multilingual contexts.

Notions of Ecology and Agency

School institutions are peopled by learners, teachers, administrators and parents' committee councils. But schools are also situated in different ecologies and the multilingual school is part of a larger multilingual ecology. For example, in the so-called 'sensitive suburbs' in France, the Ministry of Education has been supporting the schooling of children as early as age two, especially for children from a minority migrant background. The argument put forward by the Ministry for such a policy is that early schooling of bilingual or plurilingual pupils will accelerate their acquisition of the school language and their integration into dominant French culture. Teachers working in these classrooms are caught in a web of different institutional agendas, which leave them with little room to negotiate their own beliefs about language acquisition and multilingualism. As analysed by Hélot (2010), for example, in classes in Alsace it was much easier for one teacher to use German than for the other to use Turkish, although both teachers were trying to do the same thing, including the first language of their pupils in their daily activities. Therefore, when we study language policy for the multilingual school or classroom, we need to look at the language ecology in which learners' and teachers' languages are located, and how this collides or not with the larger societal ecology.

Baldauf (2008) reminds us that the issue of agency has traditionally not been investigated or regarded as important in language policy. The reason for this quite simply is that it was assumed that language policy was always carried out by central agents who made decisions that were in the best interests of the state. Who they were was of little interest, provided they had the required expertise. In fact this tendency to overlook the crucial issue of agency appears to have been endemic in all areas of social policy. More recently, however, the issue of agency has become central to the analysis of micro-contexts, where teachers, for example, are seen as central agents in language policy development at this micro/local level. As Baldauf aptly points out:

> The fundamental planning is conceptualised and carried out at the macro level with the local taking an implementation role. This is the traditional top-down approach where language policy decisions are implemented via good professional development models. By contrast micro planning refers to cases where businesses, institutions, groups or individuals hold agency and create what can be recognised as a language policy and plan to utilise and develop their language resources; one that is not directly the result of some larger macro policy, but is a response to their own needs, their own 'language problems', their own 'requirement for language management'. (Baldauf, 2008: 25–26)

Therefore, when discussing language policy for the multilingual classroom, one must take into account the complex ecologies at stake, as well as the complex interrelationships between local and global agendas and the extent to which local actors are aware of their own agency, or prepared to become agents of change engaged in contesting the power relationships in place. We would like to argue that only through taking the various dimensions and complexities of the multilingual classroom into account can school managers, administrators and teachers be led to deconstruct their traditional approaches to language teaching, to rethink critically their own relationship to language learning and to forge new pedagogies: pedagogies of the possible. A *pedagogy of the possible* means that rather than responding to the exigencies of the multilingual classroom in a negative way and waiting for centralist policies to decree new objectives, the notions of ecology and agency invite teachers and learners to see their realities in a new light and to act on this reality: in other words, to respond to all possibilities and potentialities at the classroom level, thus forging one's own policies that are locally effective and empowering.

Adopting an ecological perspective also means that reflecting on the multilingual classroom in a variety of cultural contexts will highlight both the wealth and the complexity of educational questions we need to address. Multilingual classrooms in Cameroon do not meet the same challenges as classrooms in Israel, teachers in multilingual classrooms in the United States do not share the same representations of bilingual education as their colleagues in Ireland or Colombia, students in Luxembourg classrooms experience very different language education from their peers in France, and there are no similarities in the framing of policies in Australia and New Zealand. The different chapters in this volume draw on a variety of contexts from four continents and illustrate the need to go beyond an approach of the complexities inherent to each setting that would isolate educational actors in their own ecology, rather than relate them to other actors in the world trying to grapple with similar ethical issues and forms of engagement.

Reflecting on the Possible

The studies presented in this volume are conducted from different theoretical perspectives, which address various language constellations and are situated in different cultural contexts.[1] They all ask the same questions: how can one adopt the multilingual classroom as the norm and what is the role of language policy in this change of perspective? Adopting the multilingual classroom as the norm means acknowledging diversity and changing identities in migration contexts, recognising the potential of the multilingual classroom ecology in language education, transcending the traditional sociocultural barriers in the implementation of a multilingual curriculum, defending the positioning of teachers' policies, exploiting students' metalinguistic awareness at the pedagogical level and redefining power relations in the case of minority languages in the language constellation.

The educational settings dealt with in the 10 chapters in this book include primary, secondary and tertiary contexts set in the varying cultural contexts of the United Kingdom, Ireland, France, Australia, Israel, the United States, Luxemburg, New Zealand, Colombia and Cameroon. The chapters comprising the first section of the volume present perspectives on learners followed by perspectives on teachers, which combine to underline critically the challenging complexities of the multilingual classroom. Creese and Blackledge, for example, take a language ecological perspective on the multilingual classroom in complementary schools in the United Kingdom, that is, classroom settings where community languages (in this case, Bengali, Chinese, Gujarati and Turkish) are taught outside regular school hours. Their approach throws fresh light on what it is possible for learners to achieve in a setting of such multilingual diversity. The possibilities of a pedagogy that develops the simultaneous use of languages through translanguaging (García, 2007) and flexible bilingualism (Creese *et al.*, 2006) are elucidated. The ecological approach that underpins their research illuminates the linguistic, metalinguistic and learning resources that participants bring to their classroom lives, resources that are often hidden and ignored in classrooms where multilingual learners' voices are silenced. These resources are the very ones needed for the negotiation of identity in learning: these pedagogical approaches not only give voice to plurilingual learners in the classroom, but they also engage them in the reproduction of social, community and pedagogical values, norms and goals.

The following two chapters by Mick and Hélot, respectively, illustrate what it is possible to achieve in literacy acquisition and development within the competing complexities of the multilingual classroom. Mick's research in a Luxemburgish primary school investigates learners' use of multiple semiotic resources and voices to mediate their joint learning activity. Multiple semiotics, rather than representing monolithic challenge, become the pathway to a pedagogy of the possible. Legitimating diversity is shown not to exclude but rather to foster the joint re-/co-/construction of a standard for language learning, thus empowering all implied actors to contribute actively to the construction of a community of practice.

Hélot's chapter on children reading literature in many different languages develops an innovative approach to teaching multilingual literacy. Examining how translation in children's literature may construct different relationships of otherness, while sometimes negating cultural differences, she analyses the way in which bilingual and multilingual books reflect the relationship between the languages concerned and representations of bilingual usage. The research elucidates a pedagogy of the possible where learners are confronted with works of children's literature that enable them to encounter linguistic and cultural diversity and to support the linguistic and cultural competences of plurilingual learners. The chapter shows how crucial it is to develop multilingual literacy practices from the start of schooling not only for plurilingual learners but also for monolinguals. It argues for the use of bilingual books in order to convince teachers that they should not fear working with languages they do not know. Practical examples of reading and writing activities illustrate several notions central to a better understanding of multilingual language use: language contact, transfer, code-switching and translanguaging are exemplified in some of the dual-language books studied.

The Caribbean Archipelago of San Andrés, Providencia and Santa Catalina (in Colombia) provides the multilingual context in which de Mejía explores and investigates the possibility of trilingual education. In a situation where Creole, the first language of most of the Islander community, has been generally excluded from schools, she discusses policies, curricular initiatives and classroom practices relating to education in three languages: Creole, Standard Caribbean English and Spanish. de Mejía underscores the complexities inherent in this multilingual context: while official government policy authorises the use of the students' first language(s) in bilingual and multilingual education contexts, the differing attitudes towards the three languages lead to a division of opinion about their relevance and value. While the marginalisation of Creole and the silencing of learners' voices in their L1 cause difficulties, it has been possible, nonetheless, to create certain pedagogies that legitimate that language. The creation of a Creole alphabet and the production of storybooks and textbook material have helped. Small-scale ethnographic studies on school language use point to new learning opportunities where valuable cross-linguistic strategies are used spontaneously by some of the classroom participants and are legitimised as learning approaches in the language classroom.

These studies provide critical insights into classrooms where the languages of plurilingual learners are heard, legitimated and even used as the medium of instruction. The understanding by teachers of the complexity of interrelated issues as well as their positioning vis-à-vis learners' languages act as a catalyst in transforming the classroom from a site of monolingualism to a place where plurilingualism is proactively promoted. The teachers' perspectives on the potentialities of the multilingual classroom are obviously crucial to achieving a pedagogy of the possible.

The second half of the first part of this volume focuses on teachers in the multilingual classroom. The chapter by Menken *et al.*, for example, challengingly titled 'Are We Ready? Teacher Engagement and Resistance in the Education of Emerging Bilinguals', examines the teaching practices of classroom teachers with language learners in New York City schools, where there has been a continual increase in students who come from diverse cultural backgrounds, bringing with them the asset of languages other than English. Schools there have largely responded by providing more (and only) English education, as opposed to bilingual programmes that develop students' native language and literacy skills. The study identifies instructional features that support students' bilingualism and multilingualism as well as those that constrain them. Teachers' efforts to embed explicit language and literacy instruction across content area subjects such as English language arts, mathematics, science and social studies as well as in a new course titled 'Spanish for native speakers' are examined. Examples from classroom observations illustrate how careful instructional planning can increase student learning in terms of language and content, or further leave them behind.

O'Rourke's chapter points clearly to what is achievable in the multilingual classroom if there is real teacher engagement with learners' multilingualism. Based on observations and analysis of a multilingual action research project involving teachers, pupils and parents of pupils in a primary school in inner city Dublin, the study shows how students' plurilingualism has been valued and negotiated in the classroom. By incorporating a range of multilingual and language-awareness activities into their classroom, teachers created a school environment that explicitly valued and recognised all the languages that children brought with them.

Ngomo's research on multilingual classrooms in Cameroon again elucidates what teachers can do to support their multilingual students' languages and linguistic development. The multilingual context of Cameroon poses certain challenges to teachers, stemming both from the complex linguistic situation on the ground and from historical, political and sociocultural constraints. Ngomo shows how these factors impinge on the daily micro-interactions among teachers and learners in the multilingual classroom. Drawing on research on classroom ecology, autonomous language learning and affordances, this chapter shows how opportunities provided by the multilingual environment can be exploited despite multiple constraints. Special emphasis is put on the concept of autonomy which, when promoted in the classroom, can be a catalyst for achievement.

Schools in multilingual contexts both inherit and are influenced by ideologies, politics, existing institutional practices, social affiliations and societal attitudes to bilingualism/multilingualism. The construction of language education policies in education often attempts to legitimate societal realities, institutional structures, ideologies and attitudes. However, as argued above, recent approaches to language policy conceptualise it as a process in which a variety of social actors struggle to achieve authoritative contextualisation (Silverstein & Urban, 1996): they actively engage in the planning, interpretation, modification and/or (selective) implementation of policy, in accordance with existing institutional practices, external pressures and individual preferences. It is interesting to see how language affiliations and experiences with languages can either influence behaviour or be used as a discursive resource to justify such behaviour.

We should never forget that schools are microcosms of our respective societies, and they not only reflect social values and norms but also reproduce them. Because schools act as reproductive agents of societal norms, it is difficult for teachers to implement creative and empowering pedagogies that challenge mainstream values and entrenched ideologies. Promoting plurilingualism in schools means more than offering many languages in the curriculum, or even supporting bilingual education programmes. It means:

> exerting educational effort that takes into account and builds further on the diversity of languages and literacy practices that children and youth bring to school. This means going beyond acceptance or tolerance to cultivation of children's diverse languages (whether dominant, indigenous or immigrant or autochtonous minority) as teaching languages. (García *et al.*, 2006: 14)

But a range of complex interrelating factors, whether social, historical, political, economic or linguistic, will affect the extent to which the promotion of plurilingualism can be translated into new pedagogical practices for the multilingual classroom. Even when schools manage to develop their own language policies, these are always embedded in the polity of the State, and both approaches might not intersect. These issues are addressed in the remaining three chapters of the volume.

The case that Walker makes for bi/multilingualism as a settlement outcome for New Zealand is a good example of collision between monolingual and bi/multilingual discourses. While immigration to New Zealand has been a major contributor to the country's cultural and linguistic diversity, it remains, nonetheless, a predominantly English monolingual society. The dominance of English is reflected in New Zealand's settlement policy, which aims to enhance socioeconomic integration and participation through improved English language proficiency among migrants. While this is an important goal, it also highlights a disparity between the official discourse of diversity and what is essentially a monolingual approach to settlement, which tends to overlook migrants' bi/multilingual needs in the settlement process. The case for linguistic diversity as a strategic dimension in the settlement outcome is explored, based on empirical data that illustrate the importance of migrants' languages (those other than English) in the construction of a bi/multilingual sense of self, thus affording continuity and belonging at a time of change.

Clyne's contribution shows clearly that a similar monolingual mindset dominates in Australia. Like New Zealand, there is a certain 'obsession' with monolingual English literacy. In Victoria, which has a relatively supportive languages-in-education policy and where there are opportunities to take one language other than English within day school and another after hours, only 2% of year 12 students take two languages other than English for the examination at the end of secondary school. There is also a reluctance by many primary schools in multilingual areas to teach the main community language, and some secondary schools actually prevent recently arrived students from taking a third language. This is because they think students should concentrate on 'English as a second language' even though local research based on qualitative data has pointed to the advantages of bilinguals learning a third language at school over monolinguals learning the same language.

Bekerman's chapter on an integrated bilingual Palestinian Jewish educational initiative in Israel shows that bilingual literacy is largely dependent on multiple complex contextual inputs as they evolve during classroom activity. Despite the obvious political engagement of the various actors involved in the implementation of such an education programme, the bilingual school was found to suffer from somewhat contradictory practices, perspectives and expectations in relation to its goals. This last chapter is an illustration of the need for detailed ethnographic data to understand why the intended balanced language use is dependent not only on pedagogical practices, but also on multiple other complex factors on which teachers or parents have very little leeway. In this remarkable example of integrated bilingual education in a society torn by political conflict, we are brought to understand how the teaching and learning of the 'minority language' (Arabic) is severely constrained by the sociopolitical context, and this despite the bilingual and bicultural principles and goals set out by the teachers and parents. Bekerman is right to remind us of the danger of ignoring the macro-contextual factors that frame bilingual education, of forgetting that in bi- or multilingual contexts, the different languages at stake are always in a relationship of more or less power and represent more or less cultural capital for speakers in general. Thus, the question of whether schools can contest such relationships of power remains acute. This chapter is an apposite closing one in that it points to the need for ongoing dialogue with the important questions raised in other chapters in the volume. It is not only language that offers solution for change (in this case bilingual education) but other forms of human and social solutions need to be found for people to learn to live together beyond their differences. These Jewish and Arab parents clearly want their children to learn together, to share the school day and ultimately to learn to live together. The engagement of these parents and teachers at the local level towards an alternative type of education with the presence of the two languages/cultures aims far beyond just bilingual education per se. They are searching for a model of peace education, which might be considered utopian, but it is necessary for all of us to believe education can change our lives and the lives of those who live in conflict areas.

It is somewhat idealistic to believe that schools alone can completely change societies, and yet everyday teachers in their classrooms are engaged in acts of resistance against dominant ideologies, they witness the growing social inequalities that affect the children they work with, and whom they strive to help to make sense of a fast-changing world. Many believe they can make a difference if only for a few of their pupils: we hope this volume will help them to believe they can become actors of change and that embracing multilingual education is not an impossible task.

Note

1. Most of the chapters appearing in this volume were originally presented at a colloquium at the *Sixth International Symposium on Bilingualism* in Hamburg in 2007.

References

Baldauf, R.B. (2008) Rearticulating the case for micro language planning in a language ecology context. In A. Liddicoat and R.B. Baldauf (eds) *Language Planning in Local Contexts* (pp. 18–41). Clevedon: Multilingual Matters.

Ball, S.J. (1997) Policy sociology and critical social research: A personal review of recent education policy and policy research. *British Educational Research Journal* 23, 257–274.

Bourdieu, P. (1977) *Outline of a Theory of Practice*. Cambridge: Cambridge University Press.

Candelier, M. (2003) *L'éveil aux langues à l'école primaire. EVLANG, Bilan d'une innovation*. Bruxelles: De Boeck.

Corson, D. (2009) *Language Policy in Schools*. New York: Routledge.

Creese, A. and Martin, P. (eds) (2003) *Multilingual Classroom Ecologies*. Clevedon: Multilingual Matters.

Creese, A., Bhatt, A., Bhojani, N. and Martin, P. (2006) Multicultural, heritage and learner identities in complementary schools. *Language and Education* 20 (1), 23–43.

García, O. (2007) Foreword. In S. Makoni and A. Pennycook (eds) *Disinventing and Reconstituting Languages* (pp. xi–xv). Clevedon: Multilingual Matters.

García, O. (2009) *Bilingual Education in the 21st Century. A Global Perspective*. Malden: Wiley-Blackwell.

García, O., Skutnabb-Kangas, T. and Torres-Guzmán, M.E. (eds) (2006) *Imagining Multilingual Schools. Languages in Education and Glocalization*. Clevedon: Multilingual Matters.

Fischer, F. (2003) *Reframing Public Policy, Discursive Politics and Deliberative Practices*. Oxford: Oxford University Press.

Hajer, M. and Wagenaar, H. (eds) (2003) *Deliberative Policy Analysis*. Cambridge: Cambridge University Press.

Hélot, C. (2007) *Du bilinguisme en famille au plurilinguisme à l'école*. Paris: L'Harmattan.

Hélot, C. (2010) *"Tu sais bien parler Maîtresse!"* Negotiating languages other than French in the primary classroom in France. In K. Menken and O. García (eds) *Negotiating Language Education Policies: Educators as Policy Makers* (pp. 52–71). New York: Lawrence Erlbaum/Routledge.

Hornberger, N. (2006) Frameworks and models in language policy and planning. In T. Ricento (ed.) *An Introduction to Language Policy* (pp. 24–410). Malden: Blackwell Publishing.

Jessner, U. (2006) *Linguistic Awareness in Multilinguals.* Edinburgh: Edinburgh University Press.

Kemp, C. (2007) Strategic processing in grammar learning: Do multilinguals use more strategies? *International Journal of Multilingualism* 4, 241–261.

Kenner, C. and Hickey, T. (eds) (2008) *Multilingual Europe. Diversity and Learning.* Trentham: Trentham Books.

Ó Laoire, M. (ed.) (2006) *Multilingualism in Educational Settings.* Hohengehren: Schneider Verlag Baltmannsweiler.

Ricento, T. (2006) *An Introduction to Language Policy. Theory and Method.* Malden, MA: Blackwell.

Shohamy, E. (2006) *Language Policy: Hidden Agendas and New Approaches.* New York: Routledge.

Silverstein, M. and Urban, G. (1996) The natural history of discourse. In M. Silverstein and G. Urban (eds) *Natural Histories of Discourse.* Chicago: University of Chicago.

Wagenaar, H. and Cook, S.D.N. (2003) Understanding policy, practices, action, dialectic and deliberation in policy analysis. In M. Hajer and H. Wagenaar (eds) *Deliberative Policy Analysis* (pp. 139–171). Cambridge: Cambridge University Press.

The Ecology of the Multilingual Classroom: From Complexity to Pedagogy

Perspectives on the Learners

Chapter 1

Ideologies and Interactions in Multilingual Education: What Can an Ecological Approach Tell Us about Bilingual Pedagogy?

A. CREESE and A. BLACKLEDGE

Introduction

This chapter uses the metaphor of language ecology to consider language practices and ideologies in complementary schools. Complementary schools are also known as supplementary, community language, mother tongue language and heritage language schools. They are voluntary, outside the state system, established and run by community members. There is great diversity in provision. Our particular focus is on schools that explicitly aim to teach a community language. The schools in our study are held either at the weekend on Saturdays and Sundays or after school during the week. They tend to meet for around 2–3 hours weekly and more or less keep to the same term dates of mainstream schools. Since 2002, we have researched complementary schools to look at identity, learning and linguistic repertoires of young people and teachers.[1,2] The complementary schools we researched were Bengali, Chinese, Gujarati and Turkish in Birmingham, Manchester, Leicester and London, respectively. The project aimed to explore the social, cultural and linguistic significance of complementary schools both within their communities and in wider society, and to investigate how linguistic practices of students and teachers in complementary schools are used to negotiate their multilingual and multicultural identities.

Language Ecology: An Interactional Perspective

The study of language ecology is the study of diversity within specific sociopolitical settings where the processes of language use create, reflect and challenge particular hierarchies and hegemonies, however transient these might be. An ecological perspective on multilingualism is 'essentially about opening up ideological and implementational space in the environment for as many languages as possible' (Hornberger, 2002: 30). At its heart is the dialectic between the local interactional and the social ideological. An ecological perspective warns us against too easily reaching comprehensive tidy findings. Kramsch suggests that we use an ecological framework to voice the 'contradictions, the unpredictabilities, and paradoxes that underlie even the most respectable research in language development' (Kramsch, 2002: 8; Kramsch & Steffensen, 2008).

The language ecology metaphor offers a way of studying the interaction in order to explore how social ideologies, particularly around multilingualism get created and implemented. Creese and Martin (2003, 2008) describe classrooms as ecological micro systems. They argue for the importance of exploring ecological minutiae of interactional practices in classrooms, linking these to the ideologies that pervade language choice and language policy. A similar point is made by Jaffe (2008) who describes a need for 'microecologies' of linguistic, social, political and pedagogical practice (Jaffe, 2008: 225). It is in the detail of the interactional that ideologies are formed. As Silverstein argues,

> the macro-sociological is really a projective order from within a complex, and ever changing, configuration of interdiscursivities in micro-contextual orders, some of which, it turns out, at any given moment of macro-order diachrony asymmetrically determine others. (Silverstein, 2003: 202)

Silverstein shows that the dominant macro social order is a manifestation of smaller, local and iterative micro orders some of which dominate the macro ideological order more than others. In taking a classroom ecological perspective, with a specific focus on multilingualism, we can explore how cultural reproduction is framed locally (Erickson, 1990). The purpose of this chapter is to consider how the multilingual orientation of complementary schools frame bilingual pedagogy as an ideology and how teachers and students practise it locally and interactionally. In the larger macro ideological order, which is increasingly hostile to multilingualism and multiculturalism through its enforcement of monolingualism in society (Blackledge, 2005; Rassool, 2008) complementary schools provide an alternative (Mirza & Reay, 2000), safe (Martin, 2005) and multilingual (Hornberger, 2005) space for institutional bilingualism. We consider the possibilities they present to challenge the monolingual macro order.

Participants in complementary schools have various views and practices about what constitutes bilingualism and how languages should be taught, learnt and maintained (see Creese *et al.*, 2008). One view is that language boundaries are clear and sacrosanct; in other words, in complementary schools a 'language' should be preserved and kept free from contamination by other sets of linguistic resources. A second view is that in practice, bilinguals do not make a distinction between the various signs which they use to convey meaning; that is they do not experience their language use as 'bilingual' or consisting of different languages, rather they draw on whatever semiotic signs are available to them to make meanings. Both views and practices run alongside one another in complementary schools (see Creese & Blackledge, 2010).

Complementary schools are different from other language teaching and learning contexts, such as English as an additional language (EAL) and modern foreign language (MFL) in mainstream schools because of their focus on the community context. Complementary schools are institutions which endorse multilingualism as a usual and normative resource for identity performance (Creese *et al.*, 2006; Martin *et al.*, 2006) and which strive to influence identity and cultural socializations, extending the bilingualism of the students who attend (Creese *et al.*, 2008). Complementary schools' particular concern with community values and the nature of affiliation to and expertise in the community language suggests the need for a pedagogy which responds to young people and teachers who have experience of diaspora in particular and distinct ways (Anderson, 2008; Cummins, 2005). This chapter describes aspects of the bilingual pedagogy used by participants in complementary schools and argues for a flexible bilingualism and flexible pedagogy.

Language Separation as Bilingual Pedagogy

Bilingual education has traditionally argued that languages should be kept separate in the learning and teaching of languages. We see this explained in an early text on 'language distribution in bilingual schooling' (Jacobson & Faltis, 1990).

> Bilingual educators have usually insisted on the separation of the two languages, one of which is English and the other, the child's

vernacular. By strictly separating the languages, the teacher avoids, it is argued, cross contamination, thus making it easier for the child to acquire a new linguistic system as he/she internalizes a given lesson.... it was felt that the inappropriateness of the concurrent use was so self-evident that no research had to be conducted to prove this fact. (Jacobson & Faltis, 1990: 4)

Keeping the languages separate, it is argued, helps the child. This discussion is brought up to date in the rationale behind the USA's two-way bilingual immersion programmes which are described as 'periods of instruction during which only one language is used (that is, there is no translation or language mixing)' (Lindholm-Leary, 2006: 89). According to Cummins (2005) an explanation for this separateness is the continuing prevalence of monolingual instructional approaches in our schools. He describes the assumptions behind these approaches as:

(1) Instruction should be carried out exclusively in the target language without recourse to the students' L1.
(2) Translation between L1 and L2 has no place in the teaching of language or literacy. Encouragement of translation in L2 teaching is viewed as a reversion to the discredited grammar/translation method ... or concurrent translation method.
(3) Within L2 immersion and bilingual/dual language programs, the two languages should be kept rigidly separate: they constitute 'two solitudes'. (Cummins, 2005: 588)

The 'two solitudes' to which Cummins refers above are similarly captured by others in the research literature. Heller coins the term 'parallel monlingualism' (Heller, 1999: 271), in which 'each variety must conform to certain prescriptive norms'. Heller argues that students learn to become bilingual in particular ways (and therefore not others) and that these constructions of bilingualism advantage particular groups of students. Baker (2003), building on Fishman (1967), describes bilingualism with diaglossia in which each language is used for distinct and separate social functions (Baker, 2003); Swain uses the phrase, 'bilingualism through monolingualism' (Swain, 1983: 4); Creese and Blackledge (2008) use the term 'separate bilingualism' to describe language-learning classroom contexts in complementary schools where teachers insist on the use of the target language only. Each term describes the boundaries put up around languages and represents a view of the multilingual/bilingual student/teacher as 'two monolinguals in one body' (Gravelle, 1996: 11).

There are emotional implications to insistence on separate bilingualism in educational contexts. Back in 1981 Zentella recorded one of the teachers in her study saying:

> When they don't understand something in one language, they'll go to the other, which is easier for them ... and like, then sometimes I have to be bouncing from one language to the other, which is wrong ... Puerto Rican teacher (in Zentella, 1981: 127)

The Zentella quote indicates the moral disapproval of 'mixing' languages in the classroom. Shin in her study describes attitudes towards code-switching as negative, noting that bilinguals themselves 'may feel embarrassed about their code switching and attribute it to careless language habits' (Shin, 2005: 18). Setati *et al.* (2002: 147 in Martin, 2005: 90) make reference to the 'dilemma-filled' nature of code-switching in their study of South African classrooms. Martin describing code-switching in Malaysia shows how,

> The use of a local language alongside the 'official' language of the lesson is a well-known phenomenon and yet, for a variety of reasons, it is often lambasted as 'bad practice', blamed on teachers' lack of English-language competence ... or put to one side and/or swept under the carpet. (Martin, 2005: 88)

These studies show that moving between languages has traditionally been frowned upon in educational settings with teachers and students often feeling guilty about its practice. Research shows that code-switching is rarely institutionally endorsed or pedagogically underpinned. Rather, when it is used, it becomes a pragmatic response to the local classroom context. Lin (1996, 2005) describes student and teacher code-switching practices as 'local, pragmatic, coping tactics and responses to the socio-economic dominance of English in Hong Kong, where many students from socioeconomically disadvantaged backgrounds with limited access to English resources struggled to acquire an English-medium education for its socioeconomic value' (Lin, 2005: 46). Martin (2005: 89) speaks of code-switching as offering classroom participants 'creative pragmatic and "safe" practices ... between the official language of the lesson and a language which the classroom participants have a greater access to'. Arthur and Martin (2006) argue that code-switching allows participants to better accomplish the lesson and is a pragmatic response used to annotate texts and provide greater access.

'Translanguaging' as Bilingual Pedagogy

The educational issues around parallel monolingualism described in the research above have led practitioners and researchers to question the stricture of separate bilingualism. Cummins (2005) challenges the squandering of bilingual resources in mainstream contexts. He argues for a need to articulate bilingual instructional strategies that teach explicitly for two-way cross-language transfer. Anderson (2008) has recently called for flexible approaches to pedagogy to respond to bilingual contexts which do not fit easily into existing paradigms. Lin and Martin (2005) have argued for more multilingual pedagogic and curriculum research. The research documented in Lin and Martin (2005) and Arthur and Martin (2006) describe the pedagogic potentials behind code-switching. These include increasing the inclusion, participation and understandings of pupils in the learning processes; the development of less formal relationships between participants; ideas more easily conveyed and lessons 'accomplished'. They speak of the 'pedagogic validity of codeswitching' (Arthur & Martin, 2006: 197) and consider ways in which the research might contribute to a 'teachable' pedagogic resource (Arthur & Martin, 2006: 197).

Important avenues of research have began to question the validity of boundaries around languages. García (2007: xii) shows in her work in New York schools that languages are not hermetically sealed units. García, prefers the term 'translanguaging' to code-switching to describe the usualness and normality of 'bilingualism without diglossic functional separation' in New York classrooms (García, 2007: xiii). Makoni and Mashiri (2007) suggest that rather than developing language policies which attempt at hermetically sealing languages we should be describing the use of vernaculars which leak into one another to understand the social realities of their users. As Lemke argues:

> It is not at all obvious that if they were not politically prevented from doing so, 'languages' would not mix and dissolve into one another, but we understand almost nothing of such processes ... Could it be that all our current pedagogical methods in fact make multilingual development more difficult than it need be, simply because we bow to dominant political and ideological pressures to keep 'languages' pure and separate? (Lemke, 2002: 85)

There are some examples of pedagogies which explicitly seek to develop bilingual strategies based on ecological perspectives. Hornberger (2002, 2005, 2008) describes her work on the continua of biliteracy as an ecological model in the sense that language and literacy features are nested and intersecting. One change along one point of a continuum will cause potential changes along other continua resulting in a reconfiguration of the whole educational picture (Hornberger, 2002). In terms of optimizing pedagogy, Hornberger suggests,

> bi/multilinguals' learning is maximized when they are allowed and enabled to draw from across all their existing language skills (in two+ languages), rather than being constrained and inhibited from doing so by monolingual instructional assumptions and practices. (Hornberger, 2005: 607)

Another ecological pedagogic approach is described by López (2008: 143) who uses the term 'concurrent approaches' in training prospective indigenous teachers in Latin America. He describes 'concurrent approaches' as 'generally untried but innovative use of languages used in the business of teaching and learning' (López, 2008: 143). López argues for a bilingual pedagogy which shows that 'in indigenous everyday life, the two – or in some cases three or more – languages are needed many times in connection to one another and not as discretely separate as is often supposed' (López, 2008: 143).

Cummins too makes some explicit suggestions for developing bilingual strategies. He suggests:

> (a) systematic attention to cognate relationships across languages; (b) creation of student-authored dual language books by means of translation from the initial language of writing to the L2; other multimedia and multilingual projects can also be implemented (e.g. creation of iMovies, PowerPoint presentations, etc); (c) sister class projects where students from different language backgrounds collaborate using two or more languages. (Cummins, 2005: 588)

In the United Kingdom, research has shown how bilingual children do not view their literacies and languages as separate, but rather experience them as 'simultaneous' (Kenner, 2004; Robertson, 2006; Sneddon, 2000).

However, there is also some caution expressed in the research literature regarding the development of bilingual strategies/pedagogies based on flexible methods. Martin writes,

> And yet we need to question whether bilingual interaction strategies 'work' in the classroom context.... [D]o they facilitate learning? Can classroom code-switching support communication, particularly the exploratory talk which is such an essential part of the learning process. A corollary to this is whether teacher-training programmes (both

pre-service and in-service), in multilingual contexts take into account the realities and pragmatics of classroom language use in such contexts. (Martin, 2005: 90)

Lin (1999) acknowledges the switching between English and Cantonese in her 1999 study ensured understanding and motivation but warns against notions of easy transferability to other classrooms in other contexts and the danger of participating in the reproduction of students' disadvantage. Further, the development of pedagogies which respond to the research literature will not work in any 'mechanistic generalisable way' (Arthur & Martin, 2006: 197). The importance of responding to local circumstances is made clear in the literature reviewed here. Although we can acknowledge that across all linguistically diverse contexts moving between languages is natural, how to harness and build on this will depend on the sociopolitical environment in which such practice is embedded and the local ecologies of schools and classrooms.

In the following sections we look at particular examples of flexible bilingualism in the context of complementary schools and consider some of bilingual strategies used in complementary school classrooms. Before this, we briefly describe the design of the study and the nature of the data collected.

Methods

The research project consisted of four interlocking case studies with two researchers working in two complementary schools in each of the four communities. The case studies focused on Gujarati schools in Leicester, Turkish schools in London, Cantonese and Mandarin schools in Manchester and Bengali schools in Birmingham. Each case study identified two complementary schools in which to observe, record and interview participants. After four weeks observing in classrooms using an ethnographic team approach (Creese *et al.*, 2008), two key participant children were identified in each school. These children were audio recorded during the classes observed, during break times and where possible, as they entered and left the complementary school site. Stakeholders in the schools were interviewed, including teachers and administrators, and the key participant children and their parents. We also collected key documentary evidence, and took photographs.

Flexible bilingualism as pedagogy

For this discussion we draw on data from the Gujarati and Chinese schools in the larger study. We start with an assembly in JBV, one of the

Gujarati schools in the study. Assemblies are held at the end of each Saturday morning session so that parents picking up their children can attend. The whole school attends and assemblies are always very well attended by parents. The teachers sit at the front and the side. Children sit on the floor facing the front. Parents are at the back. Each week one particular class and their teacher lead the assembly. It is also an opportunity for the head teacher to address the whole school: young people, teachers and parents. There are 200 children on roll at the school and the assembly is a busy event which requires teachers to move furniture to accommodate all participants. In the extract we see that SB, the head teacher, uses both Gujarati and English to speak to the audience. The translation is given after the text showing the use of both English and Gujarati.

Extract one

SB: ... what's going to happen here Jalaram Bal Vikasma? Holiday **nathi** ... **awata Shaniware apne awanu chhe.** we're coming here **awta shaniware** ... [several Ss put up their hands] ... Amar? ... [picks on Amar or Amit to reply] ... **Amare kidhu ne ke** GCSE presentation **chhe** ... **awanu chhe.** I know that we're finishing on Friday in mainstream school, **pun aiya agal badhayne awanu chhe** .... I know, it's a surprise. **Khawanu etlu** *fine* **chhe,** K warned me today ... it's something all of you will like, teachers will like ... something for all of us .... [points to the HB's class sitting in front of her] **a balko a varshe GCSE karwana chhe etle** next year **a badha awshe mehman thayne, mota thayne!** ... we're not going to take much time, 'cause I've got few other things to tell you as well ...
[assembly transcript]

SB: ... what's going to happen here in JBV? *It's not a* **holiday,** *we've to come here next Saturday* ... we're coming here *next Saturday* ... [several Ss put up their hands] ... Amar?...[picks on Amar or Amit to reply] ... *As Amar said, there's* GCSE presentation, *you have to come.* I know we're finishing on Friday in mainstream School, *but you all have to come here* .... I know, it's a surprise, *lovely food,* K [a parent] warned me today, it's something all of you will like, teachers will like ... something for all of us...[points to the HB's class sitting in front of her] *these children are doing GCSE this year* **so** *next year they will come as guests, all grown up!* ... we're not going to take up much time 'cos I've got a few other things to tell you as well ...
[Assembly audio and video recording]

If we break down the interaction further, we are able to identify more specifically some of the bilingual strategies SB uses to engage her audience. The following show which utterances are said in English and which are said in Gujarati. We do this, not because we wish to argue that each language is delivering different functions, but rather that in classifying them into language groups, we can argue that such classifications are meaningless for the speaker, SB.

In English
what's going to happen here Jalaram Bal Vikasma? Holiday
we're coming here
GCSE presentation
I know that we're finishing on Friday in mainstream school,
I know, it's a surprise
warned me today ... it's something all of you will like, teachers will like ...
something for all of us. ...
next year
we're not going to take much time, 'cause I've got few other things to tell
you as well ...

In Gujarati
we've to come here next Saturday
next Saturday ... As Amar said, there's
but you all have to come here ....
lovely food, K
something for all of us ... these children are doing GCSE this year so
they will come as guests, all grown up

We wish to make the following points from classifying the utterances into two languages. First, both languages are needed simultaneously to convey the information about school openings and closings. That is, each language is used to convey a different informational message but it is in the bilingualism of the text that the full message is conveyed. As López (2008), argues, both languages are 'needed' in connection to one another. The message meaning is not clear without both languages. An analysis which looks at the languages separately therefore does little to explain the way SB performs her identity as head, teacher, parent and community member. Second, it is the movement between languages that SB engages with her diverse audience. The teachers, children and parents have different levels of proficiency in both Gujarati and English. SB uses her languages to engage her audience. However, her 'languages' do not appear separate for her in this social act, but rather a resource to negotiate meanings and include as many of the audience as possible. SB's language indexes her knowledge of the social and linguistic complexity of the community she addresses. We would argue that SB's utterances are examples of translanguaging in which the speaker uses her languages in a pedagogic context to make meaning, transmit information and perform identities using the linguistic signs at her disposal to connect with her audience in community engagement. Gujarati and English are not distinct languages here for the speaker in this context. SB does not confine signs to different languages, rather her heteroglossia encompasses language forms simultaneously.

In the second extract from the Gujarati class, we see another example of flexible bilingualism as an instructional strategy to engage students. In the following extract young people in the second of the Gujarati schools have been working on a folk story. Previous to this class, the teacher had led the students in a reading and oral exploration of the narrative. In the extract below the teacher has asked students to work in pairs to make up their own version of the story. The interactions show the teacher (PB) speaking with a pair of students in front of the whole class.

Extract two

PB: ... **chalo, tame taiyar chho**? ... [talks to other Ss] .... **ek diwas** ... **chalo** ....
> *< come on, are you ready? ... one day ... come on ... >*

Ss: what?

PB: [inaudible]

Ss: we're still writing ... we have written that much [shows book to PB]. Not much, is it?

PB: **shena upper banawi chhe**?
> *< what is it about? >*

Ss: **Kootro ane wandro**
> *< dog and the monkey >*

PB: **Kootro ne wandro? Shu banawi chhe warta**?
> *< dog and the monkey? What story have you made? >*

Ss: they make friends and they go out

PB: **be mitro chhe ane-**
> *< they are two friends and ->*

Ss: they are going out

PB: **e bai mitro chhe, kootro ne wandro ne bai farwa jay chhe**
> *< they are both friends and they go out (for a walk) >*

Ss: they are going out

PB: kya farwa jay?
   < *where do they go?* >
Ss: jungle**ma**
   < *in the jungle* >
PB: jungle**ma, wandrabhai** jungle**ma jai shake?**
   < *in the jungle, can the monkey go into the jungle?* >
Ss: no, they are going out [laugh]
PB: sssh! Pachhi shu thyu?
   < then what happened? >
[Classroom video recording]

In this extract we see how despite the teacher's return to Gujarati at each turn, the students respond in English. We also see that the students' colloquial use of English creates two different interactional frames. Whilst the teacher's aim is the production of a traditional folk story, the students' aim is to give the story a more modern meaning. They use the phrase 'going out' to create a different meaning from that intended by the teacher. The students have turned the monkey and dog into lovers. The teacher does not or chooses not to understand this implication.

We wish to make several points about the bilingual teaching strategy used by classroom participants. First, the extract show participants drawing across all their existing languages (Hornberger, 2005) to stay focused on the task of story creation. That is, although the teacher mostly uses Gujarati and the young people mostly use English, the task of creating a new version of an old folk story is 'accomplished' by the classroom participants (Arthur & Martin, 2006; Lin & Martin, 2005) because they are able to move between languages. The teacher and students both 'accept' the language use of their interlocutor because it allows them to stay on task. Although the two languages appear to be more functionally distinct here than in extract eight, with the teacher using Gujarati and the young people using English, it is again the use of both languages together which makes the task meaningful and fun for the young people. Young people are able to play with 'words' showing their linguistic sophistication and double meaning of 'going out' in both English and Gujarati. The teacher allows the laughter and continues with the task. Both English and Gujarati are legitimate because both are used in the pedagogic task at hand which is learning about a traditional folk story and creating new interpretations around it. The second point to be made, is the teacher's willingness to explicitly accept a newly coined heteroglossic term. 'Junglema', which is introduced by students and accepted by the teacher is viewed as a linguistic resource which keeps the task moving forward.

The next extract comes from the Mandarin school in the Chinese case study. As in the extract above, the teacher has been working on folk stories with the young people: 'Hou'yi shoots the suns and Chang'e flies to the moon'. When this interaction takes place, the class had been involved in learning key vocabulary and reading aloud the textbook dialogue which introduces festivals and the stories associated with them. The teacher then embarks on a long process of narrating and explaining the story. We look at one short extract from this literacy event below.

Extract three

T: 有人把箭偷了 < Someone stole the arrow >因为 < because> *people, they know that they will not survive if there was no sun right? If there is no sun, they will not survive either. So people took the arrow . . . .*

Zhang: (interrupting and expressing doubt) 这个后羿不懂啊 < And this Houyi didn't know/understand? >

T: *It's a legend.*

Zhang: *Oh it's a legend. Let's just let it go. Hey . . .*

T: 然后 < Then > 后羿发现他最后一支箭不见了 < Houyi found that his last arrow disappeared >

The story-telling provides much student laughter and opportunities to question. The young people are animated. There is student consensus about the implausibility of the story. Students think it absurd that Houyi could not understand that people need the sun to live. There is ridicule but there is also engagement. In terms of bilingual pedagogy there are several interesting points to make. First, the teacher allows the interruption of the usual classroom discourse routine of 'initiate, respond, feedback' (IRF) moves. The interruption from Zhang happens in Mandarin whereas the teacher's previous utterance is in English. As with the earlier Gujarati example, we argue that because the student questioning and challenging is done bilingually it is accepted by the teacher. It appears that in the pacing of the bilingual interaction playful naughtiness is allowed because students are still involved in the learning of folk stories which is the pedagogic task in hand. The translanguaging which teacher and students engage in keeps the task moving and interrupts the usual IRF discourses of classroom life. A second point, as with the other data sets in this chapter is that both languages are needed in order for the story to be understood. That is, the teacher uses and allows the participants bilingualism in order for the story to be made complete. Each language individually is not sufficient to convey the full narrative. Our fieldnotes from one of the non-Mandarin-speaking researchers records the following in extract eleven.

Extract four

> Children seem to have got the point of the story, which I have failed to. They must do this through the teacher's code switching as it is not achievable through the English only.

A third point to be made from this short extract is that the teacher skilfully uses her bilingualism to involve students. She narrates the story in Mandarin keeping to the storyline. She explains the story in English emphasizing the story's moral tale. A final point to be made in regard to bilingual strategies is the importance of identity work for both student and teachers. The student in the extract is able to use his bilingualism in order to question and challenge the story displaying his linguistic knowledge and sophistication but also using the movement between languages to distant himself from the storyline and some of what it indexes. The teacher too is able to use her bilingualism for identity work, in her case to move between endorsing the folk story message but also 'siding' with her students notion of the ridiculousness of the story line. She uses her bilingualism to pace the teaching and get the lesson accomplished.

The fourth extract comes from the same Chinese schools. In it we see the classroom participants negotiate an interaction bilingually, through 'bilingual label quests'. Martin (2005: 11) attributes the concept of 'label quests' to Heath (1986) but extends the definition to describe bilingual label quests in which the teacher elicits labels from the student allowing for the teaching to be 'accomplished bilingually' (Martin, 2005: 11). Martin describes this as a common feature of bilingual classrooms (Martin, 2003). We see an example from the Chinese data below.

Extract five

T:　第四个词？< The fourth term? > 盼望。<'Panwang', > 盼望怎么说？< How do you say 'Panwang'?> 比如说，我们都盼望什么？< For example, what do we 'Panwang'?> 盼望，< 'Panwang'.> *expect, look forward to. Write down the explanation beside the words, in case you forget it later.* 盼望 < 'Panwang' >, *the 4th one, means look forward to.* 比如说，我们都盼望什么？< For example, what do we long for? >

In this extract we see the teacher introduce a key vocabulary item which will later appear in a dialogue which a pair of students reads to the class. The new term is 'panwang'. The teacher says it four times asking students to consider how it is said before giving a clue in Chinese that it is a verb – what do we 'panwang'? She then uses English to give the definition – 'expect, look forward'. We see that the term is given in one language and the explanation is given in another language. The 'translation' performs a pedagogic strategy of accomplishing the task of new vocabulary teaching, keeping the lesson moving forward. There are many variations of bilingual label quests in complementary school classrooms. Sometimes the teacher makes the bilingual label quest and also self answers; at other times, the teacher asks in one language and expects the students to provide the answer in the other language. In complementary schools, we see examples of bilingual quests from English to the community language and also from community language into English (for further examples, see Martin *et al.*, 2006). These bilingual quests are common in the bilingual pedagogy of complementary schools and are often used to annotate future teaching texts.

Discussion

The three data sources of interviews, fieldnotes and interactions show that at least two constructions of bilingualism exist in complementary schools: separate and flexible bilingualism. Flexible bilingualism is used by teachers and students in complementary schools as a pedagogic resource to accomplish pedagogic goals and task and for identity performance. We have argued that flexible bilingualism in assemblies and classrooms is used to engage participants in the reproduction of social, community and pedagogic values and goals.

We have suggested that as participants engage in flexible bilingualism, the boundaries between languages become permeable. We have used the terms translanguaging (García, 2007) and heteroglossia (Bailey, 2007; Bakhtin, 1984, 1986) to describe language fluidity and movement. We wish to emphasize the process by which bilingual participants in complementary schools, 'encompass socially meaningful forms in both bilingual and monolingual talk' which allow them to take up subject positions connected to past histories which are brought into play in the here and now (Bailey, 2007: 267). In other words, the bilingual teachers and students in the complementary schools in this study used whatever signs and forms they had at their disposal to connect with other participants thereby using signs to index allegiances and knowledges and create new ones.

In this chapter, we have focused on how this is achieved in the pedagogy and have argued that flexible bilingualism is used by teachers as an instructional strategy to make links for classroom participants between the social, cultural, community and linguistic domains of their lives.

Pedagogy in these schools appears to emphasize the overlapping of languages in the student and teacher rather than enforcing the separation of languages for learning and teaching. We acknowledge, however, that within complementary schools ideologies often clash with as many arguments articulated for separate bilingualism as for flexible bilingualism (Creese & Blackledge, 2010; Creese *et al.*, 2008).

Our data find much in keeping with the language ecological literature reviewed earlier in this chapter. In our research, we also find examples of the need for both languages, for the drawing across languages, for the additional value and resource that bilingualism brings to identity performance, lesson accomplishment and participant confidence. We have attempted to identify some of these through the data analysed in this chapter.

Some of the specific knowledge and skills shown by classroom participants in practising flexible bilingualism and flexible pedagogy were:

- Use of bilingual label quests, repetition and translation across languages.
- Ability to engage audiences through translanguaging and heteroglossia.
- Use of student translanguaging to establish identity positions both oppositional and encompassing of institutional values.
- Recognition that languages do not fit into clear bounded entities and that all languages are 'needed' for meanings to be conveyed and negotiated.
- Endorsement of simultaneous literacies and languages to keep the pedagogic task moving.
- Recognition that teachers and students skilfully use their languages for different functional goals such as narration and explanation.
- Use of translanguaging for annotating texts, providing greater access and lesson accomplishment.

If we are to move beyond squandering our bilingual resources and easing the burden of guilt associated with translanguaging in educational contexts, further research is needed on classroom language ecologies to show how and why pedagogic bilingual practices come to be legitimated and accepted by participants. An ecological perspective requires us to question the pedagogic validity (Arthur & Martin, 2006: 197) of separate bilingualism. Like Lin and Martin (2005) we see the need for further research to explore what 'teachable' pedagogic resources are available in flexible, concurrent approaches to learning and teaching languages bilingually.

Notes

1. ESRC: RES-000-23-1180. Investigating multilingualism in complementary schools in four communities: Creese/Baraç/Bhatt/Blackledge/Hamid/Li Wei/Lytra/Martin/Wu/Yağcioğlu-Ali.
2. ESRC: R000223949. Complementary schools and their communities in Leicester: Martin/Creese/Bhatt/Bhojani.

References

Anderson, J. (2008) Towards integrated second language teaching pedagogy for foreign and community/heritage languages in multilingual Britain. *Language Learning Journal* 36, 79–89.

Arthur, J. and Martin, P. (2006) Accomplishing lessons in postcolonial classrooms: Comparative perspectives from Botswana and Brunei Darussalam. *Comparative Education* 42, 177–202.

Bailey, B. (2007) Heterglossia and boundaries. In M. Heller (ed.) *Bilingualism: A Social Approach* (pp. 257–276). Basingstoke: Palgrave.

Baker, C. (2003) Biliteracy and transliteracy in Wales: Language planning and the Welsh national curriculum. In N. Hornberger (ed.) *Continua of Biliteracy* (pp. 71–90). Clevedon: Multilingual Matters.

Bakhtin, M.M. (1984) *Problems of Dostoevsky's Poetics* (C. Emerson, ed. and trans.). Manchester: Manchester University Press.

Bakhtin, M.M. (1986) The problem of speech genres. In C. Emerson and M. Holquist (eds) *Speech Genres and Other Late Essays*. Austin, TX: University of Austin Press.

Blackledge, A. (2005) *Discourse and Power in a Multilingual World*. Amsterdam: John Benjamins.

Creese, A. and Blackledge, A. (2008) Creese, Angela and Blackledge, Adrian. Flexible bilingualism in heritage language schools. Unpublished paper for Urban Multilingualism and Intercultural Communication, Antwerp, March 2008.

Creese, A. and Blackledge, A. (2010) Translanguaging in the bilingual classroom: A pedagogy for learning and teaching. *Modern Language Journal* 94, 103–115.

Creese, A. and Martin, P. (eds) (2003) *Multilingual Classroom Ecologies*. Clevedon: Multilingual Matters.

Creese, A. and Martin, P. (2008) Classroom ecologies: A case study from a Gujarati complementary school in England. In A. Creese, P. Martin and N.H. Hornberger (eds) *Encyclopedia of Language and Education* (2nd edn). *Ecology of Language* (Vol. 9) (pp. 263–272). New York: Springer Science + Business Media LLC.

Creese, A., Bhatt, A., Bhojani, N. and Martin, P. (2006) Multicultural, heritage and learner identities in complementary schools. *Language and Education* 20, 23–43.

Creese, A., Bhatt, A., Bhojani, N. and Martin, P. (2008) Fieldnotes in team ethnography: Research complementary schools. *Qualitative Research* 8, 223–242.

Cummins, J. (2005) A proposal for action: Strategies for recognizing heritage language competence as a learning resource within the mainstream classroom. *The Modern Language Journal* 89, 585–592.

Erickson, F. (1990) Qualitative methods. In R.L. Linn and F. Erickson (eds) *Research in Teaching and Learning* (Vol. 2). New York: MacMillan Publishing Company.

Fishman, J. (1967) Bilingualism with and without diglossia; diglossia with and without bilingualism. *Journal of Social Issues* 23, 29–38.

García, O. (2007) Foreword. In S. Makoni and A. Pennycook (eds) *Disinventing and Reconstituting Languages* (pp. xi–xv). Clevedon: Multilingual Matters.

Gravelle, M. (1996) *Supporting Bilingual Learners in Schools*. Stoke-on-Trent: Trentham Books.

Heath, S.B. (1986) Sociocultural contexts of language development. In D. Holt (ed.) *Beyond Language: Social Change and Cultural Factors in Schooling Minority Students*. Los Angeles Evaluation, Dissemination and Assessment Center, California State University, CA.

Heller, M. (1999) *Linguistic Minorities and Modernity: A Sociolinguistic Ethnography*. London: Longman.

Hornberger, N.H. (2002) Multilingual language policies and the continua of biliteracy: An ecological approach. *Language Policy* 1, 27–51.

Hornberger, N.H. (2005) Introduction: Heritage/community language education: US and Australian perspectives. *International Journal of Bilingual Education and Bilingualism* 8, 101–108.

Hornberger, N.H. (2008) Continua of biliteracy. In A. Creese, P. Martin and N.H. Hornberger (eds) *Encyclopedia of Language and Education* (2nd edn). *Ecology of Language* (Vol. 9) (pp. 275–290). New York: Springer Science + Business Media LLC.

Jacobson, R. and Faltis, C. (eds) (1990) *Language Distribution Issues in Bilingual Schooling*. Clevedon: Multilingual Matters.

Jaffe, A. (2008) Language ecologies and the meaning of diversity: Corsican bilingual education and the concept of 'Polynomie.' In A. Creese, P. Martin and N. H. Hornberger (eds) *Encyclopedia of Language and Education* (2nd edn). *Ecology of Language* (Vol. 9) (pp. 225–235). New York: #2008 Springer Science + Business Media LLC.

Kenner, C. (2004) Living in simultaneous worlds: Difference and integration in bilingual script learning. *International Journal of Bilingual Education and Bilingualism* 7, 43–61.

Kramsch, C. (ed.) (2002) *Language Acquisition and Language Socialization*. London: Continuum.

Kramsch, C. and Steffensen, S.V. (2008) Ecological perspectives on second language acquisition and socialization. In P.A. Duff and N.H. Hornberger (eds) *Encyclopedia of Language and Education* (2nd edn). *Language Socialization* (Vol. 8) (pp. 17–28). New York: #2008 Springer Science + Business Media LLC.

Lin, A.M.Y. (1996) Bilingualism or linguistic segregation? Symbolic domination, resistance, and code-switching in Hong Kong schools. *Linguistics and Education* 8, 49–84.

Lin, A.M.Y. (1999) Doing-English-lessons in the reproduction or transformation of social worlds? *TESOL Quarterly* 33, 393–412.

Lin, A.M.Y. (2005) Critical, transdisciplinary perspectives on language-in-education policy and practice postcolonial contexts: The case of Hong Kong. In A.M. Lin and P.W. Martin (eds) *Decolonisation, Globalisation: Language-in-Education Policy and Practice* (pp. 38–54). Clevedon: Multilingual Matters.

Lin, A.M.Y. and Martin, P.W. (eds) (2005) *Decolonisation, Globalisation: Language-in-Education Policy and Practice*. Clevedon: Multilingual Matters.

Lindholm-Leary, K. (2006) What are the most effective kinds of programs for English language learners? In E. Hamayan and R. Freeman (eds) *English Language Learners at School* (pp. 84–85). Philadelphia: Caslon Publishing.

Lemke, J. (2002) Language development and identity: Multiple timescales in the social ecology of learning. In C. Kramsch (ed.) *Language Acquisition and Language Socialization* (pp. 68–87). London: Continuum.

López, L.E. (2008) Indigenous contributions to an ecology of language learning in Latin America. In A. Creese, P.W. Martin and N. Hornberger (eds) *Encyclopedia of Language and Education* (pp. 141–158). *Ecology of Language* (Vol. 9). New York: Springer Science + Business Media LLC.

Makoni, S. and Mashiri, P. (2007) Critical historiography: Does language planning in Africa need a construct of language as part of its theoretical apparatus? In S. Makoni and A. Pennycook (eds) *Disinventing and Reconstituting Languages* (pp. 62–89). Clevedon: Multilingual Matters.

Martin, P. (2003) Interactions and inter-relationships around text: Practices and positionings in a multilingual classroom in Brunei. In A. Creese and P. Martin (eds) *Multilingual Classroom Ecologies* (pp. 25–41). Clevedon: Multilingual Matters.

Martin, P. (2005) 'Safe' Language practices in two rural schools in Malaysia: Tensions between policy and practice. In A.M. Lin and P.W. Martin (eds) *Decolonisation, Globalisation: Language-in-Education Policy and Practice* (pp. 74–97). Clevedon: Multilingual Matters.

Martin, P., Bhatt, A., Bhojani, N. and Creese, A. (2006) Managing bilingual interaction in a Gujarati complementary school in Leicester. *Language and Education* 20, 5–22.

Mirza, H.S. and Reay, D. (2000) Spaces and places of black educational desire: Rethinking black supplementary schools as a new social movement. *Sociology* 34, 521–544.

Rassool, N. (2008) Language policy and education in Britain. In S. May and N.H. Hornberger (eds) *Encyclopedia of Language and Education* (2nd edn). *Language Policy and Political Issues in Education* (Vol. 1) (pp. 267–284). New York: Springer.

Robertson, L.H. (2006) Learning to read properly by moving between parallel literacy classes. *Language and Education* 20, 44–61.

Setati, M., Adler, J., Reed, Y. and Bapoo, A. (2002) Incomplete journeys: Codeswitching and other language practices in mathematics, science and English language classrooms in South Africa. *Language and Education* 16, 128–149.

Shin, S.J. (2005) *Developing in Two Languages: Korean Children in America*. Clevedon: Multilingual Matters.

Silverstein, M. (2003) Indexical order and the dialectics of sociolinguistic life. *Language and Communication* 23, 193–229.

Sneddon, R. (2000) Language and literacy: Children's experience in multilingual environments. *International Journal of Bilingual Education and Bilingualism* 3, 265–282.

Swain, M. (1983) Bilingualism without tears. In M. Clarke, and J. Handscombe (eds) *On TESOL'82: Pacific Perspectives on Language Learning and Teaching* (pp. 35–46). Washington, DC: TESOL.

Zentella, A.C. (1981) *Tá bien*, you could answer me *en cualquier idioma*: Puerto Rican codeswitching in bilingual classrooms. In R.P. Duran (ed.) *Latino Language and Communicative Behavior* (pp. 109–131). Norwood, NJ: Ablex Publishing Corporation.

Chapter 2

Heteroglossia in a Multilingual Learning Space: Approaching Language beyond 'Lingualisms'

C. MICK

Introduction

'The individual voice can only make itself heard if it integrates itself in the complex choir of other voices that are already present' (Todorov, 1981: 8, referring to the Bakhtin Circle; author's translation). This hypothesis challenges the ideal of a standardising 'unitary language' (Holquist, 1981: xix, referring to the Bakhtin Circle) predominant even in Luxembourg (Mick, forthcoming). In spite of its institutional trilingualism and the important sociolinguistic and cultural diversity of its society, almost 40% of the schoolchildren do not have Luxembourgish nationality and declare not to speak one of the official languages at home.

This chapter analyses a literacy activity in German that was video-recorded in a second-grade primary classroom in Luxembourg during an exploratory ethnographic study on *Children's Plurilingualism* (Portante *et al.*, 2007). Based on Bakhtin's concept of heteroglossia, the article deconstructs language learning as a problem and investigates the observed actors' use of multiple semiotic resources or 'voices' to mediate their joint (learning) activity (Wertsch, 1991). The analysis shows that the legitimisation of linguistic diversity in the sense of the Multiliteracies Project (Gee, 2000) does not exclude but fosters the joint re-/co-/construction (Mick, 2009) of a standard (written) language learning. Additionally, it empowers (Cummins, 1996; de Mejía, 2002) all implied actors to contribute actively to the constitution of a community of practice (Lave & Wenger, 1997).

Traditionally, we have [asked] which techniques of language training produce results that most closely approximate either a standard version of a language or some idea of what a 'native speaker' might sound like, assuming that indeed the 'problem' is language, and that language education can fix it. Here we are arguing that things are probably more complicated than that. That the 'problem' may not be language at all, but that language instead may be serving as a terrain for the construction of boundaries and relations of power in ways that are legitimate within dominant discursive regimes. (Heller, 2007: 345)

Through a social approach to bilingualism, Heller (2007: 345) develops an alternative scientific perspective on language learning. Instead of focusing on single language(s), it investigates the diversity of semiotic tools in interactive meaning-making processes.

According to Heller's analyses, the concepts of 'language' or bi-/multi-/plurilingualism are often subject to ideological interpretations. In order to avoid falling into the same 'ideological trap' (without the guarantee of not falling into another), the present chapter avoids talking about languages and instead focuses on the diversity of mediational means or semiotic resources (Wertsch, 1991) in the sense of Bakhtin's (in Holquist, 1981; Todorov, 1981) reflections on 'heteroglossia'. It asks which 'voices' the observed actors in a 'language learning' classroom situation in a Luxembourgish primary school refer to, when negotiating the social reality of the learning activity and of the classroom situation they constitute. The aim of this analytical perspective is to deconstruct language learning in multilingual, multicultural contexts as an educational problem and to reconstitute it as an integrated part of social practice in any classroom. It depicts pedagogic possibilities to simultaneously legitimate children's diverse voices and to foster their learning of a linguistic standard. It argues for a critical attitude towards language learning in the sense of Pennycook's concept of 'translingual activism':

> As educators, we need to understand that the spaces and cultures our students inhabit are to be found not so much in predefinitions of cultural or linguistic background, as in the transcultural flows with which our students engage. By seeing language education as a practice in translingual activism, we open up an important space both to oppose the incursion of homogeneous discourses and to look to multiple sources of cultural renewal. (Pennycook, 2006: 114)

Our analysis aims to show that the legitimisation of children's voices not only gives them the possibility to approach dominant discourses in their own way, but also contributes to a change of the institutional reality they are communicatively re-/co-/constituting through interactions.

Scope of the Research Question

Bakhtin's concepts of heteroglossia or 'multivoicedness' (in Holquist, 1981; Todorov, 1981) challenge a materialist, essentialist ideology of singular, homogeneous and countable languages (Heller, 2007; Makoni & Pennycook, 2008), that is silently present in ideological interpretations of the concepts of bi-/multi-/plurilingualism. Instead of focusing on the formal characteristics of a linguistic variety, Bakhtin stresses the social nature of interactive language uses as meaningful practices: 'There is no such thing as a "general language", a language that is spoken by a general voice, which may be divorced from a specific saying, which is charged with particular overtones. Language, when it *means*, is somebody talking to somebody else' (cited in Holquist, 1981: xxi).

The concept of 'voice' enlarges the analytical perspective on mediational means in general by taking into consideration the social embedment or situatedness of their individual uses, as well as the dialogic nature of communication processes: 'The use of the term *voice* provides a constant reminder that even psychological processes carried out by an individual in isolation are viewed as involving processes of a communicative nature' (Wertsch, 1991: 13). According to Bakhtin (cited in Todorov, 1981: 77), utterances always stand in 'intertextual (or dialogic) relations' with other utterances that (might) have been or could/will be pronounced. Bailey (2007: 267) describes the advantages of 'heteroglossia' as an analytical concept as follows, by stressing the dimension of 'meaning':

(a) heteroglossia can encompass socially meaningful forms in both bilingual and monolingual talk;
(b) it can account for the multiple meanings and readings of forms that are possible, depending on one's subject position; and
(c) it can connect historical power hierarchies to the meanings and valences of particular forms in the here-and-now.

The current analysis is not only interested in the variety of voices as such, but studies them as mediational means for specific communicational strategies, that is, as situated social practice. It aims at interpreting the 'relations between discourse, practice, materiality and social action' (McIlvenny & Raudaskoski, 2005: 63), and questions the social reality speakers are co-/re-/constructing through the use of specific semiotic resources, be they officially considered 'languages' or not. The observations are used in order to deduce pedagogical conclusions regarding language learning in multilingual and multicultural contexts.

'Lingualisms' in Luxembourg and Its Educational System

The data for the present chapter have been collected through participant observation in an exploratory project on *Children's Plurilingualism* in Luxembourgish primary schools (Portante *et al.*, 2007). This project depicts a very relevant tension in the observed classrooms between children's heterogeneous life-world reality (Schütz & Luckmann, 1973) and an institutionally maintained ideal of a single, holistic and unitary language. Although school life in Luxembourg is officially trilingual, Portante (Portante & Mick, 2008) identifies a 'monolingual habitus' inside the educational system. The three official languages, Luxembourgish (a Moselle Franconian Germanic variety), German and French, are introduced at school as separate realities and for different contexts and subjects.

According to Weber (2009b: 136), 'monolingual identification with Luxembourgish' predominates educational policy for pre-school and also tends to become more and more popular in society in general. The Ministry of Education (MENFP, 1998: 9f) stresses the use of Luxembourgish in kindergarten (from age 3 to 5) as a means for 'integration'. Then, the official primary school curriculum (from age 6 to 12) only dedicates one hour per week to learning Luxembourgish as a subject, and constrains the use of Luxembourgish as a medium of instruction to sports, music and arts lessons. Officially, German is considered as the main medium of instruction for basic literacy. During the first three years of primary school, the curriculum allocates eight to nine hours of German language learning as a subject per week, and five lessons from the fourth year on. Learning the French language as a subject in primary school officially starts in the second year with three (during the first year of French learning) to seven hours of lessons per week (MENFP, 1998). French is meant to gradually replace German as medium of instruction in the transition from primary to secondary school, except in the technical secondary school sector. Nevertheless, according to ethnographic observations, Luxembourgish remains the privileged language for oral interaction throughout early and primary education (Fehlen, 2006), whereas German and French are mainly introduced as means for written communication (Horner, 2009).

Prevailing purist conceptions of languages and linguistic standards (Auer & Wei, 2007) as well as essentialist interpretations of language competences furthermore tend to exclude a huge variety of the social languages (Gee, 2008) students bring into school (Weber, 2009b). Everyday reality in Luxembourg is characterised by a complex sociocultural and linguistic diversity. Statistics on nationality or language may allow for a rough approximation, but they hardly grasp its most particular features, the interplay and emergence of a huge plurality of linguistic varieties, contact languages and hybrid language uses (Ehrhart, 2009): 42.6% of the resident population of Luxembourg do not have a Luxembourgish passport (2008) – a record compared to other EU member states.[1] The majority of them have a passport from another EU member state: Portugal (15.8%), France (5.5%), Italy (3.9%), Belgium (3.4%) or another EU country (7.9%); only 6.0% of the resident 'foreigners' have a passport from a non-EU country (Statec, 2008: 9). Furthermore, 40.9% of the general workforce in Luxembourg are non-resident border-crossing commuters who regularly come from France (50.4%), Belgium (25.7%) and Germany (23.3%) in order to work in the Grand Duchy (Statec, 2008: 12).

Additionally to the use of Luxembourgish, the great majority of the residing population in Luxembourg declares using French in everyday interactions.[2] According to an ethnographic study among youths with a Portuguese migration background, French tends to be the language they use most and identify with most (Weber, 2009b: 144). German, formerly the most important language in mass media, is decreasing in popularity. English is considered as the most important language on the private Luxembourgish employment market, besides French (Kingsley, 2009). Moreover, Portuguese, Italian, Spanish, Flemish-Dutch and other languages are frequently used as resources inside specific sociocultural environments of the Luxembourgish society (Fehlen, 2009). A total of 51% of the primary school children studied in the above-mentioned project (Portante *et al.*, 2007) declared that Luxembourgish is the spoken language most often used at home, for 19% of them it is Portuguese, for 14% French, as well as 16% for other languages (approximately 3% for Italian and German) (Maurer *et al.*, 2007). All children declare using more than one language at home, and as the statistics show, their home language choice does not always correspond to the official languages of Luxembourg (Portante *et al.*, 2008). Due to this sociocultural and linguistic diversity, the voices children are in contact with and develop in their everyday life are far from the institutionally maintained model of the coexistence of three unitary standard languages.

The data the present chapter is based on have to be situated in this specific contextual tension. The observed learning activity took place in a 2nd grade class in a Luxembourgish primary school. There were four actors: two children, Roberto[3] and David, as well as a project assistant, Irina, with a Portuguese family background, and Francesco, a teacher with an Italian family background. The languages used in the data excerpts are Portuguese, Luxembourgish, German and French. Roberto and David both speak mostly Portuguese at home; Roberto says he has some contact with French at home and David uses some Luxembourgish with his siblings. According to their own statements, they both started to learn Luxembourgish mainly at the kindergarten and came into contact with German when they started school.

During the observed activity, the children were working on the computer on their own narration of a European soccer championship match where Italy was playing against Portugal. First, they handwrote a draft of the text in Luxembourgish and then typed it in German on the computer. At the moment of the video-recording, Irina sat next to the children and started talking to them. Irina stated that she did not speak German, the language of the text the children were working on. Francesco joined the group from time to time, either because the children asked him to or on his own initiative. The observed activity constitutes a kind of 'third space' (Gutiérrez, 2008) inside the classroom, situated at the intersection between institutional and life-world discourses. It followed the official curriculum and aimed at learning written standard German, but also included children's home experiences[4]: the children's text referred to the European soccer championship in 2004 which took place in Portugal and which was a particularly important event for the Portuguese community in Luxembourg. The match between Portugal and Italy the children invented in their story might have been inspired by an actual encounter of these national teams in the U21 European soccer championship in 2004, or by the children's and the teacher's respective Portuguese/Italian socio-cultural family background. The specific close, protected and confidential interaction invited the children to draw on a variety of voices for their communicational aims, be they institutionally legitimated or not.

Italy against Portugal: Learning German through Soccer

The most striking feature of the data excerpt is the interlocutors' use of different languages in order to mediate their joint interaction. Switches between languages – formally highlighted in the transcript[5] – mostly seem to be motivated by the shared linguistic resources of the respective interlocutors aimed at achieving mutual understanding. Whereas the interaction with the text on the computer screen (reading, correcting) took place in German, the interactions between the children and the project assistant took place in Portuguese. Students interacted in Luxembourgish with the teacher. The two adults spoke to each other in French, and the children switched between Luxembourgish and Portuguese when talking to one another. Sometimes the specific language choice seemed to be motivated by other voices, which will be mentioned afterwards.

We identified and characterised five individual voices in the excerpt we analysed: Roberto's, David's, the project assistant's, the spell-checker's and the teacher's. These mediational means are interwoven with each other as well as with additional voices that cannot be attributed to a single person or physic entity. This will be illustrated in the following data excerpt. In the transcribed excerpt, Irina (I) joined the group of Roberto (R) and David (D) who were working on the computer. She addressed them for the first time:

1 **I: P** was there a problem?
2 **D: P** what?
3 **I: P** was there a problem; (.) are you repairing?
4 **R: P** over there.
             ((R points on the screen))
5 **I: P** or what what should be there;
6 **R: G** a:nd.
7 **I: P** Ah:: (0,2) and david what do you think (0,4) was it wrong.
8 **D: P** (no::) i think it was (0,4) because here (.) here it goes is wrong here here here here (.) because there is this thing here below.
             ((D points several words on the screen that have been underlined by the spell-checker))

Irina asked questions and tried to get general information on what was going on (1) or on what they were doing (3). She followed Roberto's respondent pointing (4) and asked for details concerning the activity they were currently accomplishing (5). She included David in the interaction asking him for his opinion (6). She was behaving as a prudent newcomer who tries to participate in the ongoing activity without imposing her way of acting.

Although David was the first one reacting to the project assistant's question (2), Roberto's voice seemed to be privileged, because he constructed himself as an expert with regard to the ongoing activity: with a resolute attitude, he showed Irina that they were actually communicating with the spell-checker's voice when she joined the group (8). While explaining this, he constantly gazed at the computer screen and pointed with his finger towards the underlined words of the text (4). In a sense, he even took over the voice of the spell-checker by pronouncing the 'correct' form of the underlined word he was pointing to (6).

Roberto's relation to the other voices can be characterised by 'ventrilo-quations' (Bakhtin, cited in Holquist, 1981), that is, by his use of other voices for his communicational aims. For example, he picked up the adjective 'magic' (195) Irina had introduced at three different moments. But by doing so, he also transforms it into his individual approach:

195	**I: P**	the teacher makes magic:, and baps

270	**D: L**	*ö. (1,0) how do we make the ö. =*
271	**R: L**	*= i know. (2,7) m:a:g:::i:c::.*
		((inserts the required letter; sings the adjective 'magic'))

387	**R: L(F)**[6]	*magi:c.*
		((F had just changed the size of the letters))

446	**R: L(F)**	*u:o:: it's magi:c. (1,0) look. (0,3) they take some sheets.*
		((looks at the printer))

Roberto not only changed the prosodic features of the pronunciation of 'magic', but also adapted it to the language he was using. He seemed to integrate Irina's word in his own voice in an individual manner.

By contrast, David's voice seems to depend to an essential degree on other mediational means available in this context: in a docile manner, he took over the voice of the project assistant when using the same verb in his answer (I: *what do you think* (7); D: *I think that* (8)). He also approached the position of the spell-checker: he translated the spell-checker's visual voice with an accompanying gesture, pointing at the underlined words (8), and adopted the spell-checker's perspective by replacing the local adverb *there*. The project assistant and Roberto used to talk about the text (1, 3, 4, 5) by its antonym *here* (8). Whereas Roberto used ventriloquations of other voices to articulate and design his own voice autonomously, David seemed to struggle with and subordinate to the voices to which he refers. The most obvious example was his constant use of the word 'fault' in German (or perhaps Luxembourgish[7]):

19	**D: P, G**	It's a <u>fault::,</u>

166	**D: P, G**	it is still (like this) <u>fault</u>- (.) still (there)- =

281	**D: P, G**	but it's a <u>fault;</u>
282	**I: P**	A?
283	**D: P, G**	it's a <u>fault;</u> =
284	**I: P, G**	=it's a <u>fault</u>? (.) what is <u>fault</u>.
285	**D**	e::m::-
286	**I: P**	it's wrong? =
287	**D: P**	= (yes) it's wrong; yes; =
288	**I**	= h::a:.

289	**R: P**	( ) it's also bad (1,5) (no) (3,9) once more.
		((R works on the computer))
290	**D: P**	it's bad. =

Due to the formal characteristics, the German/Luxembourgish word 'fault' seems to have originated from another voice that significantly influenced David's reality construction in this specific language-learning classroom context. It is the voice of the unitary standard language ideology he apparently got in contact with in German or Luxembourgish. The excerpt additionally insinuates that this word does not only lack formal integration in David's voice, but that furthermore, he seems to struggle with its meaning: He does not spontaneously find an equivalent formulation in Portuguese, but he confirms Irina's suggestion of translation. Probably, the institutional significance of a 'fault' as a mechanism of sanction David is exposed to at school (Mick, forthcoming) did not correspond to the use of the same concept in his primary socialisation.

In the analysed excerpt, this institutional concept of 'fault' was alluded to by Francesco and Irina when they talked in French, but this happened after David's first use of the concept:

119	**I: F**	**but there are some faults**;
		((to F))
120	**F: F**	[...] **let's have a look at the faults**;

The normative discourse it implies is furthermore represented in the following verbalisations of Irina and Francesco:

5	**I: P**	what what should be written there;

197	**F: L**	*how do we write* [...]

The same *normative discourse* also seemed to have guided Roberto's and David's activity from the beginning. They spontaneously interpreted Irina's introductory questions about whether there was a *problem* (1, 3) and whether they *were repairing* (3), as references to the correction of the text. The data do not show explicitly what motivated them to do so; but as David's statement (8) insinuates, the children were particularly intrigued by the fact that the spell-checker marked so many words in the text. It seems as if they considered this activity as a competition against the computer's spell-checker, and as a playful or aesthetic issue of the work they were doing: while David used the spell-checker's indications to structure the ongoing action (in Portuguese: *(now) we have to correct this one* (154)) Roberto was counting down the underlined words they were to erase (in Portuguese: *five left*, 155).

Language and orthography learning seem not to be their first and predominant aim, but it was exactly what they were concentrating on.

Two additional non-personified 'voices' further intersect with this specific plurality of mediational means: a discourse on belonging or membership and a discourse on soccer matches. The first one became relevant when Irina discussed with the children why the spell-checker underlined some of the names of the Portuguese football players in the soccer team. Roberto quickly solved this 'problem' by referring to the language difference (12). David, on the contrary, continued to consider the spell-checker as an authority and looked for a correction or a translation of the names (13, 17, 19, 369) – although he was the first one in defining the spelling of the name as correct (in Portuguese: *he::re: it's okay; (.) simão (0,4) written. (10)*). Irina ended the discussion by legitimating their collective authority regarding the spell-checker in this specific case with a *membership discourse*: (in Portuguese) *we are Portuguese and we know that simão is correctly written* (25). Through the formulation of this sentence in the first-person plural she groups different voices into one common category (*we – Portuguese*) and links the membership of this category to experience and knowledge. The same idea is also resonating in the teacher's allusion to a normative discourse previously quoted (in Luxembourgish: *how do we write*, 197). The category referred to by the personal pronoun 'we' also constructs a community of practice related to the ongoing social activity.

This membership discourse in the observed interaction was closely linked to the soccer match of the Italian and Portuguese national teams in the children's text. The story briefly mentioned that Portugal lost the game, but finished with ambiguous words about the superiority of one of the teams. The teacher drew the children's attention to this ambiguity (233) in their story, so that they were pushed to clearly define the winner as can be seen in the following excerpt:

231	**R**	Portugal. =
232	**D**	= [Portugal.]
233	**F: L, G**	[a:hh:a.] (0,4) <u>but one cannot see that. one cannot understand this here. (0,6) look (.) but Portugal against Italy, (0,3) but they will win. (0,6) Italy will win.</u>
234	**D + R: L**	*no::::.*
		((R looks at F, R + D smile))
235	**F: L**	*or not.* [(*no?*)]
236	**D: G**	<u>[bu]t (0,4) Portugal-</u> =

237	**F: F**	**= I said that one cannot understand (0,3) who will win. m?=**
		((F talks to I, laughs))
238	**I: F**	**= I understood;**
		((laughs))
239	**F: L(F), G**	*ok* <u>Portugal against Italy;</u>
		((F talks to the children))
240	**I: F**	**but I also see that the one behind, he also has some Italian features;**
		((I to F; laughs))
241	**F: F**	**some few;**
		((laughs))

The teacher's opposite suggestion to define Italy as the overall winner (233) was considered by the children as a joke. Irina interpreted it ironically and linked it to Francesco's biography and knowledge of Italian culture (240). Francesco confirmed this in an equally ironic manner (241). Later, David also used this kind of discourse on belonging in order to legitimate the definition of the Portuguese team as winner, no matter the specific score of the match their story narrated:

261	**F: G, L, G**	= <u>Portugal will (.) win</u> (0,5) *let's write* <u>Italy will win.</u>
262	**D + R: L**	*no:::.*
263		((they all laugh)) (4,2)
264	**D: L**	*i am not from [ITAly.]*

Here, David and Roberto decided to protest (262) against Francesco's suggestion and David stressed his membership in negative terms (in Luxembourgish: *I am not from ITAly* (264)) as a good reason for defining Portugal as the overall winner. Furthermore, this membership discourse was doubled through David's red sweatshirt with the design of the national soccer team of Portugal, stating *Portugal* in big yellow letters on the back. The 'Portuguese team' finally won in a twofold sense, because David and Roberto succeeded in imposing their version of the text. The written story maintained its ambiguity, because it declared Italy as the winner of this specific match, but evaluated Portugal as the superior team (330–334):

330	**F: L, G, L**	= *here we are.* (1,7) <u>when Portugal (plays) against Italy, Italy (0,3) will win.</u> (1,0) *no?*
331	**R: L**	*n:o[o:].*
332	**D**	[Po:rt]u:g:al:. =

333	**R**	= Por[tugal:.]
334	**F: L**	*[a: ok.] (0,6) then write Po:rtugal:.*
		((F leaves))

The children – particularly David – were experts in many more dimensions of this *soccer discourse*. They knew all the names of the Portuguese players (Simão (10, 18, 62, 64), Nuno Gomes (35, 36, 40, 44), Figo (33, 38), Ricardo (48), Luis (15), Deco (67, 69)) and they were able to identify the name Totti (374) as the name of a player from the Italian team. Despite the teacher's suggestion, they decided to exclude this name from their text (376).

Additionally, David was an expert regarding the symbolic function of colours in the soccer and membership discourse. It became relevant when Roberto, at the end of the correction process, demanded to colour the heading of the text:

413	**R: L**	*and:: colour there; (0,2) again?*
		((R points something on the screen))
414	**F: L**	*yes. (0,5) do you want to colour the title. =*
415	**D: L**	*= yes. (.) we want red. =*
416	**R: L**	*= gr:een.*
417	**F: L**	*or blue like Italy.*
418	**R: L**	*gre- [(0,6) em:] (0,5) or:ange. (0,2) orange.*
419	**D**	*[n::]*
420	**D: L**	*no no no. red. (0,9) red. (0,5) [it is with Portugal.]*
421	**R: L**	*[green green green.]*
422		((F works on the computer)) (2,2)
423	**R: L**	*That is better. green.*
424	**D: L**	*no:. (.) that is from sporting. (1,2) but.*
425	**R: L**	*but I want- (0,8) orange like- (1,4) like- =*
426	**D: L**	*no =*
427	**R: L**	*= like Portugal.*
428	**D: L**	*no. (0,5) no.*
429	**F: L**	*which colour do you want. =*
430	**D: L**	*= e::m::: (.) red.*

Roberto proposed two different colours (green (416, 421, 423) and orange (418, 425)), but he could not legitimise his choice in the same quick and convincing manner as David did (*we want red*, 415). The latter did not only present his choice of colour as a collective decision (*we want*), but also used an elaborated argumentation for and against other colours. He knew that green was the colour of another Portuguese soccer club (424) and stressed that the Portuguese national team uses red (420) – and this after the teacher had proposed to colour the heading in *blue like Italy* (417). Apparently, Roberto was not as informed about this specific soccer discourse as David because he defined orange (the official colour of the Dutch soccer team) as the colour of Portugal (425, 427). David finally succeeded in imposing his choice because he was the first one to answer the teacher's question *which colour do you want?* (429). The letters of their text's heading were consequently formatted in red.

Heterogeneity of the Ongoing Social Action

The analysis of heteroglossia in the observed excerpts can be used to re-/co-/constitute the heterogeneous diversity of the social actions taking place in the classrooms. A main interest of all the participants was to correct the text, that is, to make it conform to standard. Even before explicitly being asked to correct the text, the children had already tried to get rid of the words underlined by the spell-checker. In David's case, the main motivation seemed to come from his submission to the unitary language ideology, as the continuous use of the German word 'fault' shows. Besides, the competition against the spell-checker seemed to present an important incentive, and Roberto then linked the whole activity to aesthetic questions, because he made the teacher format the text nicely (font size (389), 392; colour (413)). These last motivating factors become particularly important because the whole activity was linked to questions of authorship and membership, that is to the interlocutors' interactive individual and collective identity construction.

While correcting this text, the interlocutors were simultaneously negotiating their respective social roles as teachers and pupils, members or non-members, experts or novices, newcomers and insiders, authors of the text and reviewers, winners or losers, fans or opponents. The voices used as mediational means were as heterogeneous as the different social roles the children assumed: whereas David presented himself as an expert regarding the symbolism of colours in the soccer discourse (413–430), Roberto acted as superior in correcting (and translating (33–77)) the text. The children imposed their interpretation of the superiority of the Portuguese team on the teacher, but at the same time they let the Italian team win in their story. The teacher 'lost the struggle' regarding the children's final evaluation of the two soccer teams, but he remained an expert when making the children discover correct orthography (128–145, 156–158, 197–205, 302–307, 360–362, 381–383). The spell-checker was constructed as an authority in identifying errors, above all by David; however, regarding the spelling of Portuguese names, the children noticed that its 'knowledge' was constrained. David was an expert at finding strategies to exploit the spell-checker's functions for his own aims. He subsequently typed various alternatives of the underlined words and let the spell-checker decide which one was correct (169–185, 213–224). Roberto was an expert at using the keyboard of the computer; he found the key for writing the letter 'ö' (271) for which David had been searching for quite a long time (268–272).

The analysis of the project assistant's position showed that the roles of newcomers and old-timers also had to be negotiated. The boundaries of the interactively re-/co-/constructed community of practice (Lave & Wenger, 1997) are not only predefined through former social practice but are constituted together with other social roles. Irina at the beginning took over a novice attitude regarding the children (1, 3, 5, 7, 9, 18, 25, 30, 32, . . .), but she also emphasised an old-timer role concerning the collective knowledge of 'the Portuguese' (25). She gave executive power to the children in domains that apparently were reserved to the teacher (406), when she accepted David's proposal to print the text (111, 114) and almost executed it. Although David seemed to respect Irina as an authority, since at the beginning, he followed her advice and work assignments (7, 32), he overtly questioned her role as an expert in the discussion about the spell-checker's authority (19, 373). Francesco reconstructed Irina's expert role at the expense of the spell-checker by asking her for a confirmation concerning the spelling of a name (397). Interestingly, this deconstruction of the spell-checker's authority provoked David's laughter (402).

The project assistant's presence also seemed to promote the re-negotiation of the relationship between Roberto and David and between the teacher and the children, by legitimating Portuguese and a membership discourse as additional mediational means for interaction. Although the children jointly protested against the teacher's suggestion to declare Italy as the winner of the soccer match, they did not always behave as a unanimous collective. For example during the translation of the German text into Portuguese Irina had asked for (33–77), Roberto seemed to be competing with David. He corrected him, interrupted him, made him reconsider sentences he had already translated and so forth (33–77). But, at the end of the excerpt, it was David who imposed his suggestion to colour the heading (413).

The teacher at the same time accepted Roberto's suggestion to colour the heading and David's choice of a colour. He also accepted the children's definition of Portugal as the better soccer team and made them write this on the computer. Thus, he symbolically joined the children's collective identity construction and contributed to the constitution of an equal, symmetrical relationship, although giving them instructions. He also actively contributed to the inclusion of the project assistant in this interactively constructed community.

By negotiating social roles and social relationships, all the interlocutors also negotiate (i.e. learn to negotiate) their individual and collective identities as insiders or outsiders of a community that emerges from this interactive practice. Nobody is stuck in an institutionally imposed identity according to her/his performance of the standard language (Mick, forthcoming), but everybody is invited to negotiate his/her social position, personal preferences and identity inside the group through the use of various semiotic tools for their communicational aims, based on individual biographies and lived experience. They learn to defend their own opinion, position and identity through arguments that take into consideration the specific situated context of the ongoing interaction and of the community as it is being shaped through these negotiations. And by being accepted as equal participants, no matter what semiotic tools they use, they also (learn to) contribute actively to the joint re-/co-/constitution of a community of practice and thus to 'integration' in the sense given by Touraine (1994: 209; author's translation): 'For integration to exist, an individual or collective subject must be able to modify a social or cultural entity, which means that the importance lies as much on identity as on participation'.

Multilingualism and Heteroglossic Approaches to Language Learning

An approach to language learning through Bakhtin's concept of heteroglossia helps to deconstruct language learning and language or linguistic diversity as a problem, and to propose an alternative approach. Our analysis shows that linguistic diversity and diversity of voices do not cause any problem to the observed primary school children. They are capable of simultaneously using (and thus learning to use) a huge variety of 'voices' and to integrate different, even competing discourses, languages and realities in their communicational strategies. It may be a problem for them to deal with an imposed discourse as David's specific references to 'faults' indicate. But if they are allowed to draw on individual resources, strategies and preferences they are empowered to approach other, even institutionally dominant discourses in their own way. In the observed excerpt, even David approaches the normative discourse, through its embedding in a huge diversity of interacting and mutually fostering voices. This corresponds to Todorov's (1981: 8, referring to the Bakhtin Circle; author's translation) conclusion regarding the necessarily heteroglossic nature of communication processes: 'The individual voice can only make itself heard if it integrates itself in the complex choir of other voices that are already present.'

In combination with theories on learning in general, the observations we made allow for drawing pedagogical conclusions regarding heteroglossic learning contexts. The legitimisation of various 'voices' in the learning process allows children to contextualise the activity in their specific, situated biographies and to integrate new voices in their prior experience and individual expertise: for example, in domains like soccer, spelling, computer literacy, narration, translation and so on. It thus increases their motivation and allows for episodic learning, two factors with positive effects on the memorisation process as has been shown in neuroscience research (Spitzer, 2007). It gives children the possibility to re-/co-/construct knowledge and reality and not just to reproduce them. According to constructivist theories, this is a vital feature for learning processes to take place (Bruner, 1996).

It is also important to notice that in the context of our observation, children were not only legitimated to draw on their individual semiotic resources, but they were also accepted as equal participants in the re-/co-/construction of social reality. None of the voices were *a priori* defined as privileged (Wertsch, 1991: 14), in spite of the institutional context of the observed interaction. Of course, the correction activity was an important concern for all the interlocutors in the observed excerpt, but the specific interaction did not construct it as more important than the discussions about membership, the negotiations of roles or relationships or the development of expertise in other fields. This specific kind of heteroglossic learning context increases children's possibilities and the motivation of participation in interaction processes, which Lave and Wenger (2007) consider the most important factor of learning. It makes it possible for the children to participate in the negotiations of almost all features of the classroom reality, and simultaneously allows for individual and collective identity construction inside an emerging community of practice. Interlocutors thus contribute actively to construct bridges between themselves and the community they jointly constitute, in the same way as in the multi-literacies project (Gee, 2000; New London Group, 1996). They are allowed to play a part in the co-/re-/construction of the community of practice, its hierarchies and dominant discourse, as in critical pedagogy approaches (Freire & Macedo, 1987). Heteroglossic learning contexts consequently foster the cohesion and 'integration' of learning communities and thus promote ideal conditions for joint social (learning) practice.

Finally, we would like to clarify the relation between heteroglossia and multilingualism: The analysis insinuates that in a multilingual learning environment, the emergence and valorisation of heteroglossia are essentially linked to legitimating the social languages (Gee, 2008) children bring to the classroom. It requires a questioning of the ideology of a unitary language through legitimating the children's ventriloquation of various voices, whether or not they conform to the standard. This attitude simultaneously implies a critical deconstruction of ideological concepts of 'languages' as a tool for the maintenance of historically grown social hierarchies in the sense of Gee:

> It is through attempts to deny this inevitable multiplicity and indeterminacy of interpretation that social institutions (like schools) and elite groups in a society often privilege their own version of meaning as if it were natural, inevitable, and incontestable. It is by stressing this multiplicity and indeterminacy – in the context of searching and ongoing investigations of meaning – that the rest of us can resist such domination. (Gee, 2008: 129)

Legitimating multilingualism in this broad sense described above, allows for reconstituting the social role of language beyond unitary language ideologies (Makoni & Pennycook, 2008). It does not mean denying the pragmatic sense of linguistic standards for communication in larger communities of practice. However, it means looking carefully at social power relations that are fostered and co-/re-/reproduced through ideologically motivated uses of 'language' for social exclusion, domination or subordination. It re-/co-/constitutes language as a means for communication, dialogue and mutual understanding in the sense of Bakhtin, or 'integration' in the sense of Touraine. A heteroglossic approach to language learning questions the one-to-one analogy between language and community: The membership discourse in the observed excerpt constructs a link between community membership and knowledge and might tend to reproduce such a one-to-one analogy. However, the specific features of the observed social practice invite the interlocutors to co-/re-/construct the community of practice inside a classroom through the joint accomplishment of a task, irrespective of their individual language experience, their family background or their institutionally attributed role. A heteroglossic approach to language learning considers communities, that is collective as well as individual identities, as interactively re-/co-/constructed through the use of semiotic tools, be they officially considered 'languages' or not. If some of these resources are forbidden and others privileged, some voices are excluded from the interactive construction of reality – and thus from learning processes. But if the linguistic standard is pragmatically considered as only one semiotic tool among others, whose ideological and social implications are critically questioned, and if a 'broad' sense of multilingualism, is considered as 'normal', children are invited and empowered to take part in social interaction, collective meaning-making processes, and thus engage in learning processes.

Transcription conventions

[	overlapping
:	syllabic lengthening
(..... 1,0)	very short/short/medium break/break of 1,0 sec
, ?; .	rising/falling intonation
( )	unsure transcription
(( ))	comment
=	agglutination

Notes

1. From the 1960s onwards, a steady immigration of workforce started, with an important increase in the 1970s (Statec, 2008).
2. Only 3% of the population declares to speak only one language, the Francophones being the majority of them (14%) (Fehlen, 2009: 79).
3. The names in this chapter have all been replaced by pseudonyms.
4. The general task of writing a story in German was part of the children's weekly 'work plan' which they were allowed to organise on their own. The field notes do not permit an exact reconstruction of the choice of the subject of the story, but in general, the teacher tried to take into consideration the children's own experiences and preferences when designing a task or when giving them the possibility to fulfil a task on their own.
5. The letter(s) after the abbreviation for the speaker indicate(s) the language(s) that is (are) used. "I: P" means that Irina is speaking in Portuguese, L is used for Luxembourgish, G for German and F for French. The language choices are also indicated through underlines (German), italics (Luxembourgish), bold (French) or 'normal' formatting (Portuguese) in the transcribed text.
6. The indication L (F) is chosen when the choice of vocabulary is the expression of a variety of Luxembourgish that is more influenced by and oriented on the French lexicon.
7. The pronunciation of the German and the Luxembourgish word 'Fehler' is very similar. The audio-recording of the observed interactions do not allow for an accurate differentiation.

References

Auer, P. and Wei, L. (2007) Introduction: Multilingualism as a problem? Monolingualism as a problem? In P. Auer and L. Wei (eds) *Handbook of Multilingualism and Multilingual Communication* (pp. 1–14). Berlin: Mouton de Gruyter.

Bailey, B. (2007) Heteroglossia and boundaries. In M. Heller (ed.) *Bilingualism: A Social Approach* (pp. 257–274). New York: Palgrave Macmillan.

Bruner, J. (1996) *The Culture of Education*. Cambridge: Harvard University Press.

Cummins, J. (ed.) (1996) *Negotiating Identities: Education for Empowerment in a Diverse Society* (1st edn). Ontario: California Association for Bilingual Education.

De Mejía, A-M. (2002) *Power, Prestige and Bilingualism: International Perspectives on Elite Bilingualism*. Clevedon: Multilingual Matters.

Ehrhart, S. (2009) Wie viele Köpfe soll der Drache tragen – oder: Wie mehrsprachig sind Schule und Gesellschaft in Luxemburg [Electronic Version]. *metaphorik.de*, 16 (Metapher und Wissenstransfer), 29–46. http://www.metaphorik.de/16/Ehrhart.pdf. Accessed 01.09.09.

Freire, P. and Macedo, D.P. (1987) *Literacy. Reading the World and the World*. Westport: Bergin & Garvey.

Fehlen, F. (2006) Réformer l'enseignement des langues. A propos de la nouvelle politique linguistique du Ministère de l'Education Nationale [Electronic Version]. *SATDE Working Paper, 1-06*. www.uni.lu/content/download/7990/132517/file/PROFIL%20LANGUES.pdf. Accessed 16.04.08.

Fehlen, F. (2009) *BaleineBis. Une enquête sur un marché linguistique multilingue en profonde mutation*. Luxembourg: SESOPI Centre Intercommunautaire.

Gee, J.P. (2000) New people in new worlds. In B. Cope and M. Kalantzis (eds) *Multiliteracies. Literacy Learning and the Design of Social Futures* (pp. 43–68). London: Routledge.

Gee, J.P. (2008) *Social Linguistics and Literacies: Ideology in Discourse*. London: Taylor & Francis Ltd.

Gutiérrez, K.D. (2008) Developing a sociocritical literacy in the third space. *Reading Research Quarterly* 43 (2), 148–164.

Heller, M. (2007) The future of 'bilingualism'. In M. Heller (ed.) *Bilingualism: A Social Approach* (pp. 340– 345). New York: Palgrave Macmillan.

Holquist, M. (ed.) (1981) *The Dialogic Imagination. Five Essays by M.M. Bakhtin*. Austin: University of Texas Press.

Horner, K. (2009) Language policy mechanisms and social practices in multilingual Luxembourg. *Language Problems & Language Planning* 33, 101–111.

Kingsley, L. (2009) Explicit and implicit dimensions of language policy in multilingual banks in Luxembourg. An analysis of top-down and bottom-up pressures. *Language Problems & Language Planning* 33 (2), 152–173.

Lave, J. and Wenger, E. (2007) *Situated Learning. Legitimate Peripheral Participation*. New York: Cambridge University Press.

Makoni, S. and Pennycook, A. (2008) *Disinventing and Reconstituting Languages*. Clevedon: Multilingual Matters.

Maurer, M.P., Fixmer, P. and Boualam, R. (2007) *Language Uses in Family Contexts of 3 to 9 Years Old Children in Luxembourg*. Unpublished draft report. Luxembourg: University of Luxembourg.

McIlvenny, P. and Raudaskoski, P. (2005) Mediating discourses of transnational adoption on the internet. In S. Norris and R. H. Jones (eds) *Discourse in Action. Introducing Mediated Discourse Analysis* (pp. 62–72). London: Routledge.

MENFP (1998) Pour une école d'intégration. Constats – questions – perspectives [Electronic Version]. http://www.men.public.lu/sys_edu/scol_enfants_etrangers/pour_ecole_integration.pdf. Accessed 16.04.08.

Mick, C. (2009) *Diskurse von 'Ohnmächtigen'*. *Identitätskonstitution peruanischer Hausangestellter in Lima im Spannungsfeld ideologischer Strukturen*. Frankfurt am Main: Peter Lang Verlag.

Mick, C. (forthcoming) The social construction of 'school failure' and 'language problems'. In J-J. Weber (ed.) *Festschrift für Dominique Portante*. Luxembourg: Editions Phi.

New London Group (1996) A pedagogy of multiliteracies: Designing social futures. *Harvard Educational Review* 66, 1–27.

Pennycook, A. (2006) Language education as translingual activism. *Asia Pacific Journal of Education* 26, 111–114.

Portante, D. and Mick, C. (2008) *Multilingual Classroom Practices: Learning Integration from Children*. Paper presented at the Multilingual Europe Seminar on Integration and Achievement in a Multilingual Europe: Languages for Learning and Life.

Portante, D., Arend, B., Boualam, R., Fixmer, P., Max, C., Elcheroth, S., Maurer-Hetto, M.P., Roth-Dury, E. and Sunnen, P. (2007) *Children's Plurilingualism up to 9 Years: Linguistic Diversity, Learning Luxembourgish and Emergent Literacies. Final Report*. Luxembourg: University of Luxembourg and National Research Fund.

Portante, D., Arend, B., Bodé, S., Elcheroth, S., Jaminet, J. and Mick, C. (2008) Littératies plurilingues: diversité et avenirs socioculturels des enfants. Défis – ressources – opportunités. *d'Land*, 14–15.

Schütz, A. and Luckmann, T. (1973) *The Structures of the Life-World*. Evanston: Northwestern University Press.

Spitzer, M. (2007) *Lernen. Gehirnforschung und die Schule des Lebens*. München: Elsevier GmbH.

Statec (2008) Luxemburg in Zahlen [Electronic Version]. http://www.statec.lu. Accessed 02.09.09.

Todorov, T. (1981) *Mikhaïl Bakhtine. Le Principe Dialogique*. Paris: Editions du Seuil.

Touraine, A. (1994) *Qu'est-ce que la démocratie?* Paris: Librairie Arthème Fayard.

Weber, J.J. (2009a) *Multilingualism, Education and Change*. Frankfurt am Main: Peter Lang.

Weber, J.J. (2009b) Constructing Luxobourgish ethnicities. Implications for language-in-education policy. *Language Problems & Language Planning* 33, 132–152.

Wertsch, J.V. (1991) *Voices of the Mind. A Sociocultural Approach to Mediated Action*. Cambridge, MA: Harvard University Press.

Chapter 3

Children's Literature in the Multilingual Classroom: Developing Multilingual Literacy Acquisition

C. HÉLOT

Introduction

The aim of this chapter is to investigate the role of children's literature in bilingual and multilingual pedagogy and more precisely to look at the way in which authors, publishers and pedagogues deal with linguistic diversity and multilingualism. Through the analysis of translated, bilingual or dual-language books, we will try to uncover their representations of bilingualism and to explore the notion of multilingual literacies (Martin-Jones & Jones, 2000). The context of the research is the education of primary teachers working in both bilingual programmes and multilingual classrooms in France. The overall question we are investigating is how teachers can be educated to understand linguistic and cultural diversity and plurilingual practices in order to move beyond monoglossic ideologies of language and language use (García, 2009).

Our reflexion concerns teachers working in monolingual as well as bilingual programmes because, (1) we consider most mainstream classrooms as multilingual by the mere fact that many students speak languages other than the language of schooling, and as we have argued elsewhere (Hélot, 2008) we believe that all teachers today are concerned with multilingualism, and (2) bilingual education programmes still tend to be based on the principle of linguistic separation or *the two solitudes assumption* as expressed by Cummins (2007), where instructional strategies lead to a form of double monolingualism rather than real bilingual language use in the classroom.

This research is part of a wider project aiming at transforming the monolingual habitus of French primary schools (Hélot, 2007) and it looks more specifically at the literacy education of primary teachers in relation to multilingualism. Our main objective concerns student teachers; how they can be encouraged to develop different representations of linguistic and cultural diversity, and how they could be brought to envisage their multilingual classrooms as a safe space where they feel confident working with languages and cultures they do not necessarily know. Again, we need to stress that bilingual programmes are not very different from monolingual programmes: they do not necessarily cater for the plurilingual repertoire of all learners and some languages can be silenced in bilingual classrooms just as in monolingual classrooms. We are thinking in particular of minority languages spoken by immigrant populations which tend to remain on the margins of curricula for foreign or second-language teaching as well as in most bilingual education models in Europe.

While our previous work focused mainly on the analysis of various language-awareness projects (Hélot, 2008; Hélot & Young, 2006) as a first approach to developing plurilingual education, in the present chapter we are investigating the use of children's literature in translation and of bilingual and dual-language books by teachers and students in multilingual primary classrooms. Our objective here is to go beyond the celebration of linguistic and cultural diversity to actually encouraging teachers to use languages other than the school language in their literacy teaching; in other words, to help them to explore the literary world beyond national borders, to reflect on the process of translation and to start developing multilingual literacy practices in their class; that is reading and writing activities in languages other than French.

In the first part of the chapter, we will discuss the importance of looking at a work of literature as a product of a cultural and historical context, and the role of translation as offering an encounter with otherness through the mediation between different cultures. We will give some examples of the various ways in which the translation of children's literature can construct different relationships of alterity and in some cases negate cultural differences. In a second part, we will further analyse the role of translation in bilingual and multilingual books and explain how they can be used to welcome a multiplicity of languages and cultures in the classroom as well as provide support for the literacy acquisition of bilingual students. The last part will look at several multilingual children's books where no translation is offered: we will discuss the notion of translanguaging and analyse the way authors and publishers envisage language mixing and to what purpose. We will then argue for these books to be used as an incentive for students to write their own creative texts using several languages according to their own linguistic repertoires.

Our approach is interdisciplinary because our reflexion is framed within several fields: sociolinguistics, children's literature, translation, intercultural education and pedagogy. For example, the notions of language contact and translanguaging are useful to investigate the way in which languages are presented and distributed in bilingual and dual-language books and we argue that such choices for children's books reflect dominant representations of bilingualism, plurilingual practices and language learning. Because bilingual books imply the process of translation, we will refer to researchers working in the field of translation studies: we are interested in particular in the way they bring to light the interplay of relationships between different cultural contexts and literary productions in order to explore how translation mediates between different visions of the world and reveals different ideologies of language.

We consider literary translation as a form of intercultural experience, where the transfer from one language to another expresses different types of relationships between the two cultures involved as our example in the next section shows. In a sense, formal education is also about the negotiation of different cultural worlds, of more or less distant visions of the world and representations of knowledge and we know that the gap between home and school can be more difficult to negotiate for some children than others (Hélot, 2006). Our approach to intercultural education sees the negotiation between knowledge acquired in the home context and knowledge acquired at school as central to the learning process and to language and literacy acquisition (Gregory *et al.*, 2004; Kenner, 2000). This is the reason why, from a pedagogical point of view, we argue for the use of bilingual children's books: on the one hand they are a way of including bilingual learners and of supporting their home language and on the other, they give the opportunity to monolingual students to be challenged by difference; they also provide teachers with a chance to challenge ethnocentricism and to overcome their fear of having to deal with languages they do not know.

Moreover, we would like to make teachers aware that reading books in translation will open up the reading experiences of their students. Translations of children's books often underestimate the abilities of young readers to make sense of an unknown universe or of different cultures. In the case of bilingual teachers, as we have argued elsewhere (Benert & Hélot, 2007, 2009, 2010), it is most important that they are made to reflect on the translation process involving the cultural mediation of the two learning languages of their students. For example, working with both versions of a story and discussing it in both languages can provide an opportunity for the class to function in a bilingual mode, not to mention exploring difference and similarities and engaging in metalinguistic reflexion. We hope to show here that translated as well as bilingual and dual-language books can offer new pedagogical possibilities for teachers to venture into more creative approaches of literacy teaching and more specifically to start implementing multilingual literacy practices.

Children's Literature in Primary Education: Encountering Otherness through Translation

Since 2002, children's literature has been a major component of literacy acquisition in the French curriculum at primary level. Apart from the more formal acquisition of reading and writing the French language through the help of specific pedagogical readers and grammar books, the objectives of the ministerial directives insist on the development of a literary culture based on various works of children's literature. Spanning traditional tales to more contemporary authors and various genres, lists of recommended works for the three different 'cycles' of primary education have been published, and teachers are advised to select a number of books to read and study in class and at home.

These lists of children's books give authors' names, publishers and titles. Interestingly, a substantial number of books are translations into French of works originally written in different languages, but nowhere is there any mention that the book has been translated. We interpreted the inclusion of 'foreign' authors as a sign of cultural opening, a vision of literature going beyond national borders, a literary recognition of works produced in other countries and of their translation into French. However, when preparing trainee teachers to use some of these books in class, we noticed that their reception of translated works was no different from that of books written by French authors. For example, a very popular book in France is Anthony Browne's *Voices in the Park* (1998), rendered in French as *Histoire à quatre voix*.[1] When the student teachers chose this book to prepare literacy activities, they read it as if it had been written originally in French. They made no comments about the name of the author and did not ask any questions as to where he might come from. Apart from the park as a setting to the story, they made no references either to the location of the park (Central Park in New York), although it can clearly be deduced from the illustrations. In other words, the cultural context of the book did not strike the student teachers as specific to a particular culture and they read the book as if it were a French literary product.

One should not be surprised by such reading strategies on the part of our students, because none of them knew the original English version and it is generally believed that the aim of a translation is to make the process invisible. However, on looking more closely at the translation of this particular book, one might question the translation approach chosen, as we will see below. It should be stressed that we are not arguing at this point for the use of children's books in their original language. On the contrary, we would like to defend the role of translation in making many literary works available to a maximum of readers, but we also believe that translation should not necessarily be an invisible process (Oittinen, 2000). By making no mention of translation (and translators) in the lists proposed to teachers, the Ministry of Education probably wishes to insist on the universal value of children's literature published in different parts of the world; but, in practice, it makes teachers unaware of different literary traditions, not to mention of the dominance of the English-speaking world in children's books.

Browne's *Voices in the Park* was presented to the student teachers in its original English version and was going to reveal many surprises as compared to the French version. Apart from the translation of the title in French, which uncovers the whole point of the story and loses the sense of mystery expressed in English, we gave them page 4 of both books and asked them to compare the two versions. Our objective was to make teachers aware of the distance between the two texts and to reflect on the reasons that could have motivated the translator. The illustration is exactly the same in both editions and shows the mother in the park suddenly realising that she cannot see her son any longer. Table 3.1 presents the two texts.

Table 3.1 Comparison of the English and French versions of Brown's *Voices in the Park*

Language	*English*	*French*
Titles	*Voices in the Park*	*Histoire à quatre voix*
Extract from page 4	I was just planning what we should have to eat that evening when I saw Charles had disappeared. Oh dear! Where had he gone?	Je réfléchissais au menu du déjeuner – j'avais un joli reste de poulet, je pouvais le servir agrémenté d'une salade, ou bien décongeler l'un de mes délicieux potages –, lorsque je remarquai tout à coup que Charles avait disparu ! Mon Dieu ! Où était-il passé?[a]

[a]Which could be retranslated as 'I was reflecting upon the menu for the day. I had some lovely chicken left over. I could serve it along with a salad, or again defrost one of my delicious soups, when suddenly I noticed that Charles had disappeared! Oh dear! Where had he gone?'

Upon comparing both texts we would like to make an initial remark: the source text does not present any particular translation difficulty into French and a literal approach would not have robbed the story of any meaningful detail. The long digression in French about the meal (no longer dinner but lunch), is a perfect example of adaptation, domestication[2] (Oittinen, 2000) or foreignisation (Venuti, 1995): what we see here is the target text being placed in a linguistic and cultural context which is familiar to the target text reader, and through this process the experience of foreignness is negated. Adaptation or domestication happens to be a very common process in the translation of children's literature, and is often justified by pedagogical reasons. It reveals two things: the vision translators (or publishers) have of children as readers and the representations they have of the relationship between the two cultures. It is particularly striking in our example where the digression concerns meals and food. Does the translator think a French mother has more elaborated thoughts about the coming meal than an English-speaking mother? Do only French mothers think in terms of 'menus' and need to describe them at length?

Indeed, we know how the process of translation is the result of a series of choices made by a translator in order to bring a text written in a source language accessible to a reader in a target language; we also know how complex this process can be because it is linked to various theories of translation, different ideologies of language, different times in history and to editorial constraints imposed by publishers. An addition such as the one analysed above could be justified by a strategic choice to mark further the distinct narrative styles in French. However, in this particular example, we would agree with Cordonnier's analysis of adaptation in children's literature when he writes:

> [Children] are protected in a kind of closed world. They are considered as particularly fragile human beings who cannot understand and consequently who should not be made to have any experience of otherness. How? With adaptation, which is the main word as far as the translation of children's literature is concerned.[3] (Cordonnier, 1995: 179)

For Cordonnier, adapting a literary text is a form of mutilation, it robs the texts of its strangeness and it reveals an ethnocentric attitude, an impossibility to think one's relationship to the other. He sees translation as a process, which reflects our relationship to otherness, to 'foreignness' and thus which should be conceived as the expression of successful relationships of alterity. Whereas adapting a source text to the target culture is synonymous with a form of annexion or assimilation and, as explained by Cordonnier, is the product of a monoglossic ideology because the translator identifies with the national language and culture and the other is negated.

In a similar vein, Venuti (1995: 20) proposes to use a 'foreignisation' strategy in translation, which he opposes to domestication. Domestication he writes is 'an ethnocentric reduction of the foreign text to target language cultural values' whereas foreignisation is a 'tool to restrain the ethnocentric violence of translation'. He argues for foreignisation as a strategy to cultivate a heterogeneous discourse and variation in literary culture. Before him, Berman had also deplored the general tendency to negate the foreign in translation and believed that 'The properly ethical aim of the translating act is receiving the foreign as foreign' (Berman, 1992: 285). Both authors/ translators insist on the necessity to develop an ethical approach of translation, which shows more respect for cultural differences.

The translation of Brownes's *Voices in the Park* into French is particularly interesting to study because the aim of the author is to get readers to understand the notions of point of view and narrative voice. The story is very cleverly told through the four voices of four characters of different gender, age, colour and social class. Even the two dogs are different and the typesetting for each of the four parts of the book is also different. The wonderful illustrations and seasonal changes expressed in colour contrasts give a strikingly rich parallel narration to the text and help to engage the reader in various points of view on the encounter between the two children. Because the same event is depicted through four narrative voices, the reader experiences a form of decentering which is most interesting as a literary device, even if the presentation of the chapters makes this very clear. This is no doubt one of the main reasons why French teachers like the book so much. This said, the French translation of the title robs the reader of her own discovery of the narrative structure, of the very experience of discovering alternative view points and of making one's own meaning of the story.

We believe that adaptation or domestication is particularly counterproductive in the case of a text in which the central theme is the difference of perspective. Such a translation approach expresses a very narrow view of cultures in contact. The various translation choices into French of this particular book remind us that translation choices are ideological, they reflect the translator or publisher's child images: through aiming their work at children, writers, translators and publishers not only express their own view of childhood but society's values and beliefs as well. Because literature for children is 'a body of literature which belongs simultaneously to two systems, the literary and the pedagogical, it is a literature in which the dominant social cultural and educational norms are inscribed' (O'Sullivan,

2002: 38). This point seems to us most important to explain to student teachers, who should be made aware of the role of literature in the socialisation of children. The confrontation with the two texts in English and French was used as a strategy to raise all the above questions and more specifically to question translation strategies that underestimate the child as a reader, that rob children of the possibility of constructing their own meaning of a text and of extending their experiences of otherness.

A more detailed analysis of the style of language used by each character to mark their social class and the way the difference is far less subtle in French are illustrations of the domestication of the text. Comparing the two versions helps to see how and why the adaptation in French of this wonderful story betrays the intention of its author who trusted children all over the world to understand his story and to appreciate the rich emotions portrayed both in the text and in the illustrations.

This is the reason why we wanted to make student teachers aware of the process of translation as more than just the transfer from one language into another, more than the negotiation of one culture with another, but as an expression of the relationships between the two cultures; and in the specific case of children's literature, the process of translation reveals a representation of the child reader as more or less autonomous in her encounter with literature. However, it was not our intention to reinforce a stigmatized vision of translation (Venuti, 1998), which would stress the idea that texts should be read in their original language; on the contrary, our objectives were to get trainee teachers to acknowledge and understand that the process of translation is marked by ideologies of language and childhood. We also wanted to make them aware of the intercultural dimension of translation, because translating an author means encountering another vision of the world which is rooted in another culture, in a given space and time, and offering to readers who do not know the source language the experience of a new cultural encounter, another chance to confront one's own cultural understandings to others', and thus to live a new experience of otherness.

We will now turn to the pedagogical value of translation when used in bilingual texts and books.

Bilingual and Multilingual Books for Children: Understanding the Role of Translation

As explained above, translation is a process that puts into contact two languages belonging to two different cultures marked by historically determined relationships. But as Bokiba (2007) argues, the sociolinguistic dimension of the relationship between the two languages cannot be ignored. For example, the two languages in question can be languages of international communication with more or less the same status in society, or one language can be a dominant language and the other a minority language. In the latter case, the process of translation as transfer of human experiences and ideas from one culture to another will bring about a different outcome depending on which is the source language and which is the target language. When translation involves the transfer of a dominant language into a dominated language, the process can play a very important part for the minority language because it will enrich the language and give it access to modernity. In the reverse case, when a dominated language is translated into a dominant language, the process of translation will provide a wider visibility to the minority language, possibly more influence and prestige because its culture will gain access to universality.

More importantly, as Bokiba explains for African languages, the process of translation shows that all languages can be the source of literary creation and all languages can express human experiences, even languages that have not been written down before. In other words, translation is more than just a transfer from one language into another it is a form of literary acknowledgement, which allows for the circulation of literary works across the world and the development of a global literary heritage.

Encountering linguistic and cultural diversity

We would like to illustrate the above idea with the example of a book of poetry published in France for young readers by the well-known publisher 'Rue du Monde'. The book is titled *Tour de terre en poésie. Anthologie multilingue de poèmes du monde* (Henry & Vautier, 1998) and contains 50 poems in their original language with their translation into French presented on the same page or in some cases on the opposite page. The back cover sums up the book in the following way: 'Fifty poems from fifty different cultures in their original languages and in French, tell us about humanity: love, family, imagination, war, nature, others ... Like a window of poetry to open onto the world'.

We like the book for many reasons, not only for the great variety of languages presented but for the choice of languages it offers: from Romani to Berber, Basque, Arabic, Vietnamese, Turkish, Albanian, Inuktitut, Malgache, Nahuatl, Armenian, Breton, Corsican, Catalan, Occitan, Cheyenne, Navajo, Hindi, Kurdish, Georgian, Letton, Quechua, Amharic, Tibetan, Telugu, Creole, Hawaïan, Rundi, Tamoul, Singhalese, Peul, Wolof, Hebrew, Greek, Chinese, Japanese and Korean and several European languages. This choice of languages is obviously an editorial strategy to include a range of languages reflecting varied sociolinguistic contexts: regional minority languages spoken in France as well as immigrant minority languages, lesser-used languages as well as endangered languages, discriminated languages like Romani, first-nation languages from different regions in the world, African languages and languages from Asia, as well as more familiar European languages, which are taught in schools.

The presentation of the various languages and of the many different writing systems and scripts as well as the short notices explaining where these languages are spoken give an ecological vision of linguistic diversity where all the languages are ascribed the same recognition and where beyond linguistic difference, all the poems work in a complementary fashion to express human emotions. The preface by Henry makes this clear:

> Through the singularity of their music and of their writing system, more than 5000 languages participate in the beauty of the world, enriching one another from their respective differences. But like animal and plant species, the languages of the world are fragile. If some of them dominate, it is at the expense of those that disappear, sometimes without leaving any traces. Yet there are no big or small languages: each language carries within itself a poem that speaks to us, an emotion that looks strangely like us. (Henry & Vautier, 1998: 7)

Moreover, the table of contents not only gives the name of each language but also adds a note about its affiliation (e.g. Letton, Baltic language spoken in Latvia) and in many cases makes reference to more than one country (Kurdish, Irano-Aryen language spoken in Turkey, Iran, Iraq and Syria). Although the information is brief, it refers to historical factors such as Quechua being spoken at the time of the Inca Empire, or geographical precisions such as Navajo being the language of Indian people in Arizona and New Mexico, or again acknowledging sociolinguistic varieties as in the case of Creole being spoken differently in Martinique, Guadeloupe, Haiti or Reunion.

Apart from giving readers (and teachers) useful information about many less well-known languages, the book offers a choice of poems (or extracts in some cases), which are easy to understand for young learners yet with enough literary qualities to help them develop an appreciation of poetry. The names of each translator are also included since translation in this case is the central purpose of the book: it is thanks to the work of translators that other languages and cultures are made available to the French reader. Thus, the book is also an illustration of what translation means and that communication is possible between people speaking different languages. This is an important point because teachers often assume that children understand the process of translation, but it is not the case. For example, we have witnessed young students being told by their teacher that they were going to be read an English or Spanish story in French: they reacted at once by saying they were not going to understand anything. Indeed, because our classrooms are so monolingual and because approaches to the teaching of foreign languages often forbid the use of translation, children have a rather vague understanding of the process. Rarely are they given the chance to witness in class someone translating from one language to another in order to help a non-French-speaker. Yet, we know that from a very young age children are aware of linguistic difference: we heard a three-year old in a kindergarten in France comment most positively on her teacher switching to German in order to communicate with a German-speaking pupil who did not know any French (Hélot, 2010).

Supporting bilingual learners

In the case of bilingual students, who are used to switching from one language to another in their home environment and in their community, they quickly understand that common practices in their out-of-school environment such as translanguaging are not allowed at school where home languages tend to be silenced, all the more so when they are immigrant minority languages. And as well as silencing home languages, schools tend to ignore or undervalue the competences that are part of being bilingual and bicultural. Many bilingual children live everyday situations where they need to translate for some member of their family, yet their ability to negotiate two or more languages and cultures goes unnoticed at school where monolingualism is the rule. This is particularly so in the case of children from immigrant backgrounds whose parents will tend to be stigmatized for their lack of competence in French, and rarely will these students be praised for their translation skills.

In our opinion, the multilingual anthology of poems we have just discussed is a good example of pedagogical material, which can be used to develop a first awareness of linguistic and cultural diversity combined with an education to multilingual literacy. It is particularly suitable for the multilingual classroom where teachers have to deal with a variety of languages they do not know. The large choice of languages represented makes it possible to find poems in the languages spoken by most bilingual pupils in a classroom. For example, choosing a poem in the home language of a newcomer at school is a way of welcoming the pupil and of acknowledging her home language, and because the whole class learns the poem in French, it is also a way of sharing the newcomer's culture. Translation in this case is the process that helps to bridge different languages and cultures and which makes it possible to develop a form of socialization where openness to others and solidarity can develop. Because the translation is available in French, the teacher does not have to know the home languages of bilingual pupils, but can begin to learn about them, to discover their writing systems and even how they sound. One can imagine asking the student's parents to come and tell the poem in class or to record it orally so that pupils discover new sounds and develop a curiosity for other languages (see Hélot & Young, 2006 for language-awareness projects involving the collaboration of parents).

It is with such multilingual strategies that teachers can begin to develop an inclusive approach to their teaching, while taking into account the singularity of each of their pupils. Using multilingual books can sharpen their sensitivity and respect for linguistic diversity and help their bilingual students to be proud of their bilingualism and thus see their bicultural identity in a positive light. At the same time, monolingual students will be confronted by other languages and will learn to go beyond a feeling of strangeness, or lack of understanding, and slowly will be brought to decentre, that is, to understand that it is possible to see the world differently. And through this process, the language competences of bilingual students become an asset for the whole class and for the teacher. Finally, learning a poem by heart should also involve creative writing activities and again the multilingual anthology could be used as an example: bilingual students could be invited to write in their own language, as well as in French, and in the process strengthen their acquisition of both languages (see Cummins, 2006, for the production of what he calls 'identity texts' in classrooms in Canada). One could imagine a multilingual class producing its own anthology of bilingual poems or stories based on the various languages spoken by the students and subsequently published on the web, or distributed to families so as to signal to parents the importance of valuing and developing their bilingual heritage (Sneddon, 2009).

From bilingual books for children to multilingual literacies

Bilingual books for children offer another opportunity to look at the way the relationship between different languages is envisaged and represented. The denomination 'bilingual books' covers different configurations: books where two languages are present in the same volume, with the two languages on the same page or facing each other on alternate pages, books with a reversed double entry for each language (see the recent Toon books collection by Casterman[4] for example), books published simultaneously in two languages (Éditions du Jasmin[5]), and 'dual books' where one chapter is written in one language and the next in another language (Talents Hauts editions[6]). The originality of the different formats is no doubt revealing of the importance given to 'foreign' language learning in France and of the need for publishers to target buyers such as parents and teachers. Our analysis does not intend to be exhaustive here, but rather to focus on a few examples, which seem to us to be revealing of a general trend in recent publications; that is, exposing young readers to texts written in languages other than French.

A critical analysis of language distribution in bilingual books

The main questions we are interested in relate to the representations of multilingualism in bilingual books; for example, the way the two languages are presented: which language comes first or takes precedence over the other, which language is the source language and which is the target one, and in the case of some languages like Arabic, for example the way script directionality is handled. We would like to argue that all these points are relevant from the reception point of view, for even if readers and teachers are not necessarily aware of precedence given to one language over another, such choices are the expression of representations towards different languages, they reveal unequal relationships between them and they reproduce these ideologies in children's books.

The small publishing house 'Editions du Jasmin' has caught our attention because its aim is to publish bilingual books in order to sustain the advantage of bilingualism developed in the home context. In an interview given on their website,[7] Saäd Bouri, who created the publishing house, explains that he started several bilingual collections in French and Arabic for young readers because he could not find any books in Arabic to read to his young daughter. Apart from the fact that books for children in Arabic are indeed very rare in France,[8] the collections are interesting because of their editorial choices. They comprise two different kinds of bilingual books for different ages: for older readers, the books include both languages in one volume, and for very young children, a series of small hard-cover books published in two versions, one in French and the other one in Arabic.

While both formats are referred to as bilingual books they do not offer the same reading experience: the bilingual books read just like a French book, whereas the two books published in different languages show at once that directionality of writing in French and Arabic is not the same. In the case of the book in Arabic, one will turn the pages from left to right and notice that the illustrations are oriented in an opposite way to those in the French version. In the bilingual books, although both languages are present on the same page, precedence is given to the French language, which comes first on the page above the Arabic. For example, in *'Jade et l'armée des poules'* by B. al-Maari[9] (2007), one notes that the cover page shows the title in Arabic above the title in French, but the title page inside the book is the reverse with the French title above the Arabic one. The subtitle states that it is a French–Arabic bilingual tale, and on the inside cover two translators are thanked, without stating the source language. The beautiful illustrations and the names of the main characters refer quite clearly to an Arabic cultural context, yet the editor has chosen to give the book the same format as books in French. Inside the book, all pages show the French language above the Arabic, except for one page (page 6) where the text in Arabic comes first on the left page and is followed by the French on the opposite page.

We make the hypothesis, based on the order of languages mentioned in the subtitle; that is, a French–Arabic bilingual tale, that this is the reason why the book has been given a French format, and yet we believe respecting directionality of the Arabic language would have offered readers a further experience of different literacy practices. In our opinion, the fact that the source text is French does not justify the language priority on the page, particularly when the tale comes from the Arabic tradition. While it seems obvious that these bilingual books are intended for a bilingual audience, one wonders why the publisher has made the choice to give precedence to French. In the case of a language like Arabic, which still has the status of a minorised language in French schools, one would like to find more than traditional tales from Arab countries, more than bilingual books featuring the Arabic language, but bilingual books where this language is prioritised, meaning that the book is bound so as to be read turning pages from left to right.

This is indeed what the bilingual collections for very young readers provide, because in this case two books are offered, one in each language. And the Arabic version reads like an Arabic book and therefore gives readers a form of authentic literary practice. However, the illustrations and texts depicting various common professions or situations (the postman, at the crèche) reflect a European or French cultural background, which gives the impression that the Arabic language as a target text is just there as a pretext, that the Arabic version has been thought of after the French version. So that the positive dimension of giving the Arabic language a visibility, is counterbalanced by the illustrations, which are clearly Eurocentric. Is the reason for this that the age group targeted is thought by publishers to be too young to be exposed to a less familiar environment? We do not mean to say here that the Arabic language should always be accompanied by illustrations depicting life in Arab-speaking countries, for it could also reinforce cultural stereotypes: children should indeed be exposed through books, to cultural worlds they share. But again, we wonder whether children's ability to understand a text with pictures are not underestimated as is so often the case, particularly when books are translated.

From a pedagogical point of view, we would like to argue that the Arabic version is most useful not only for Arabic speakers but for all children to understand that stories can be told and written in any language. Very handy for pre-readers, the two books can be observed and compared, the two scripts being very different but the illustrations being the same, yet oriented differently. Through comparison, beginner readers can be brought to understand the importance of directionality in their own language and in others, and that all languages are not read the same way. The two books also allow for the direct experience of handling page turning differently and from the beginning of schooling confront very young children with the diversity of literacy practices. And again, a link can be made between home and school for children who see their parents reading in Arabic at home.

Multilingual Literacy Practices: Bilingual Books without Translation

Stories to learn to read and write a new language

Other experiences of multilingual literacy practices are offered in a series of books written by Lisa Bresner (2001, 2003) and illustrated by Fredérick Mansot. The books tell traditional Chinese stories in French but the text includes some Chinese ideograms, which the readers will learn to decipher as they progress through the story. First, the ideograms are placed right next to a French word (e.g. moon, sun, toad, etc.), but on the following page, the French word is replaced by the ideogram, asking the reader to remember visually what they mean. The number of ideograms is not exhaustive, they do not figure on each page but the key words are given in Chinese throughout the story. Apart from the exquisite illustrations, it is interesting to notice that the author has taken care to present the Chinese words vertically on the illustrated page, whereas in the French text they are aligned horizontally next to French words. Bresner studied Chinese and was a translator as well as an author. It is clear her intention in these books is to guide readers into the world of Chinese stories and also of its written language. The last 10 pages of the book titled *Le secret d'un prénom*, for example, give a short Chinese lexicon of the names in the story, their meaning and their pronunciation, as well as explanations about the way ideograms combine. In the story itself, vertical columns of seven squares illustrate how one writes Chinese ideograms in a series of strokes placed precisely inside the pre-divided squares. At the end of the book, the author offers readers the opportunity to choose a Chinese name and to learn to write it, having given short explanations about calligraphy, and cultural notes about names in China.

Again what these books offer is a chance for young readers to be confronted with another culture through a story with beautiful illustrations and also through a first introduction to the Chinese language. The way the ideograms are integrated into the French text is particularly motivating for children and demystifies the idea that learning Chinese is very difficult. As well as taking children into the world of reading Chinese ideograms the book also encourages them to learn to write the language and to discover the role of calligraphy in Chinese culture. Nothing is simplified and vertical combinations of ideograms are proposed, offering some examples of language-awareness activities, which are contextualised and which combine reading in two languages and writing in an unknown language. In our opinion, Brezner's books have a pedagogical dimension, which has been constructed as a real literary experience combined with a new literacy experience where the unknown language is woven into the text and the illustrations, so as to awaken children's curiosity for other languages. Perhaps the lasting impression these books give is that the author herself loves the Chinese language and that she wants to share her passion with young readers by making their first encounter with reading and writing ideograms an artistic experience as well as a first approach to multilingual literacy.

Multilingual Books, Dual-language Books and Translanguaging

More rare and difficult to find are books for children (or for adults) where several languages are present in one story or poem without translation. Whereas translanguaging and hybrid language use (García, 2009) are very common in multilingual communities, in technology-enabled communication as well as often heard today in popular music,[10] few authors dare to venture into such practices in writing. We have referred elsewhere (Benert & Hélot, 2010) to the Austrian author Jandl and his multilingual poem *Chanson* (1966) where he mixes French, English and German nouns and articles to produce a kind of linguistic fireworks, freeing each language from all constraints and more importantly of normatively imposed linguistic barriers. As we explained in our article, we used Jandl's text with teachers involved in bilingual education in Alsace where the model in place separates the two languages to such an extent that the teachers are obliged to function in a monolingual mode and are thus prevented from doing cross language activities in German and French. We have analysed this model of bilingual education as double monolingualism (Benert & Hélot, 2008) based on what Cummins calls 'the two solitudes assumptions' (Cummins, 2007: 229). He writes:

> ... it does seem reasonable to create largely separate spaces for each language within a bilingual or immersion program. However there are also compelling arguments to be made for creating a shared and interdependent space for the promotion of language awareness and cross-language cognitive processing. The reality is that students are making cross-linguistic connections throughout the course of their learning in a bilingual or immersion program, so why not nurture this learning strategy and help students to apply it more efficiently. (Cummins, 2007: 229)

Like Cummins (2006) and many other researchers working in the field of literacy acquisition (Gregory, 2008; Gregory *et al.*, 2004; Kenner, 2000), we would argue for bilingual learners to have the right to use both their languages simultaneously in class and we believe it is important to show teachers that language contacts can be a source of creativity. Therefore, we are interested in books for children, which offer a different representation of multilingualism; that is books where the two languages (or three) are included in the narration without translation. One such example is Leyla Torres's *Subway Sparrow* published in 1993 by Farrar, Straus and Giroux.[11] *Subway Sparrow* is the story of a sparrow trapped in a car in the New York subway and how an English-speaking girl, a Polish-speaking woman and a Spanish-speaking man, as well as a silent adolescent boy, cooperate to free the bird. It is striking to discover that each character in the story speaks their own language and to see on the page the three languages intermingling, giving an authenticity to the depiction of life in a multilingual city. The main language of the book is English and when Spanish or Polish are used no translation is given, because the reader does not need any translation to understand what is being said. Apart from the presence of the three languages next to one another on some of the pages, the beautiful illustrations show four characters of different gender, age and colour. The three languages give some information on their different backgrounds or cultures, so that the book is not only multilingual but also presents a multicultural vignette. One could analyse further the role of the beautiful watercolours that support the caring tone of the story, which is about cooperation among people of different cultures.

The presence of the three languages next to one another gives an authenticity to the multilingual context in which the story is set but more importantly it represents an excellent example of what García refers to as 'translanguaging' (García, 2009: 45). García defines the term as 'multiple discursive practices in which bilinguals engage in order to make sense of their bilingual worlds' (García, 2009: 45), and she goes on to explain that bilingual families and communities must translanguage in order to construct meaning, and that 'bilinguals translanguage to include and facilitate communication with others, but also to construct deeper understanding' (García, 2009: 45). This is exactly what Torres has decided to do in her book: she gives her characters the right to express themselves in their own language in order to construct a deeper meaning to her story and indeed it is through the choice of translanguaging that she can make the main point of the story understood; that is that people can communicate and work together beyond linguistic difference.

We would argue that this point is far more important than just including different languages to expose readers to other linguistic systems, because it legitimizes translanguaging. This is perhaps what teachers have the most difficulty with, including bilingual teachers. Thus, the book is another example of legitimate multilingual writing and could serve as a kind of model for writing activities in class: for example, learners could write stories in groups, inserting in their texts some words or expressions from their home languages. Through the use of translanguaging in the classroom, the competence of bilingual speakers would be supported and valued as a source of learning for themselves and their peers. Multilingual and multicultural understandings of the same text can be developed through such instructional strategies, which can also generate different understandings from multiple perspectives. Through the creation of a new space for literacy activities where multilingualism can flourish, bilingual students are offered the possibility to make full use of their plurilingual repertoire, and monolingual students are made to cross linguistic and cultural barriers and thus understand that 'literature although not written in the same language can speak the same language' (Bokiba, 2007: 111).

Finally, *Subway Sparrow* is a story for teachers because it illustrates convincingly that they also, can work and cooperate with their bilingual students and they can learn from them. And apart from the need to support bilingual students, letting other languages enter the classroom through bi- or multilingual books or writing activities using several languages, is a way of taking some distance with the language of schooling, of going beyond a monolingual mindset, of envisaging other languages in a complementary fashion or ecological balance, rather than as a possible threat for the dominant language.

We would like at this stage to give two more examples of books featuring examples of translanguaging. The first is O'Sullivan and Rösler's (1990b) *I like you – und du?* published in German and English and the second Causse's *Romeo@Juliette* published in French and English in 2006. While both books are part of a series published to encourage young second-language learners of English to read in this language, the authors' – or publishers' – choices are quite different. In the case of the book published in France, the story is organised in several short chapters, one chapter written in French the following one in English. The narrator's point of view is the criteria for the switch of language: one character lives in France the other in the United Kingdom and both protagonists exchange emails in their 'native' language.

The book published in Germany offers a more audacious experience of translanguaging: the two languages are both present and intermingle in the narrative; in other words the text switches from German to English from one paragraph to the next and even from one sentence to the next, again, according to the point of view of the characters who speak their first language. Because the story is set in Ireland, Irish also figures in the narrative. Of further interest in this story is the theme of mobility: the characters, a German girl and an Irish boy both live in families that have to move to different countries for professional reasons and the story also dwells on their intercultural experiences.

Although it is not stated explicitly, the characters in both books are obviously bilingual since they understand one another; but in the German book the language is more complex and has not been simplified like in the French book, the back cover of which mentions a target audience of readers having studied English for at least two years. The reading experience in the German book is quite different from the French book because the switching of languages takes place much more frequently in the story, indeed it is an integral part of the story, and in a sense, although there are two languages on the page, after a while, one forgets about the change of language. So that one could say that there is a kind of continuum from one language to the other and a blurring of linguistic borders in the German/ English text, which is similar to what bilinguals experience when they speak. For when bilinguals communicate with other bilinguals who share the same languages, they switch languages without necessarily being aware of the switch. In the German/English book, the pace of the story is such that one cannot imagine the English language posing any problems to German readers, so that the reading experience involves some learning of the language but in a less obviously pedagogical orientation than in the French book. One can surmise that readers construct the meaning of the story based on their knowledge of their stronger language and this very knowledge helps them to understand the other language. In other words, the learning process is such that the two languages support one another in a relationship of solidarity to bring the reader to be involved in the story.[12] In the French/English book, one could argue that the French chapters give some motivation to the reader to go on reading the next chapter in English but the relationship between the two languages is more distant than the relationship between German and English in O'Sullivan and Rösler's story. Admittedly, German and English are two languages which are closely related historically, but there are also many similar cognates in English and French.

In any case, in both examples, readers are offered a new experience of reading while being exposed to two languages, an experience of multilingual literacy that allows them to enter into fiction marked by a plurality of languages which does not hinder comprehension, at least for the targeted readership. Translation in these cases is not necessary; readers can access the new language based on their inter-language and learn to make sense of a story without necessarily understanding every word. Perhaps most motivating, is the experience of being able to function like a bilingual person and of having the freedom to go from one language to the other without too many difficulties.

Conclusion

It is interesting to note that such books are often referred to as 'dual-language' books rather than 'bilingual' books, a term reserved for books where the same text is present in both languages through translation. But we believe dual-language books, which use two languages to tell one story reflect bilingual language practices more exactly. As we know, bilinguals do not live the same experience twice in two different languages, and there are no clear cut boundaries between the languages they use, but rather a languaging continuum that they access according to their needs and their environment. However, as we have argued throughout this chapter, translation cannot be disassociated from multilingualism, since it is the very process by which we can have access to a multiplicity of languages and cultures in the world, and share with others our values and imaginary. This is one of the reasons why the translation skills of bilingual students should be acknowledged and supported at school. Despite the development of a global language like English, we will always need translators to bridge cultural differences and to confront readers to otherness. Therefore, translators of literature for children should not be made to negate the dimension of alterity inherent to all literary work by publishers underestimating children's abilities to understand difference. Publishers should be reminded that young readers are not only curious and open, they have a thirst for knowledge which is well matched by the creativity of many authors and illustrators writing for children. As to teachers working in multilingual classrooms, we hope that through the use of multilingual children's books they could challenge their hesitation to work with languages they do not know, they would develop an understanding of bilingual language use and above all become aware of how much they can learn from their own bilingual students. And last but not least, that children's books are written to help children grow up and make sense of the world they live in; therefore, bilingual students should have access at school to literature in their own languages.

Notes

1. *Histoire à quatre voix*: the French title translated from the English *Voices in the Park* when retranslated literally means 'Four voices to tell a story' and thus reveals explicitly what the author wants the reader to understand implicitly.
2. Berman (1984) used the term 'naturalization' to describe this translation strategy.
3. Our own translation from French. The following translations from French are also our own.
4. See website at http://jeunesse.casterman.com/Search_result.cfm. Accessed on 14.01.11.
5. See website at http://editions-du-jasmin.pagesperso-orange.fr/diff.htm. Accessed on 14.01.11.
6. See website at http://www.talentshauts.fr/ Accessed on 14.01.11.
7. See website at http://www.editons-du-jasmin.com. Accessed on 14.08.09.
8. See, however, the very rich collection of bilingual books in many different languages published by L'Harmattan Jeunesse at http://www.editions-harmattan.fr/jeunesse/index.asp. Accessed on 12.01.11.
9. Boutros al-Maari is from Syria, he has been working as an illustrator in France since 1997. See website at http://boutros-almaari.com/bio.php. Accessed on 12.01.11.
10. See, for example, the song by the French group La Tordue, titled '*Le pétrin*' and sung in 18 different languages. See website at http://www.dailymotion.com/video/xw4fp_la-tordue-le-petrin_creation. Accessed on 2.02.11.
11. Torres could also be the illustrator, as the book makes no mention of an illustrator.

12. On the point of interdependence across languages, see Cummins' interdependence hypothesis 1981, Cummins (2001), as well as Baker (2001) and Genesee *et al.* (2006).

References

al-Maari, B. (2007) *Jade et l'armée des Poules.* Paris: Éditions du Jasmin.

Baker, C. (2001) *Foundations of Bilingual Education and Bilingualism.* Clevedon: Multilingual Matters.

Benert, B. and Hélot, C. (2007) Tomi Ungerer: homo viator. Trois langues et quatre récits pour penser la notion d'identité. In J. Erfurt, H. Hart, H. Klein and K. Middell (eds) *Grenzgänge 14, H. 28. Beiträge zur einer modernen Romanistik* (pp. 167–188). Germany: Leipziger Universitätsverlag.

Benert, B. and Hélot, C. (2009) Traduction et Altérité. In V. Lalagianni (ed.) *Children Literature Studies and Literary Theory Today.* Neohelicon, Acta Comparationis Literarum Universalis. Dordrecht: Springer Publishers.

Benert, B. and Hélot, C. (2010) Littérature de jeunesse et plurilinguisme. A la rencontre de deux auteurs polyglottes en formation bilingue: Tomi Ungerer et Ernst Jandl. In S. Ehrhart, C. Hélot and A. Le Nevez (eds) *La formation des enseignants en contexte plurilingue: Une approche critique* (pp. 115–144). Frankfurt: Peter Lang.

Berman, A. (1984) *L'épreuve de l'étranger. Culture et traduction dans l'Allemagne Romantique.* Paris: Gallimard.

Berman, A. (1992) *The Experience of the Foreign: Culture and Translation in Romantic Germany.* Trad. S. Heyvaert. Albany: University of New York Press.

Bokiba, A-P. (2007) La traduction littéraire, vecteur d'interculturalité. Synergies Chili Numéro 3 – Année 2007, Revue du GERFLINT. http://ressources-cla.univ-fcomte.fr/gerflint/chili3/chili3.bobika.pdf. Accessed 8.08.09.

Bresner, L. (2001) *Les dix soleils amoureux des douze lunes.* Arles: Actes Sud Junior.

Bresner, L. (2003) *Le secret d'un prénom.* Arles: Actes Sud Junior.

Brown, A. (1998) *Voices in the Park.* London: Picture Corgi Books.

Causse, M. (2006) *Romeo @Juliette.* Paris: Talents Hauts.

Cordonnier, J-L. (1995) *Traduction et Culture.* Paris: Didier.

Cummins, J. (2001) *Negotiating Identities. Education for Empowerment in a Diverse Society* (2nd edn). Los Angeles: Californian Association for Bilingual Association.

Cummins, J. (2006) Identity texts: The imaginative construction of self through multilingual pedagogies. In O. García, T. Skutnabb-Kangas and M. Torres-Guzman (eds) *Imagining Multilingual Schools. Languages in Education and Globalisation.* Clevedon: Multilingual Matters.

Cummins, J. (2007) Rethinking monolingual instructional strategies in multilingual classrooms. *The Canadian Journal of Applied Linguistics,* Special Issue 10, 2. In R. Lyster and S. Lapkin (eds) *Multilingualism in Canadian Schools* (pp. 221–240) Canada. http://aclacaal/org.

García, O. (2009) *Bilingual Education in the 21st Century. A Global Perspective.* Chichester: Wiley Blackwell.

Genesee, F., Paradis, J. and Crago, M. (2006) *Dual Language Development and Disorders.* Baltimore: Paul Brookes.

Gregory, E. (2008) *Learning to Read in a New Language*. London: Sage.

Gregory, E., Long, S. and Volk, D. (eds) (2004) *Many Pathways to Literacy*. London: Routledge Farmer.

Hélot, C. (2006) De la notion d'écart à la notion de continuum. Comment analyser le caractère inégalitaire du bilinguisme en contexte scolaire? In C. Hélot, E. Hoffmann, M-L. Scheidhauer and A. Young (eds) *Ecarts de langue, écarts de culture: A l'école de l'Autre* (pp. 185–206). Frankfurt: Peter Lang.

Hélot, C. (2007) *Du bilinguisme en famille au plurilinguisme à l'école*. Paris: L'Harmattan.

Hélot, C. (2008) *Mais d'où est-ce qu'il sort ce bilinguisme?* La notion de bilinguisme dans l'espace scolaire français. In J. Erfurt, G. Budach and M. Kunkel (eds) *Zweisprachig lehren und lernen. Ziele, Konzepte und Erfahrungen* (pp. 72–97). Frankfurt: Peter Lang. Europäischer Verlag der Wissenschaften. Reihe: Sprache, Mehrsprachigkeit und sozialer Wandel, Bd. 7.

Hélot, C. (2010) Tu sais bien parler, Maîtresse. Negociating languages other than French in the primary classroom in France. In K. Menken and O. García (eds) *Negociating Language Policies in Schools: Educators as Policy Makers* (pp. 52–71). New York: Lawrence Erlbaum.

Hélot, C. and Young, A. (2006) Imagining multilingual education in France: A language and cultural awareness project at primary level. In O. Garcia, T. Skutnabb-Kangas and M. Torres-Guzman (eds) *Imagining Multilingual Schools. Languages in Education and Globalisation* (pp. 69–90). Clevedon: Multilingual Matters.

Henry, J.M. and Vautier, M. (1998) *Tour de Terre en Poésie. Anthologie multilingue de poèmes du monde*. Voisins-Le-Bretonneux, France: Rue du Monde.

Jandl, E. (1966) *Laut und Luise*. Olten: Walter.

Kenner, C. (2000) *Home Pages. Literacy Links for Bilingual Children*. Stoke on Trent: Trentham Books.

Martin-Jones, M. and Jones, K. (2000) (eds) *Multilingual Literacies*. Amsterdam: John Benjamins.

O'Sullivan, E. (2002) Comparing children's literature. *German as a Foreign Language. GFL-journal* no. 2, 33–56. On WWW at http://www.gfl-journal.de/2–2002/osullivan.html. Accessed on 13.08.09.

O'Sullivan, E. and Rösler, D. (1990) *I Like You – und du*? Hamburg: Rotfuchs Rororo.

Oittinen, R. (2000) *Translating for Children*. New York: Garland, Inc.

Perrot, J. (2008) *Mondialisation et Littérature de Jeunesse*. Paris: Éditions du Cercle de la Librairie.

Sneddon, R. (2009) *Bilingual Books, Biliterate Children. Learning to Read through Dual Language Books*. Trentham: Trentham Books.

Torres, L. (1993) *Subway Sparrow*. New York: Farrar, Straux, Giroux.

Venuti, L. (1995) *The Translator's Invisibility. A History of Translation*. London: Routledge.

Venuti, L. (1998) *The Scandals of Translation: Towards an Ethics of Difference*. London: Routledge.

Chapter 4

Multilingualism and Pedagogical Practices in Colombia's Caribbean Archipelago

A-M. DE MEJÍA

Introduction and Historical Background

The Archipelago of San Andrés, Providencia and Santa Catalina (with a total landmass of 52 km²) is located in the Western Caribbean sea, around 480 km northwest of the Colombian mainland and 180 km east of Nicaragua (Sanmiguel Ardila, 2006).[1] Like many other Caribbean islands, the Archipelago has had a chequered past. The island of Providencia was originally colonised by English Puritan settlers in 1629, fleeing from religious persecution in England. Four years later, a group of these settlers moved to the nearby island of San Andrés. Pirates and buccaneers were active in this area at different times during the 17th century and at the beginning of the 18th century, cotton plantations were started on the islands by English settlers from Jamaica. Labour for these was provided by slaves brought over, for the most part, from West Africa, as well as from other parts of the Caribbean (Sanmiguel Ardila, 2006).

After the Spanish conquered the islands in 1786, the English-speaking native inhabitants were allowed to remain, provided they swore allegiance to the Spanish Crown, converted to Catholicism and communicated in Spanish. While there was nominal acquiescence to these demands, in reality language and religion became a means of resistance to Spanish domination (Dieck, 1998).

In 1822, the Archipelago became part of the newly independent Republic of Colombia and slavery was officially abolished throughout the country in 1851. The Baptist Church gradually became a pillar of island culture, even though there were attempts on the part of the State to strengthen Catholicism and the use of Spanish in official domains, such as education. This was particularly noticeable after the designation in 1953 of San Andrés as a free port, which led to massive immigration of Spanish speakers from mainland Colombia (Mainlanders or 'Panyas'[2]).

This contact of the islands with diverse religious, linguistic and cultural influences has meant that there has been a long tradition of multilingualism among the *Isleño* ('Islander') communities. However, in spite of a series of well-meaning initiatives, recognition of multilingualism has not been generally incorporated within the education system. In this chapter, I will argue that in order to propitiate the development of multilingual education in the Archipelago, it is necessary to incorporate a wider Caribbean perspective within the discussion.

Sociolinguistic Context

According to linguists and sociolinguists working in the area, the islands are characterised as being a multilingual context, where three main languages are spoken: Spanish, Standard Caribbean English and English Creole, sometimes known locally as 'Islander English' (Dittmann, 2006; Flórez, 2006; Sanmiguel Ardila, 2006). These languages are generally in a diglossic relationship with each other. Spanish is the usual language of commerce, government and education, while Standard English is restricted to religious services, particularly in the Baptist communities. Creole, on the other hand, is the language used in informal or family and community contexts among the native Islanders.

A great boost was given to the status and use of Creole as a native minority language by the Colombian Constitution of 1991, where it was officially recognised, for the first time, that Colombia is a multiethnic and pluricultural nation (Article 7) and that the languages of the minority communities would be co-official with Spanish in the areas where these were spoken.

Although official recognition was hailed by the communities as a great step forward, this did not immediately change ingrained attitudes towards these minority languages, particularly the Creole languages,[3] which have often been considered examples of badly spoken, or 'broken' English or Spanish. However, as noted by Dieck (1998), there is recent evidence of change in this area, in that the English Creole speakers of San Andrés and Providencia are beginning to revalue their languages as part of their cultural heritage which needs to be preserved.

The Afro-Colombian communities in Providencia and Santa Catalina, the two most traditional of the islands, use Standard Caribbean English (strongly associated with their regional historical patrimony), as well as Creole and Spanish, although it seems that, as Standard English is not used as frequently as might be expected, fluency levels are declining. As Abouchaar *et al.* (2002) maintain,

> In contrast to many places in the Caribbean (Jamaica, Trinidad, Grenada and Guyana) where English, in the form of Standard Caribbean English, used in education and for State formalities, coexists with the Creole language, used for everyday communication, in Providencia the space for English has gradually been taken over by Spanish. It is probable that the lack of contact between Creole and the lexifying language leads to greater interaction between Creole and Spanish.[4] (Abouchaar *et al.*, 2002: 77)[5]

San Andrés shows a similar picture of multilingual decline, according to a recent study (Andrade, 2004; cited in Sanmiguel Ardila, 2006). Spanish monolingualism is rapidly increasing on the island and the use of Creole is decreasing in the face of the mass use of Spanish by Colombian immigrants from the mainland.

However, in a recent small-scale study, this time on language attitudes in San Andrés and Providencia carried out by Flórez on the islands, there is a more optimistic vision presented. The researcher notes, 'on both islands respondents' attitudes can be considered favourable to the three languages and to multilingualism' (Flórez, 2006: 140). In addition, it seems that the researcher found that attitudes to Creole and Standard English were slightly more favourable in Providencia, than in San Andrés.

Yet, Sanmiguel reminds us that although there may be signs of positive attitudes towards language diversity on the islands, 'The absence of a language policy which recognises the value of language and cultural diversity and the trilingualism of its inhabitants in everyday contexts, will end up positioning languages like Creole in San Andrés society' (Sanmiguel Ardila, 2006: 81).[6]

Language and Educational Policy Initiatives and Implementation

The multilingual reality of language use is reflected, to a certain extent, in different spheres of the education system. The majority of schools cater for Spanish-speaking 'Mainlanders' and use Spanish as the medium for teaching and learning. Most Islander teachers, however, speak Creole as a first language and have an appropriate level of oral Spanish, but have difficulties with Standard English, as can be seen in the following observation:

> 99% of the teachers and administrators have Creole as their mother tongue. Their proficiency in Spanish as a second language is sufficient for normal communicative purposes. Throughout the research, some difficulties about writing in Spanish in academic documents were noted (...) If bilingual education involving English were to be implemented, the majority of the teachers would need intensive preparation in this language.[7] (Abouchaar *et al.*, 2002: 74–75)

This is hardly suprising if we take into account that in the 1970s English had practically disappeared from the island schools, after its predominance in the education system during the 19th century, even though Creole remained a marker of cultural and social identity among the Islanders (Abouchaar, 2002; cited in Sanmiguel Ardila, 2006).

Recent legislation has reinforced the emphasis on the rights of minority communities in Colombia to develop educational programmes based on the principles of Ethnoeducation, known in other parts of Latin America as 'Intercultural Bilingual Education'. The Education Law of 1994 decreed that 'the teaching of ethnic groups who have their own linguistic tradition will be bilingual'. This was followed in 1995 by Decree 804, which stated that,

> Education for ethnic groups is part of the public education service and is supported by a commitment of collective development, where the different members of the community in general, exchange knowledge and experience aimed at maintaining, recreating and developing a global life project according to their culture, their language, their traditions and their own autochtonous jurisdiction. (Article 1: 1)[8]

Within the support provided by the officially sanctioned Ethnoeducation policy, there have been a series of bilingual and multilingual initiatives over the years aimed principally at the Afro-Colombian or Islander population. Dionisio Brown (1999) in the Office of Ethnoeducation in San Andrés proposed 'a bilingual methodological approach' based on the use of the students' first language (defined as either Standard Caribbean English or Spanish) as the main language of initial literacy, while the second language was to be introduced orally at first. Later, in 4th and 5th Grade a modified form of Preview–Review would be introduced, in which a short review of teaching and learning would be given in the 'other' language, that is the language not used during the main part of the lesson. The status of Creole was seen as a 'platform ... from which to project students towards the target language, which is the standard form of English' (Brown, 1999: 146). However, this was not considered an appropriate language for teaching and learning, as Brown states, 'We maintain that Creole is only spoken by a few people and will never acquire prestige and power' (Brown, 1999: 146).[9]

Part of the reason for this relegation of Creole to informal, family domains, or subsidiary school contexts, such as recreation, disciplinary talk, fights, etc. (Abouchaar, 2006, personal communication, Abouchaar & Moya, 2005) was the fact that it was an oral language with no written alphabet. However, in 1997, the Christian University of San Andrés, a private confessional institution, under the auspices of the Baptist churches of the Southern United States, together with representatives of the Summer Institute of Linguistics,[10] began a community project for the development of an alphabet for Creole, based on the orthographic system developed for English Creole in Belice.

In 1998, a pilot project was designed for the production of pedagogical material in 'Islander English' (Creole) to be used in three Baptist primary schools on the Island at the level of preschool and Grade 1. The basic hypothesis was that,

> native San Andres, Providence and Santa Catalina Island children (i.e. children who learn to speak Islander English at home as their first language) who, during their pre-first and first grade of school are taught in their mother tongue and are given mother tongue support in subsequent grades, will do better academically in the content areas such as mathematics, social science and natural science. (Morren, 2001: 230)

The trilingual programme also aimed at helping the students to use English and Spanish as second and third languages as well, or better than other native Island children, who did not receive initial teaching and learning in Creole.

The idea was to begin literacy in Creole and then change to reading and writing in Standard English in Grades 2 and 3. Literacy in Spanish would begin in Grades 3 and 4, ending up with approximately 50% of teaching and learning in English and 50% in Spanish in Grade 5. This developed into the Pilot Trilingual Project in 2001. Three public schools, under the auspices of the Baptist Church were chosen as experimental schools where a trilingual education programme could be developed and implemented (Morren, 2001).

According to Morren (2001: 235), the pedagogical model would be developed in the following manner (see Table 4.1).

Table 4.1 Pedagogical model/scope and sequence: Trilingual Education Project 2000, San Andrés, Providence and Santa Catalina Islands

1999 Pre-prim A	1999 Pre-prim B	2000 1st Grade	2001 2nd Grade	2002 3rd Grade	2003 4th Grade	2004 5th Grade
Everything in Creole ABCs	Everything in Creole ABCs	Reading and writing in Creole	Reading and writing in English	Reading and writing in English	Reading and writing in English	Reading and writing in English
Numbers	Numbers	Math in Creole	Math in English	Math in English and Spanish	Math in English and Spanish	Math in Spanish and English
Social Science concepts	Social Science concepts	Social Science in Creole	Social Science in Creole	Social Science in English and Creole	Social Science in English and Spanish	Social Science in Spanish
Natural Science concepts	Natural Science concepts	Natural Science in Creole	Natural Science in English	Natural Science in English	Natural Science in English and Spanish	Natural Science in Spanish and English
Environmental print in Creole	Environmental print in Creole	Oral English	Oral Spanish	Reading and writing in Spanish	Reading and writing in Spanish	Reading and writing in Spanish

Source: Taken from Morren (2001: 235)

As an integral part of this project 32 'Big Books' written in Creole were developed: nine of these were focused on the area of social science, four on natural science and three on mathematics (Moya Chaves, 2004).

Preliminary results indicated that both teachers and students felt more motivated working in Creole on familiar topics, which were easily understood by pupils. Teachers were encouraged to produce other materials using Creole and felt proud of 'being able to write in their family and community language, using their cultural knowledge and feelings' (Bowie & Dittmann, 2007: 71–72).[11] The project also helped them to become more consciously aware of separating their use of Creole from Standard English in the classroom.

The immediate problems noted in the project had to do with the lack of real financial support from the local Educational Authorities, as well as the need to familiarise both parents and members of the local government with the aims and methodology of the project. There was also the need to provide better physical conditions and equipment for the participating schools.

However, in a later reflection on the difficulties encountered, Marcia Dittmann observes, 'There is still resistance on the part of large sections of the Islander community and teachers to the use of writing in Creole and the teaching of the same in the schools' (Dittmann, 2006: 95).[12] She notes great insecurity in the teachers' use of Creole to teach initial literacy, such that it was mainly reserved for oral use only, while the teaching and learning of literacy processes were mostly carried out in Spanish. As she says, there was a noticeable 'jump from oral use [of Creole] and the use of stories written in Creole to writing in Spanish in Grade 1 Primary' (Bowie & Dittmann, 2007: 73).[13]

Nevertheless, in 2004, the Colombian Education Ministry and Islander Pedagogical Commission signed an agreement for the development of a model called 'Intercultural Trilingual Ethnoeducation for the Islander People'. This called for the development of a type of education based on the sociocultural context, and the Creole language, which is today 'the dominant language and supreme for the Islander'[14] (Mitchell *et al.*, 2004 quoted in Sanmiguel Ardila, 2006: 78).

So what can we conclude from this brief review of language and education policy and practice on the islands? First of all, there seems to be support, at least in theory, for the principle of the use of the students' first language as the basis for future bilingual development. The problem is to decide which are the languages accepted as legitimate for this purpose in the education system. Furthermore, calls for the use, or not, of Creole within the education system are usually a political issue, associated with the preferred construction of identity of the Islander community.

However, as Flórez warns us, 'It is not infrequent in Creole speaking communities that even speakers themselves deny the existence of the Creole language and claim that they only speak the lexifier' (Flórez, 2006: 145),[15] a phenomenon that I myself have been a witness to in the Archipelago. The situation is further complicated, as Sanmiguel Ardila (2006) recognises, by the fact that English is the language of highest prestige among the inhabitants of the islands and thus, it is difficult for many to accept the idea of the inclusion of Creole in the education system, particularly as it is not seen as useful for social mobility.

Multilingual Students and Current Classroom Practices

One of the few studies carried out recently in the islands to focus on actual language use of students and teachers within the educational system is a participatory action research project, aimed at changing students attitudes towards the use of Creole, 'by the creation of a medium to write it down ... a trilingual school newspaper' (Moya Chaves, 2004: 34–35). This study is interesting in that it is the only one I know of that has taken a participatory, ethnographic stance to language use in one particular school context on the Islands. For this reason, I propose to discuss some aspects in more detail in this section.

The school where the project was carried out, *Flowers Hill School*, is officially classified as a bilingual institution, formed by three Baptist schools: *Emmanuel School*, *Christian Mission* and *Central Baptist School*. Students come from a variety of family origins: Nicaragua, the United States and mainland Colombia, particularly Chocó, Barranquilla, Cali, Medellín and Bogotá. Thus, some of the students are mainlanders and do not speak Creole; others are sometimes referred to as 'fifty-fifty', where one parent is originally from mainland Colombia and the other is a native Islander; while others are known as *raizales* or Islanders and usually live in one of the more traditional neighbourhoods. The tensions of these different origins are evident in some of the student comments reported:

> I don't feel rejected because I am not Islander or *Panya*. But there are some people that do feel so.

> There are people who say that the Islanders are closed and sometimes I think, without wanting to offend, that it is true.[16] (Moya Chaves, 2004: 28)

In her classroom observation, the researcher noticed that there was constant codeswitching between Spanish, English and Creole reflecting the mix of students, some coming from monolingual (Spanish) schools and others, Creole-speaking Islander students. Spanish and Creole were the dominant languages of oral interaction in the institution, the former for classroom control and the latter for explanations, even though teachers tried to talk to Islander students mainly in English. The Islander students often acted as unofficial translators for their Spanish-speaking peers, who showed little inclination to interact in English.

One of the English teachers referred to the bilingual status of the school in the following way:

> I think it has no more than a name of a bilingual school, but I think we are working on it ... and for our native people this is a great privilege, as right now, as far as I know, there are only two institutions which are still professing bilingualism: us and Brooks Hill. (Moya Chaves, 2004: 43)

The trilingual newspaper project, *FiWii News*,[17] developed with students from Grades 8 to 11, involved them in finding out about local culture, language use, oral history, jokes, riddles and so on and writing reflections and articles in Spanish, English and Creole. The reaction to the finished project was generally positive, but the researcher reflected on just how permanent the effect of this initiative would be:

> Students and teachers seemed to be pleased with the result of the newspaper, but I still wonder whether Creole is going to be kept in the newspaper, in the class, or if 'FiWii News' is going to be another tide that came to San Andrés, just leaving temporary traces. (Moya Chaves, 2004: 52)

She came to the conclusion that it was important to encourage writing in Creole but that a longer process was necessary to consolidate this. She recognised, however, that many teachers consider Creole as a primarily oral language and consider that it is this characteristic which keeps local traditions and culture alive. They also believe that using this language in the curriculum will cause confusion for the students in the learning of Standard English and they question the learning of Creole when they see it as unlikely that students will find speakers or contexts in which they can use their native language when they leave school.

Conclusion

What I have tried to do in this chapter is to discuss several key issues arising from policies, curricular initiatives and classroom practices relating to trilingual education in the Archipelago of San Andrés, Providencia and Santa Catalina in order to show some of the tensions and complexities inherent in this multilingual context. While it is interesting to note that official government policy authorises the use of the students' first language(s) in bilingual and multilingual education contexts, the differing attitudes towards the three languages in play leads to a division of opinion about their relevance and value. In particular, the marginalisation of Creole as a legitimate classroom language causes difficulties for many Islander children, especially in the early years of schooling (Dittmann, 2006).

However, there are some recent developments which would seem to be promising with regard to developing students' potential trilingualism on the Islands. One of these is the creation of a Creole alphabet and the production of story books and text book material in Creole, as the basis for a trilingual curricular proposal under the auspices of the Christian University of San Andrés. Another is the carrying out of small-scale ethnographic studies on school language use which helps to recognise some potentially valuable cross-linguistic strategies used spontaneously by some of the classroom participants, such as the constitution of Islander students as 'language brokers' in the multilingual classroom setting referred to in this chapter.

The concept of 'language ecology' (Creese & Martin, 2003; Reyes & Azuara, 2008) as applied to multilingual classrooms on the Islands can help to show, 'how languages exist and evolve in an eco-system along with other languages, and how they [their speakers] interact with their socio-political, economic and cultural environments' (Hornberger, 2002: 35 cited in Creese & Martin, 2003: 163). This would imply analysing multilingual classroom language use in San Andrés, Providencia and Santa Catalina, not as an isolated phenomenon, but as part of a linguistic and cultural continuum which involves home and community settings as well as institutions and official bodies.

Iliana Reyes (2008) in a recent study which adopted an ecological perspective to language use, carried out on home biliteracy practices involving Latino families in Arizona, focused on two key research questions:

- How do young emergent bilinguals develop biliteracy in their everyday sociocultural contexts (home, school, communities)?
- How do different sociocultural factors influence the ways in which teachers and parents support children's potential to become bilingual and biliterate?

I think it is quite possible to reformulate these questions to reflect the trilingual potential of the Islands, but it would also be necessary to ask in what ways school and education administrators support students' potential to become trilingual and triliterate.

In her conclusions, Reyes (2008) maintains that a complex interplay between L1 and L2 belief systems in the different contexts will affect acquisition of L2. She also outlines some of the implications of adopting an ecological model in relation to the areas of theory, research and practice. With regard to theory, she maintains that an ecological approach to language must adopt a dialogical point of view; in research, she sees a need for longitudinal studies of language ecologies and socialization in bilingual or multilingual classrooms; while in practice, there is need to extend the focus to include political discourse. She also makes a plea for the transfer of successful strategies from 'naturalistic' to classroom settings, highlighting the importance of recognising the 'funds of knowledge' (Moll, 1992) that multilingual children bring to the classroom. These are valuable recommendations for future developments in language and education policy and practice on the Islands.

This is one final vision which has only been briefly touched upon in this discussion: the question of which frame of reference should be used to contextualise the use of Creole as a valid communicative resource: Spanish-speaking Colombia, or a wider Creole-speaking universe in the Caribbean. In this respect, the Reverend Ricardo Gordon May, Secretary of Education in the Archipelago in an impassioned speech in 2003 argued for the inclusion of Creole in the school system by indicating an extra national frame of reference: other Creole-speaking nations in the Caribbean. Having just returned from a congress in Barbados on Creole languages, he said this to his fellow Creole-speaking Islanders,

> But I want you to realize, because sometimes they will tell you, 'Well, we don't need Creole; Creole you can only use here in San Andrés'. That is a lie: in twenty five countries in the Caribbean you have people who look just like you, with a similar history like ours, and they are going through the same process.

Sanmiguel Ardila in a similar vein, but from a more academic standpoint, recognises one of the challenges for the islands as that of

> Accepting, rather than rejecting the composition of the multilingual classroom, based on pedagogical and intercultural principles ... The multilingual and pluricultural classroom reflects the sociolinguistic composition of the island [San Andrés], which is not distant from the real dynamics of the makeup of multiethnic societies, characteristic of the Caribbean, where conceptions of the world are as diverse as they are enriching in their meeting.[18] (Sanmiguel Ardila, 2006: 83–84)

Perhaps this change of referent is what is needed to help to legitimise the use of Creole within a trilingual education system in the multilingual and pluricultural context of San Andrés, Providencia and Santa Catalina in the future.

Notes

1. There is some discrepancy about these distances. Flórez (2006) quoting the World Wildlife Fund (2001) refers to 620 km and 150 km, respectively.
2. This expression, still commonly used on the Islands, derives from the word 'Spaniard' (Moya Chaves, 2004).
3. The other Creole language used in Colombia is Spanish-based Creole known as *Palenquero*, spoken in the community of Palenque San Basilio, near the coastal city of Cartagena.
4. A diferencia de muchos lugares del Caribe (Jamaica, Trinidad, Grenada, Guyana) donde coexisten la lengua inglesa – bajo la forma de inglés estándar caribeño – para efectos de la educación y las formalidades del Estado, y la lengua criolla para la comunicación cotidiana, en Providencia el espacio de la lengua inglesa ha sido gradualmente ocupado por la lengua española. Es probable, entonces, que esta falta de contacto entre la lengua criolla y su lengua lexificadora facilita aún más la interacción entre la lengua criolla y la lengua española' (Abouchaar *et al.*, 2002: 77).
5. Author's translation of this and other quotations in this chapter from Spanish to English.
6. 'La ausencia de una política lingüística que reconozca el valor de la diversidad de lenguas y culturas, y el trilingüismo de sus habitantes en ámbitos de cotidianidad, terminará por afecto el posicionamiento de lenguas como el creole en la sociedad sanandresana'.
7. 'El 99% de los maestros y directivos tienen en la lengua criolla su lengua materna. El dominio del español como segunda lengua es suficiente para propósitos de la comunicación ordinaria. Se percibieron a través de la investigación algunas dificultades para la redacción en español de documentos de carácter académico (...) En caso de que se implementara un programa de educación bilingüe que incorporara el inglés, la mayoría de los docentes requeriría formación intensiva en esta lengua' (Abouchaar *et al.*, 2002: 74–75).
8. 'La educación para los grupos étnicos hace parte del servicio público educativo y se sustenta en un compromiso de elaboración colectiva, donde los distintos miembros de la comunidad en general, intercambian saberes y vivencias con miras a mantener, recrear y desarrollar un proyecto global de vida de acuerdo con su cultura, su lengua, sus tradiciones y sus fueros propios y autóctonos'.
9. 'el criollo puede ser usado como plataforma para lanzar a los estudiantes a la lengua objetiva, que es la forma estándar del inglés ... Sostenemos que el criollo es hablado solamente por unas pocas personas y nunca adquirirá prestigio y poder'.
10. Now known as the 'Wycliff Bible Institute'.
11. 'su orgullo al poder escribir en su lengua familiar y comunitaria, empleando sus conocimientos y sentimientos culturales'.

12. 'Aún hay una resistencia por parte de amplios sectores de la comunidad raizal y del magisterio raizal al empleo de la escritura en creole y la enseñanza de la misma en las escuelas'.
13. 'el proceso actual saltó desde lo oral y la utilización de las historias escritas en "creole" a la escritura en español en primero de primaria'.
14. 'la lengua dominante y suprema para el raizal'.
15. In this case, English.
16. 'Yo no me siento rechazada porque no soy ni isleña ni *panya*. Pero hay una personas que sí . . . ' 'Hay gente que dice que los isleños son cerrados y a veces yo creo, que sin ánimo de ofender, es cierto'.
17. In Standard English this means 'Our News'.
18. 'Acoger más que rechazar la composición del aula multilingüe con base en principios pedagógicos e interculturales . . . El aula multilingüe y pluricultural refleja la composición socio-lingüística de la isla la cual no es ajena a las dinámicas reales de conformación de sociedades multiétnicas, características del Caribe, cuyas concepciones del mundo son tan diversas como enriquecedoras en su encuentro'.

References

Abouchaar, A. and Moya, S. (2005) Dominio de la lengua española entre estudiantes del grado quinto en la Isla de Providencia. *Cuadernos del Centro de Estudios Sociales* 9, 8–12. Bogotá: Universidad Nacional de Colombia.

Abouchaar, A., Hooker, Y. and Robinson, B. (2002) Estudio lingüístico para la implementación del programa de educación bilingüe en el municipio de Providencia y Santa Catalina. Número especial de *Cuadernos del Caribe* No. 3. San Andrés Islas: Universidad Nacional de Colombia.

Andrade, J. (2004) *Una aproximación al atlas socio-lingüístico de San Andrés, Isla.* Tesis de pregrado, Departamento de Lingüística Universidad Nacional de Colombia, Sede Bogotá-Sede Caribe.

Bowie, P. and Dittmann, M. (2007) El proyecto piloto trilingüe de la Universidad Cristiana de San Andrés en las Escuelas Emmanuel Bautista y Bautista Central en la Isla de San Andrés. In A.M. Truscott de Mejía and S. Colmenares (eds) *Bialfabetismo. Lectura y Escritura en dos Lenguas en Colombia* (pp. 67–87). Cali: Universidad del Valle.

Brown, D. (1999) Un enfoque metodológico bilingüe para San Andrés. In A.M. de Mejía and L.A. Tovar (eds) *Perspectivas recientes del bilingüismo y de la educación bilingüe en Colombia* (pp.141–148). Cali: Universidad del Valle.

Creese, A. and Martin, P. (2003) *Multilingual Classroom Ecologies: Inter-relationships, Interactions and Ideologies.* Special Issue of the *International Journal of Bilingual Education and Bilingualism* 6, 3–4.

Dieck, M. (1998) Criollística afrocolombiana. In L.A. Maya (ed.) *Geografía Humana de Colombia: Los Afrocolombianos* (pp. 303–338). Bogotá: Instituto Colombiano de Cultura Hispánica.

Dittmann, M. (2006) La importancia de la lengua materna en el aprendizaje de una segunda lengua y en la educación bilingüe: el caso de la comunidad raizal del archipiélago de San Andrés. *Memorias del Segundo Simposio Internacional de Bilingüismo y Educación en América Latina* (pp. 73–86). Universidad de los Andes, Bogotá 5, 6 y 7 de octubre de 2006.

Flórez, S. (2006) A study of language attitudes in two Creole-speaking islands: San Andrés and Providence (Colombia). *Íkala, Revista de Lenguaje y Cultura* 11, 119–147.

Mitchell, D., Dittmann, M. and Forbes, O. (2004) *Propuesta de Etnoeducación Intercultural Trilingüe para el Pueblo Raizal*. Documento de trabajo.

Moll, L.C. (1992) Bilingual classroom studies and community analysis. *Educational Researcher* 21, 20–24.

Morren, R.C. (2001) Creole-based trilingual education in the Caribbean archipelago of San Andres, Providence and Santa Catalina. *Journal of Multilingual and Multicultural Development* 22, 227–241.

Moya Chaves, D.S. (2004) Going up and down the hill with 'Fi Wii News', or the production of a bilingual newspaper for Flowers Hill Bilingual School, San Andrés. Unpublished monograph. Bogotá: Universidad Nacional de Colombia.

Reyes, I. (2008) *Bilingualism in the Americas: Toward an Ecological Model for Theory, Research, and Practice*. Presentation during the Thirteenth Round Table in Applied Linguistics, Universidad Distrital Francisco José de Caldas, Bogotá, 29–30 May 2008.

Reyes, I. and Azuara, P. (2008) Emergent biliteracy in young Mexican immigrant children. *Reading Research Quarterly* 43, 374–398.

Sanmiguel Ardila, R. (2006) Mitos, hechos y retos actuales del bilingüismo en el Archipiélago de San Andrés, Providencia y Santa Catalina. *Memorias del Segundo Simposio Internacional de Bilingüismo y Educación en América Latina* (pp. 55–72). Universidad de los Andes, Bogotá 5, 6 y 7 de octubre de 2006.

Part 1

The Ecology of the Multilingual Classroom: From Complexity to Pedagogy

Perspectives on the Teachers

Chapter 5

Teachers at the Epicenter: Engagement and Resistance in a Biliteracy Program for 'Long-Term English Language Learners' in the United States

K. MENKEN, A. FUNK and T. KLEYN
with L. ASCENZI-MORENO, N. CHAE and N. FLORES

Introduction

The United States is in the midst of an unprecedented demographic shift, as the number of minority students and those learning English grows at an exponential pace (National Clearinghouse for English Language Acquisition, 2007). Despite these increases in students who come from diverse cultural backgrounds with the asset of languages other than English, schools have largely responded by providing more (and only) English education, as opposed to bilingual programs that develop students' native language and literacy skills as English is added to their linguistic repertoire. Although New York City has historically been supportive of bilingual education, in recent years there has been a drastic decline in bilingual programs due to a convergence of language policies within an overall context of language restriction in the United States (Menken, 2008).

This chapter shares findings from research about emergent bilinguals[1] who have attended US schools for seven or more years and whose prior schooling has been linguistically subtractive – in the United States, these students are referred to as 'long-term English language learners' (or LTELLs). In this chapter, we document our efforts to implement a new biliteracy program to meet the needs of these students in two New York City high schools. Prior to our work in these schools, the native languages of long-term ELLs were not used in their education. In the 2008–2009 academic year, by contrast, both of our research sites implemented a new program for Spanish-speaking LTELLs as a way to increase their literacy skills in English and Spanish and subsequently improve their academic performance.

This chapter focuses on the complex role of teachers in implementing new language programming that essentially changes schools from institutions that promulgate monolingualism to those that utilize and, ideally, embrace their multilingualism. More specifically, we examine the teaching practices of the classroom teachers involved in this project, most of whom had never received prior preparation to work with emergent bilinguals, and document both their efforts and resistance to meeting the needs of these diverse students. We identify institutional and instructional features found to support the students, and those that stood in the way of their success. Specifically, we consider the teachers' efforts to embed explicit language and literacy instruction in the following subjects: English language arts (ELA), English as a second language (ESL), mathematics, science and social studies as well as in a new course titled 'Spanish for native speakers'. And, we examine these teachers' collaboration with one another across the subject area divide; in traditional high schools, few opportunities are provided for collaborative planning, particularly across subjects. Examples from classroom observations illustrate how thoughtful instructional planning can increase student learning of language and content, and likewise how the absence of such planning can further leave these students behind. Moreover, in this chapter we highlight the tensions that arise in educational contexts where multilingualism is being brought from the periphery toward the center of student learning.

Language Policy in the United States and New York City

In the United States, approximately 47 million people – 18% of the population – speak a language other than English at home and, if current immigration rates continue, this number will increase to about 40% by 2030 (National Council of Teachers of English, 2008; Shin & Bruno, 2003). Emergent bilinguals are thus the fastest-growing population in US schools – in 1990, one in 20 public school students in grades K–12 was an emergent bilingual while today the figure is one in nine; it is estimated that in 20 years this figure will be one in four (Goldenberg, 2008).

In spite of this growing diversity, or more likely in reaction against it, schools in the United States are increasingly likely to restrict the use of immigrant languages and instead teach emergent bilinguals solely through the medium of English (García, 2009; Menken, 2008). Zehler *et al.* (2003)

estimate that national enrollment in bilingual education programs has dropped from 37% to 17% over the past decade. Crawford (2007) among others attributes this loss of bilingual programs to the following policy changes: (1) the states of California, Arizona and Massachusetts have in recent years passed antibilingual education legislation; and (2) on a national level, federal education policy has promoted English-only schooling since the passage of *No Child Left Behind* in 2001, in particular due to the law's emphasis on high-stakes testing in English (Gándara & Baca, 2008; Hornberger & Johnson, 2007; Menken, 2008; Wiley & Wright, 2004). Thus, the vast majority of US-emergent bilinguals are educated only in English, in spite of ample research support for the argument that students who develop and maintain their native languages in school typically outperform their peers in English-only programs and experience academic success over time (Baker, 2006; Krashen & McField, 2005; Thomas & Collier, 2002).

New York City is one of the most diverse cities in the world, and city schools reflect that extreme diversity. Over 40% of public school students in the city speak a language other than English at home, and 14% are currently English learners (New York City Department of Education, 2008). In some cases, over 50 languages are spoken within a single school (García & Fishman, 2002). Thus, the city boasts a wide range of educational programming options for emergent bilinguals, including those in which students are taught bilingually and others in which they are taught monolingually.

Although New York City has historically been supportive of bilingual education, and many such programs have proliferated since the 1970s, in recent years this has begun to change as the city echoes national trends. In the 2002–2003 school year, 39.7% of all emergent bilinguals were enrolled in bilingual education programs, while 53.4% were enrolled in ESL programs. By the 2007–2008 school year, however, just 25.2% of emergent bilinguals were in bilingual programs while 69.2% were in ESL (New York City Department of Education, 2008).

Research on LTELLs

The findings reported in this chapter are the most recent from a three-year research project that we conducted in New York City about LTELLs. In the city, such students comprise one-third of all emergent bilinguals at the secondary level (New York City Department of Education, 2008). Prior to our research, however, little was written or known about these students and programming for them in high schools was not differentiated in any way from that of other emergent bilinguals. As such, we found that high schools are generally not prepared to meet the needs of these students, and instead LTELLs typically attend ESL courses intended for new arrivals. One of the major findings reported in our earlier research is that the prior schooling of these primarily US-educated students has been linguistically subtractive, in that their native languages have not been fully developed in school and instead largely replaced by English (Menken & Kleyn, 2010).

We find that LTELLs typically fall into three main categories: (1) transnational students, who move back and forth between the United States and their family's country of origin; (2) students who – while attending US schools – have shifted between transitional bilingual education, ESL programs and mainstream classrooms with no language support programming; and (3) students who have received consistent subtractive schooling, due to enrollment in subtractive models of bilingual education and/or ESL throughout their educational careers. Thus, these emergent bilingual students have had limited opportunities for academic language development in either English or their native languages. As a result, although LTELLs are orally bilingual when using language for social purposes, they typically have limited academic literacy skills in English or in their native languages. As bilingual education programs in the city decrease overall, it is likely that more emergent bilinguals will experience linguistically subtractive schooling and over time become LTELLs.

Methods

Based on our prior research, we developed a program focused on academic language and literacy development both in English and Spanish, and implemented it in two New York City high schools serving Spanish-speaking LTELLs in the 2008–2009 academic year. In the city, small, specialized high schools where all the students are emergent bilinguals have been proven successful (as in the International High Schools, cited in Ancess, 2003; Fine *et al.*, 2007). Unlike these high schools, our research project was implemented in schools where emergent bilinguals comprise only a minority of the total student population, and their needs are tangential to the school's central focus.

We sought to support the development of students' academic language and literacy skills in English and Spanish through a three-pronged approach, implementing the following course structure for 9th- and 10th-grade students:

(1) Spanish Native Language Arts (NLA) courses, to help students develop a strong foundation in academic Spanish language and literacy.

(2) ESL courses, in which LTELLs are taught separately from new arrivals so that instruction can focus on academic literacy in English rather than on the development of basic language proficiency.

(3) Content-area courses – such as mathematics, science and social studies – that focus simultaneously on content, language and literacy learning (for further description, see Menken & Kleyn, 2009).

As part of this biliteracy project, teachers plan collaboratively throughout the year to create units of study that foster language and literacy skills in all subjects. They also participate in professional development meetings focused on theory, pedagogy and application.

A total of 42 students were included in our final sample: 13 at School 1, 15 at School 2 and 14 at School 3. School 3 served as our control school, as it did not implement the program described above. School 1 is a large vocational high school, while School 2 is a small high school. As such, there were variances in the implementation of the program model, in that the student participants at School 1 were 9th graders, while School 2 enrolls combination 9th/10th-grade classes due to the school's small size. School 1 offered ESL, ELA and Spanish NLA to a cohort comprised solely of LTELLs, while for their mathematics, science and social studies classes LTELLs were mixed with other students. At School 2, LTELLs were mixed in with other students for all their courses.

The findings reported in this chapter focus on the essential role of educators in program implementation. Our research findings are based on classroom observations, interviews and professional development meetings, with 10 teachers at the two school sites, conducted repeatedly throughout the year. Conducting periodic classroom observations was central to our research, as doing so allowed for the documentation of teachers' usage of specific pedagogical approaches and their outcomes, and also their efforts to support the content and literacy learning of LTELLs (Genesee & Upshur, 1996).

Over the course of the school year, each teacher was observed four to five times by one member of our research team with content expertise in the subject area observed. We documented the extent to which teachers infused language and literacy methods specifically focused on the educational needs of LTELLs into their instruction; following each lesson, the observer gave the teacher two scores ranging from 0 to 1 (with 0.25 increments) – one for the teacher's effort and the other for the teacher's implementation of language and literacy strategies. Two types of teacher interviews were conducted throughout the year-long study. First, following each classroom observation, the research team member and teacher had a post-observation debriefing session where they discussed the lesson. In addition to the four to five debriefing interviews, each teacher participated in a year-end interview in which they reflected on the successes and challenges of the biliteracy program as a whole, as well as their own work with LTELLs in particular. The principal investigator (Menken) met periodically with administrators at each school to learn their perceptions of the program's implementation. At the end of the year, an in-depth semistructured interview was also conducted with administrators. Interviews were audio-recorded, transcribed, coded and analyzed according to themes that arose most frequently (Creswell, 1998; Miles & Huberman, 1994).

Findings: Teacher Engagement, Preparedness and Barriers

One of the most significant factors impacting the efficacy of our biliteracy program was the level of teacher engagement with the program's ideals and practices. After the project began in Fall 2008, we soon realized that we had underestimated the great impact of teacher engagement and preparedness on our efforts at language education policy implementation. There were also several institutional barriers that arose over the course of the project period, as a result of decisions made by school administrators, which impacted programming. Our program was in fact successful overall, in that the LTELL students at the two schools involved in our study made substantial gains in their reading comprehension in English and Spanish, and gains were greater than those made at the control school (as we report in Menken *et al.*, 2009). That said, the program would have been more successful with greater engagement and preparation of the educators involved. Moreover, here we identify factors that should be considered in language education policy implementation efforts, particularly in schools that have for years promulgated monolingual ideology and pedagogy.

Over the course of the school year spent in the two participating schools, we found that teachers fell into one of the three main categories when asked to change their programming and practices to meet the needs of LTELL students. The first group was comprised of several teachers at both schools who demonstrated enthusiasm from the outset; throughout the year, these teachers were eager for insights about the LTELL population and proactive in developing, implementing and evaluating effective classroom strategies to meet their needs. Other instructors fell into the second group, in that they proved reluctant to modify or expand upon the teaching methods they employ with other student populations; consequently, the instruction they provided to the LTELLs in their classrooms departed in principle and practice from our model, and was not differentiated to meet the specialized needs of LTELLs. A third group of teachers made signifi-cant efforts to infuse a focus on language and literacy development into their lessons, but were not always effective in implementing their plans.

In order to quantify this observable level of teacher 'fidelity' to the bilit-eracy project, two evaluation measures were incorporated into our class-room observations: Teacher effort (at infusing language and literacy) and effectiveness (of the language and literary strategies they implemented), both of which were evaluated by our team during our observations on a scale of 0–1 at quarter-point intervals (as described in the Methods section). Scores are shown in Table 5.1.

The findings presented in the table support the existence of the three groups of teachers outlined above. The teachers in the top two rows received the highest scores, in that no teacher in this group received an effectiveness score below 0.75 in any single observation. Conspicuously, these three instructors – who consistently strove to implement language and literacy strategies and did so most effectively – were those for whom English language and literacy were already central to the curriculum: the ELA and ESL teachers. In contrast, no teacher in the other four subject areas ever received a single-observation effectiveness score *above* 0.5, with the lowest scores belonging to the mathematics and science teachers at School 1, who consistently displayed strong resistance to the aims and

Table 5.1 Teacher effort/literacy strategies: Average scores

	School 1		School 2	
	Effort	*Effectiveness*	*Effort*	*Effectiveness*
English language arts (ELA)	1.00	0.90	1.00	1.00
English as a second language (ESL)	0.88	0.75	n/a[a]	n/a
Spanish native language arts (NLA)	0.40	0.35	0.25	0.13
Social studies	0.13	0.06	0.63	0.44
Mathematics	0.00	0.06	0.81	0.25
Science	n/a[b]	n/a	0.44	0.31

[a]The ESL teacher at School 2 co-taught with other teachers, mostly in global studies (social studies); there was no independent ESL class. While his fidelity to the model was high throughout the year, only the teachers with whom he taught were evaluated.
[b]School 1 decided to eliminate 9th grade science for the cohort involved in this study, presumably due to scheduling pressures.

approaches of the program. The other five teachers – spread among the four 'non-English' subject areas – represent the third group mentioned above, whose various levels of effort yielded mixed results. Ms H,[2] for example, made strong efforts to infuse literacy into her classroom, but found a number of obstacles in her way:

> I feel like there are very few [ELL/LTELL] resources out there. I feel like people don't consider math a literacy area. It's like English, then global, the two main ones. Then science and math, like you don't need to read to do math. Yes, you do. (Ms H, Math Teacher, School 2, Interview Transcript)

These and other challenges to teacher engagement – as well as key factors that foster it – are considered in detail below.

'Language vs. content'?

At first glance, the higher scores for ELA and ESL teachers might seem only natural. The teachers of these subjects (whom we call 'Ms K', 'Ms D', 'Ms S' and 'Mr N') had stronger backgrounds in explicit language and literacy pedagogy, through both their training and prior teaching experience. Therefore, the changes they made to how they taught prior to participation in this project were more minor. In addition, language and literacy learning are central to the state-determined curricula that they must cover. The teachers of other subject areas (called 'Ms N', 'Mr A', 'Ms H', 'Mr M' and 'Mr L') faced the dual challenges of less experience with this type of instruction, and the need to teach content that was less explicitly focused on language and literacy (e.g. historical figures and events, mathematical and scientific formulas). The clear demarcation (see rows 4 and 5) between content teachers who put in significant effort and those who did not is worth noting here; teacher 'buy-in' to the very concept of language and literacy infusion was a factor that mitigated (School 2) or compounded (School 1) the difficulties already inherent in language planning for the content areas.

What about native language arts?

What the 'language vs. content' divide does not easily account for are the lower evaluations of both Spanish teachers, whose pedagogical backgrounds presumably centered on language and literacy as much as those of the ESL and ELA teachers. Part of the explanation is that Spanish teachers are not prepared to teach Spanish to native speakers of the language who have experienced language loss, and who have low literacy skills in the language as a result. Additionally, neither school previously offered native language arts (NLA) courses. At School 1, Spanish had previously only been offered as a foreign language arts course to be taken by native-English speakers; at School 2, Spanish had not been offered at all and the Spanish teacher had been teaching ESL. While the ESL and ELA teachers needed to adapt their previous curricula for LTELLs, Ms C, the NLA teacher at School 1, could draw only from her experience teaching native-English speakers in a foreign language course, while Mr R at School 2 was faced with creating an entirely new NLA curriculum from scratch. Mr R spoke of this pressure early on when asked where he needed additional support:

> The curriculum itself. I can plan a good lesson, but I need to organize that. I want to sit down with someone who is used to doing it. I have a curriculum that I have that I've been working on with my mother-in-law (who was a teacher). I want to make it meaningful to me. What are the learning points, the four modalities [speaking, writing, listening, reading]? (Mr R, NLA Teacher, School 2, Interview Transcript)

Ms C did not settle on a textbook until several weeks into the school year, and felt much more effective after she did:

> We tried to get a book that would fit all of my students' needs. I met with Ms J and [teacher name] and we came up with the idea that *Navegando* is good for them, because it has a lot of activities. They practice talking, reading and writing ... I feel now that the follow-up is more specific. [The textbook]'s guided towards their needs. (Ms C, NLA Teacher, School 1, Interview Transcript)

There were also significant individual differences between the two teachers that emerged over the course of the year. Mr R expressed interest in LTELLs and their particular needs in early conversations, but proved somewhat less dedicated to actually implementing new strategies for his LTELL students as the year went on; in his final class observation, Mr R's effort was assessed at 0. By contrast, Ms C overcame initial unfamiliarity with how to help her students develop foundational native language literacy skills, and by spring was starting to receive 0.5s in both of her observation scores. Ms C's description of one of her later lessons reflect the work that she had done, both on her own and in collaboration with the ELA and ESL teachers at her school:

> [What's working is] the fact that the [students] are writing and they have to write in English class and they have to organize thoughts,

they're writing narrative. They were writing that in the English class, it's connected all the time. What they are writing in one class, they are writing in this class. (Ms C, NLA Teacher, School 1, Observation 4 Notes)

The Assistant Principal also noticed Ms C's growth over the course of the project period:

[Ms C] made the greatest growth, the greatest leap. I think working with [researcher (Ascenzi-Moreno)] was a great help. I saw a strong leap ... someone who didn't have a lot of experience, who struggled with some of the activities in class ... to someone who was very confident in the classroom ... [who] would do her thing, and do what she had to do, who felt very confident. So I saw tremendous growth, a tremendous change in Ms C! (Ms J, Assistant Principal, School 1, Interview Transcript)

Undoubtedly, differences in disposition among the various teachers involved in the study – for example Ms C's open-mindedness and work ethic, as well as the willingness of School 1's other teachers to collaborate with her – impacted their levels of engagement.

Teacher Engagement

Positive effects of heightened teacher awareness about LTELLs

It is has been about five years since the New York City Department of Education began requiring schools to disaggregate the data they gather about emergent bilinguals by subgroup, including LTELLs. One of our primary findings has been that simply increasing teachers' awareness about this population has improved the quality of services being provided to them. Before we began our study, the teachers in the participating schools had little to no awareness about long-term ELLs, and schools citywide had no educational programs in place specifically tailored to the needs of this population. This limited attentiveness is expressed by Ms S:

To be honest, I don't think that we had ever given an actual direct thought to the idea that there are ELLs and there are long-term ELLs. Are we doing anything specific for those long-term ELLs? So the study certainly helped us to focus our energy and focus our strategies on them. (Ms S, ELA Teacher, School 2, Interview Transcript)

Over the course of the biliteracy project period, teachers received on-going professional development from members of the research team in formal group sessions and also in the one-on-one classroom observations and subsequent discussions described above. Toward the end of the year, Ms K had come to the following understanding about LTELLs:

> They need a lot of structure, a lot more scaffolding, a little bit at a time. You can't overwhelm them with too much ... They need people to understand that they are LTELLs, to be patient with them, that it's okay to use their native language, they still need to. I've learned for myself that there's such a wide spread of LTELLs, there are those that are not as academic. They are not miscategorized or misprogrammed. They are not special education. (Ms K, ELA Teacher, School 1, Interview Transcript)

Ms K noticed that although there were differences in the students' abilities, as a group they require additional support structures and time. She also noted that some LTELLs do not perform well academically, but not as an outcome of learning disabilities, such as those evident in students assigned to special education classes.[3] Ms K understands that what this population of students requires most is their teachers' awareness and appropriate modification of teaching strategies.

Mr N, the ESL teacher at School 2, provides an example of what the 'scaffolding' for LTELLs that Ms K refers to above looks like in the Global History classroom where he co-teaches with the social studies teacher:

> What we did in Global was instead of giving them entire textbook chapters to read, which is something that a lot of teachers still do, we would take chunks that were important from the chapter and we would turn those chunks into double-entry journals where they'd have a chunk and had a question beside it. They had to read that chunk and then answer that question. I found that when we did that the LTELLs were able to access the text more. (Mr N, ESL Teacher, School 2, Interview Transcript)

In this excerpt, Mr N clarifies how instruction is modified for LTELLs.

Ms N utilizes a similar scaffolding approach based on questioning in her science course, only she has students pose the questions. In her classes, students take notes, often by copying what is on the board, overhead or PowerPoint presentation. Because this approach does not guarantee students actually comprehend what they write, Ms N has success with an activity she calls 'know your notes'. Instead of the teacher asking students questions about what they copied, it is the students who must ask questions based on their notes and then pose them to their peers. This activity places students in the position of not only answering questions, but also asking them, which can be even more demanding. Further pedagogical strategies the teachers found successful with LTELLs in their classrooms include: activating prior knowledge, oral language development, attention to vocabulary and active read alouds (described further in Menken *et al.*, 2009).

Moreover, by simply clarifying for teachers the diversity of the student population they serve, and highlighting the specialized learning needs of LTELLs, the teaching practices of several teachers changed in positive ways at the schools involved our study. As a result of this increased awareness, they identified and refined teaching strategies such as those described above, which they found were successful for their LTELL students.

Teacher collaboration

Although collaboration among high-school teachers is typically uncommon, and collaboration across content areas is even less prevalent at this level, our biliteracy program required teachers to plan together. In the summer of 2008, before the program began, the ELA, NLA and ESL teachers from both schools met with a few members of the research team to plan a linked curriculum, whereby different courses would reinforce and build upon each other. This was meant to set the tone for the remainder of the year, during which unit planning was intended to be collaborative across all three language teachers and courses.

The collaboration process took on different formats at each school. In School 1, the ESL, ELA and NLA teachers continued to work together during their scheduled planning time, although the ELA and ESL teachers were in actuality able to work more closely with each other than with the NLA teacher. Nevertheless, the three teachers taught the LTELL students in back-to-back periods (with the ELA teacher having a double-period block). Ms D speaks to the effectiveness of this working relationship, which was entirely new for the teachers at School 1:

> It's been great collaborating with the ELA teacher. I don't collaborate as much with the Spanish or other teachers. I needed to learn the ELA strategies, so that helped me a lot. Ms K and I were just teaching point of view at the same time, so the students had just done it and they were like 'I know that'. That was great to hear that ... but also working that time into our meetings you know, it became necessary because of the study. But it was necessary anyway. (Ms D, ESL Teacher, School 1, Interview Transcript)

As Ms D mentions, the collaboration was very helpful, but did not equally involve all the teachers in the biliteracy program, largely due to scheduling issues. Nevertheless, even though she and Ms K did not have the time to meet with the NLA teacher on a regular basis, their collaborative planning positively impacted the students in Spanish as well.

The similar focus embedded into course curricula allowed students to create connections around literacy in English and Spanish and to see how skills transfer across languages. Ms C explains, 'Students were reintroduced to the writing process in Spanish. This lesson is a review of what has been done in ELA, to connect students' understandings of the writing process to NLA'. Thus, even a minimal level of collaboration positively affected students. Ms J, the assistant principal at the school, summarizes the power of teacher collaborative planning and the discussions they had about their students:

> Conversations, the teachers, like, with Spanish and English and ESL they taught along the same theme. And they planned together and they talked about the kids together, that this child did this in my room. This child is very quiet in my class. And this child does this. Just to have a conversation. And they also visited each other. That was great. (Ms J, Assistant Principal, School 1, Interview Transcript)

While collaboration was new at School 1, as it was a required component of the biliteracy program, it was already part of the school culture at School 2 prior to the start of our project. The teachers across all the content areas at School 2 select a common skill to teach each month, and address it in their own subject area. For example, teachers focused on comparing and contrasting one month and word sorts to develop content vocabulary another month. However, while the teachers at School 2 did come together to collaborate, their efforts were not centered on the needs of emergent bilinguals or long-term ELLs. It was not until the LTELL biliteracy program started and we began coming into the school for professional development sessions that the specific focus and collaboration around LTELLs began.

With the smaller size of School 2 and teachers' closer working proximity, they were able to co-plan and also to co-teach. This was the case with the ESL and content teachers. In this collaborative team-teaching structure, the ESL teacher focused on the explicit literacy skills required to make the content accessible to students. Ideally, both teachers worked together as equals to bring language and content instruction to students in a consistent and uninterrupted manner. However, this was not always easy, especially if the ESL teacher lacked content knowledge, or if the content teacher was not open to having another teacher in their room; at times, content teachers can see the ESL teacher simply as a paraprofessional or assistant there solely to help beginner students (for further discussion of this common downfall of co-teaching, see Creese, 2005). Nonetheless, there were instances of successful team-teaching at School 2. The lesson summary below shows how the mathematics and ESL teacher collaborated:

> Both teachers taught equally throughout the lesson. The focus on literacy was explicit through a sorting activity that centered on applying prior knowledge and specific vocabulary as it applied to the content of solving 2-step equations. The teachers worked together seamlessly so it seemed as if both were the math instructor, despite one of them being the ESL specialist. The students were quite engaged in the activity and the lesson appeared to be successful. (Ms H and Mr R, Math and ESL Teachers, School 2, Observation Notes)

Although challenging in terms of the time commitment required and interpersonal relationships between teachers, collaboration at both schools was viewed as a positive aspect for instruction and student learning. For LTELLs, the reinforcement of skills across their different courses allow for purposeful connections to be made rather than those that arise simply by coincidence. Also, co-teaching can ensure that students receive content and literacy instruction simultaneously. It is likely that an expansion of such collaboration, already in place to different degrees in both schools, would only deepen its positive impact on LTELLs.

Teacher Resistance

In all likelihood, every school (if not every professional institution) counts among its members both those amenable to new ideas and those less open to change, and neither school in the study was an exception to this rule. Given the creation of a new LTELL student cohort apart from other emergent bilinguals, a new program of study involving the addition of Spanish courses, and the explicit objective of developing unique classroom strategies for that cohort, our program was bound to meet a certain level of resistance from teachers of the second type, and this was indeed the case. Some teachers were relatively open about this:

> The way we've been told now is maybe you have them in groups ... with the curriculum we have now, I don't know how we can do that. You will never be able to cover the curriculum. (Mr M, Math Teacher, School 1, Interview Transcript)

Student collaboration was indeed something our team suggested for the LTELL classes, but, while perhaps not finding this particular approach problematic per se, Mr M was in general resistant to new ideas. Mr L presents an entirely different justification for avoiding group work:

> I can't do group work. That idea is not going to translate. There's this belief that young people can work together. They're so caught up in this self-entertainment that group work ... is a non-starter. (Mr L, Social Studies Teacher, School 1, Interview Notes)

It should be noted that these views of student collaboration are at variance with those of other teachers in our program, but again, perhaps more significant are the phrases 'will never', 'is not going to' and 'nonstarter', which indicate *a priori* rejection of the viability of group work with LTELLs, as opposed to consideration of its relative value after actually attempting it. Indeed, as far as could be told from classroom observations, Mr M and Mr L succeeded in avoiding group work throughout the course of the year. The lessons of both teachers were strikingly and consistently teacher centered: students were given problems or questions to do independently and silently, and then had their answers checked by the teacher. In several cases when time grew short for the completion of a worksheet, the teacher hushed the students in order to spoon-feed them – orally or on the board – the answers they were supposed to have found but had not. 'Crowd control' was often mentioned as a reason for avoiding group work; interestingly, however, classroom management was a salient challenge in both classrooms, despite (or perhaps because of) this teacher-centered focus.

Mr L and Mr M demonstrated similar resistance to 'razzle-dazzle' (i.e. various methods of infusing language and literacy instruction into content areas) from the start of our research project, and this resistance also lasted throughout the project period. When asked to consider methods of developing students' vocabulary beyond mere impromptu, oral glossing of difficult words as he came across them in a text, Mr L replied:

> If I were to start doing razzle-dazzle, it's going to raise the [students'] anxiety levels. I tried that a couple times [before the start of this program], but it didn't work. (Mr L, Social Studies Teacher, School 1, Interview Notes)

Occasionally, apparent resistance or reluctance on the part of teachers in the program contradicted their outward affinity for the ideas behind the project. Mr R, the NLA teacher, has already been mentioned in this regard: while never expressing the type of firm opposition to student collaboration seen above, he maintained strongly teacher-centered practices, with little student talk and minimal modeling or scaffolding for whatever independent work the students were required to do. Indeed, at one time or another, all of the teachers involved in the project expressed support for the concepts of native language support, additional scaffolding/ modeling and in general developing programming and instruction with the needs of LTELLs in mind. In spite of this 'lip service' to the ideals of bilingualism and language learning, some teachers never moved their support of these ideals from theory into practice. Additionally, as described in the section that follows, there were several external barriers that inhibited the engagement of the educators in the program.

Institutional Resistance

School culture

The two schools we worked with had different climates. While the administration at School 1 began the school year stating a strong commitment to collaboration among the teachers, in actuality the only teachers who regularly collaborated were the ELA, ESL and NLA teachers (with the NLA teacher less frequently involved). Over time, we found that limited opportunities for collaboration negatively impacted teacher engagement. The roots of this difficulty were both logistical – for example, few or no designated periods for co-planning, either during or after school – and cultural in nature. By cultural we mean that School 1's teachers had evidently not been encouraged to work together in the past, and many were reluctant to do so for this program.

This was most notable in professional development sessions at the school, in which discussion of theories and practices for LTELLs were met with indifference from some of the faculty and administration alike, while model lessons demonstrating effective strategies were greeted more enthusiastically. Little value, in effect, was attached to the exchange of ideas among teachers: professional development was perceived as an exclusively top-down affair. Participants arrived late, wandered freely in and out of the discussion to attend to other business (e.g. cell phone calls), and – when one session ended at 5:03 instead of 5:00 sharp – a teacher asked the Assistant Principal in apparent seriousness if they would be paid overtime for the indiscretion. These behavior patterns indicated, in our view, a trickling down of an institutional ethos that devalued teacher collaboration and did not prioritize the needs of LTELLs.

On the other hand, School 2 paid greater logistical and cultural attention to the value of collaboration, with teachers participating more actively in discussion and viewing professional development and planning meetings as serious, worthwhile activities (though even more collaborative planning might have helped; see Mr R's comments below). It seems entirely reasonable to think that the lack of lowest-quadrant Teacher Effort scores (cf. Table 5.1) at School 2 might be related, at least indirectly, to this institutional culture.

Programming/scheduling issues and Spanish instruction

Several difficulties with class scheduling and programming resulted in decreased teacher engagement, and a disproportional number of these problems pertained to support for the Spanish language programming that was such a crucial component of our efforts. Although both schools incorporated NLA classes into the LTELL program, sustained school support for these classes was lacking, reflecting a perception among school administrators and sending students a strong message that learning Spanish was less important than other subjects. Both schools scheduled NLA classes either first period or last period, times when students were most likely to be absent – particularly given that LTELLs tend to be disengaged in schooling. Teachers referred to first period as 'a buffer' (Mr R); students came in late or left early because they did not consider it 'cutting', and generally perceived that classes at those times were not as serious as others.

Scheduling, of course, was not the only root of this perception; the institutions nourished it in other ways. While conducting student interviews at School 2 in early February 2009, our research team was surprised to learn that the LTELL students had taken an NLA course in the fall, but were no longer taking it and would not be taking it any more. The students had, in fact, lost their NLA class with the change in marking period; although the class was reinstated shortly thereafter, roughly a month had transpired without it, and another message had been sent to students about the class's (un)importance.

At School 1, another institutional challenge arose when the integrity of the LTELL cohort was not maintained: new students were matriculated into the Spanish class throughout the year, requiring the NLA teacher to constantly deal with new class dynamics, the task of familiarizing herself with the language abilities of each new student, and meeting student needs in an increasingly heterogeneous classroom. In some cases, these new students were not LTELLs at all, a fact that cut against the very aim of the project. Although this phenomenon was unfortunately not limited to the NLA class, it was most acute in this class, and it contributed to the undermining of the Spanish class's already fragile validity in students' minds.

Absenteeism was a consistent problem in NLA classes at both schools, a fact that in its own way affected institutional 'fidelity' to the program model.

> When I started with them the first period in the morning, that was in the beginning of the year, a lot of them were coming late. The other thing is they keep on sending me students to that class. I had one last week. There is one student in that class who I don't know yet. He was absent today. I would say almost every month a new student comes to that class. (Ms C, NLA Teacher, School 1, Interview Transcript)

Another challenge was the lack of materials and planning time needed to successfully implement the NLA class. Teachers at both schools, but Mr R in particular, felt alone in the planning and implementation of the program. Since the students were LTELLs, and therefore highly proficient oral speakers of Spanish (for social purposes) with low academic reading and writing skills, the class could not be taught as a foreign language class. Nor could the class be conceived as a literature class, since the students had widely varying Spanish literacy skills, inclusive of those with very rudimentary levels. These two modes – Spanish as a Foreign Language and Spanish Literature – are usually how Spanish is taught at the secondary level in the United States, and so both NLA teachers in our program needed significant support in developing a meaningful and skills-rich curriculum from scratch, one that was appropriate for LTELLs. However,

> One challenge that really burns me is not having the support of the general school ... the general school community. It's pretty much on your own. And I think it's something that the students have experienced, not having support from everyone. So that was a challenge. Also [another challenge] is engaging them. A lot of them went into class and said to themselves: I know this, I don't need this. Students also get the message that the school does not prioritize the Spanish program. (Mr R, NLA teacher, School 2, Interview Transcript)

Mr R's views stand in apparent opposition to our previous discussion on school culture: he teaches at School 2, which we described as significantly better at fostering teacher collaboration than School 1. In direct contradiction to its otherwise collaborative ethos, School 2, interestingly, displayed a lack of institutional support for the teaching of Spanish to LTELLs. Moreover, neither school administration saw NLA as an essential subject, reflected in their making decisions that in many ways undermined Spanish instruction altogether.

Class size and cohort consistency

School 1 was, as just mentioned, inconsistent at maintaining the LTELL cohort. While the group of students remained more or less intact throughout the year in ELA and ESL classes, enrollment in the NLA, social studies and mathematics classes changed dramatically from marking period to marking period. This became abundantly clear in Mr L's social studies class, which swelled to 34 students by spring.

> The powers that be decided to put them [ELLs and LTELLs] together, and it's basically a joke. (Mr L, Social Studies Teacher, School 1, Interview Notes)

This poorly considered expansion had an effect on engagement – both of teacher and students – that is easy to imagine; the program was institutionally declared to be of low value. Moreover, larger class sizes reduced the possibility that a teacher already resistant to change would try new approaches:

> 34 kids to a room. There's not even enough room for group formation. (Mr L, Social Studies Teacher, School 1, Interview Notes)

The impact of testing: Language vs. content, revisited

All high-school students in the state of New York need to qualify a set of Regents exams (in mathematics, science, social studies and ELA) in order to graduate. Teachers in our sample – particularly those of science, social studies and mathematics – mentioned the pressure of preparing students for Regents examinations as a primary obstacle to their implementation of explicit language and literacy activities. When asked how she planned for the content and literacy needs of LTELLs in her first observed lesson, School 2's math teacher (Ms H) replied that the content had been based directly on a mock Regents exam, and that she had not planned for literacy at all. As the year progressed, Ms H agreed in principle with the possible benefits of emphasizing literacy in her content area, but felt unable to deviate from her standard plan of 'drill and kill'.

> When I know something will work [for the Regents] with literacy, I'll insert it. (Ms H, Math Teacher, School 2, Interview Transcript)

Mr A, a first-year social studies teacher at School 2, had a similar aware-ness of the fundamental value of explicit literacy instruction for LTELLs – even as a key to performing well on standardized tests – yet found the need to cover the content necessary to pass the tests directly at odds with the time needed to focus on language and literacy development. Both social studies teachers at his school received prods from the admini-stration for falling behind the set pace of the Regents curriculum, a pace which Mr N, School 2's ESL teacher, referred to as 'ridiculous'. By the end of the year, Mr A had come to see literacy as a precondition for this content-building with LTELLs:

> [Over the course of the LTELL program I've learned that] LTELLs lack basic literacy skills needed to access information and do well on state tests, and these skills must be built <u>before</u> students can fully demon-strate their knowledge and understanding of concepts and informa-tion, or do well on such tests. (Mr A, Social Studies Teacher, School 2, Interview Transcript, emphasis added)

The views of these two teachers to some extent bookend the ways instruc-tors cope with the difficulty of preparing LTELLS for Regents exams, with Ms H viewing literacy as something one might 'insert' if given more time or concrete proof of it bearing fruit on the Regents, and Mr A viewing the content 'concepts and information' as something LTELLs demonstrate knowledge of only after their literacy skills are sufficiently developed. Both teachers face a similar challenge, one that no content teacher in our program felt trifling.[4]

The looming specter of the earth science Regents exam obliged Ms N to hurry through a Regents-centered curriculum, as well as to herd her students through the requisite number of labs (experiments) in order to sit for the test. 'Completing' a lab meant, for official purposes, having the right answers written down in the right places; the class's lab sessions, which might otherwise have furnished an opportunity to explicitly teach science literacy and the metacognitive skills that go into scientific think-ing, instead centered around the spoon-feeding of answers to finish within the allotted class time. Ms N was under direct pressure from the admini-stration to do this; she would hear from superiors if too few students completed labs. When asked what worked for her LTELL group in a particular class period, she replied:

> They all completed the lab and made the connection to their lives. They have to complete a certain number (30) to take the Regents, so it is good that they finished. (Ms N, Science Teacher, School 2, Interview Notes)

As the year progressed, Ms N reported success with vocabulary development, graphic organizers and developing oral language as a springboard to academic language; but, throughout the program, Regents pressure provided a barrier to infusing attention to language and literacy development in her classroom.

In each of these instances, we see high-stakes testing force even those teachers expressing support for explicit language and literacy instruction to emphasize rote coverage over in-depth analysis, not necessarily because they think this is effective for LTELLs but because they feel pressure from administrators to cover content, and understandably want their own students to perform well on the exams. In the case of those teachers with predisposed resistance, standardized testing provides another incentive for leaving literacy and language to the English teachers.

Discussion and Conclusion

This chapter documents the essential role of teachers in efforts to re-envision schools from subtractive institutions that cause multilingual students to become monolingual over time, to those that actually embrace multilingualism and build upon the diversity of their students. Specifically, our work focuses on schooling for 'long-term English language learners', primarily US-educated secondary students who, because of their prior schooling experiences, are orally bilingual when language is used for social purposes, but who have limited academic literacy skills in either of the languages they speak. In an effort to reverse some of the language loss these students have experienced and improve their school performance, we highlight efforts to change the programming and pedagogy these students received over the course of an academic year in two New York City high schools. In specific, our project involved infusing explicit attention to academic language and literacy development into all subject areas and developing the students' Spanish language skills.

While it might seem that promoting multilingualism would be easy within contexts of extreme diversity, such as New York City, our findings dispel such expectations. Our research examines the responses of teachers to new language education policies in their schools, involving professional development and teacher collaboration, as well as changes to programming, pedagogy, curricula and materials. While these changes were found to have had a positive impact on student performance, a significant result after years of programming that failed to serve this student population well, we also lament that our outcomes were more modest than they might have been, due to the absence of a full commitment to the program on the part of all teachers involved. As stated at the outset, and further detailed in Menken *et al.* (2009), the students in our sample made greater gains in their reading comprehension in both Spanish and English than the students in our control school, who actually performed worse in both areas over the course of the project period.[5] These findings suggest that our project benefitted the student participants, in spite of the limitations that we highlight in this chapter.

Although our project was successful in this regard, our findings lead us to believe that it would have had an even more positive impact had all the teachers fully bought into the program model we asked them to implement. Instead, we found that the teachers participating in our biliteracy project fell into three categories, which highlight the extent to which they embraced or rejected the model: (1) those who made great efforts to infuse explicit language and literacy instruction into their courses, and were effective in doing so; (2) those who resisted the model and would not make any effort to focus on language or literacy development in their instruction; and (3) those who made an effort but experienced limited or no success in their implementation.

Moreover, we argue that changing schoolwide approaches to language entails an identity shift among certain teachers, as well as a shift in overall institutional culture. As highlighted above, the teachers who embraced our program and were most successful in their efforts to focus on the needs of LTELLs in the classroom were the teachers of ESL and ELA. Over the course of the project, they were highly engaged and collaborative, planned consistently for language and literacy development, and they successfully identified and implemented strategies to meet the needs of their students. All these teachers self-identified as language teachers, had been prepared to teach language in institutions of higher education, and had experience working with LTELLs prior to their involvement in our program.

While the Spanish NLA teachers also self-identified as language teachers, they did so as *foreign* language teachers rather than as *native* language teachers, and had no prior experience teaching Spanish to LTELLs. Thus, they felt better prepared to teach grammar, vocabulary, verb conjugation and basic conversation to native-English speakers than they did to teach Spanish literacy skills to native-Spanish speakers. As described above, institutional culture was an added challenge that particularly affected the Spanish teachers, who faced scheduling problems and cohort inconsistency, which sent students and teachers a very clear message that Spanish instruction was of lesser value than other subjects at both schools – even though these two schools had volunteered to participate in our biliteracy project.

The greatest resistance toward our program was from teachers of such subjects as mathematics, science and social studies. These teachers self-identify as content teachers and typically perceive of content as separate from language. Thus, many found it difficult to carve out time for language and literacy instruction within already tight schedules, while others rejected outright the notion that they were responsible for teaching both language and content, and would not try new approaches. Although many teachers came to see language and content as interconnected over the course of our project implementation period, they did not have the preparation necessary to explicitly teach language and literacy in their content areas. Within the United States, content teacher preparation in institutions of higher education does not typically involve preparation to teach language and/or literacy, particularly at the high-school level. This oversight is compounded by the structure of traditional US high schools, in which teachers are segregated by content area and receive few opportunities to collaborate across disciplines.

Our findings therefore have implications for teacher preparation programs as well as for research in language policy. First, in light of the focus of this volume, we suggest that all teachers – beyond only language teachers – must be prepared to face the realities of the multilingual rather than the monolingual classroom. In the United States, this involves ensuring that teachers of languages other than English are prepared to teach native speakers as well as nonnative speakers; and this involves preparing all teachers to teach the language and literacy skills required for their content area (Ramirez *et al.*, 2008; Short & Fitzsimmons, 2007). Moreover, we must make certain that *all* teachers perceive of themselves as teachers of both language and content. Second, we argue that promoting multilingualism in classroom settings relies on teachers, who are at the epicenter of language policy implementation in schools. Although the central role of teachers has traditionally been overlooked in language education policy research (Menken & García, 2010), teachers must receive the attention they deserve in order for real change to occur.

Notes

1. 'Emergent bilinguals' are defined here as students who come from homes where a language other than English is spoken, and who are receiving specialized instruction to learn English at school. While typically these students are termed 'English language learners' in the United States, as García *et al.* explain, 'English language learners are in fact *emergent bilinguals*. That is, through school and through acquiring English, these children become *bilingual*, able to continue to function in their home language as well as in English, their new language and that of school' (García *et al.*, 2008: 6).

2. All teacher names are pseudonyms.
3. Of the LTELLs who participated in this study, none were identified as special education students or those with an Individualized Education Plan (IEP). However, we do recognize that there are LTELLs who were simultaneously labeled as special education students. It is likely that their needs go beyond the approaches we describe here.
4. Mr A resorted to a significant amount of Regents drilling and rote memorization with his 10th graders in the month leading up to the exam.
5. The findings from the control school are consistent with a study by Yang *et al.* (2001), who found that without proper programming, LTELLs do not continue to improve, and that they may perform worse over time.

References

Ancess, J. (2003) *Beating the Odds: High Schools as Communities of Commitment.* New York: Teachers College Press.

Baker, C. (2006) *Foundations of Bilingual Education and Bilingualism* (4th edn). Clevedon: Multilingual Matters.

Crawford, J. (2007) The decline of bilingual education: How to reverse a troubling trend? *International Multilingual Research Journal* 1, 33–37.

Creese, A. (2005) *Teacher Collaboration and Talk in Multilingual Classrooms.* Clevedon: Multilingual Matters.

Creswell, J.W. (1998) *Qualitative Inquiry and Research Design: Choosing among Five Traditions.* Thousand Oaks, CA: Sage.

Fine, M., Jaffe-Walter, R., Pedraza, P., Futch, V. and Stoudt, B. (2007) Swimming: On oxygen, resistance, and possibility for immigrant youth under siege. *Anthropology & Education Quarterly* 38, 76–96.

Gándara, P. and Baca, G. (2008) NCLB and California's English language learners: The perfect storm. *Language Policy* 7, 1–16.

García, O. (2009). *Bilingual Education in the 21st Century: A Global Perspective.* West Sussex: Wiley-Blackwell.

García, O. and Fishman, J. (eds) (2002) *The Multilingual Apple: Languages in New York City* (2nd edn). Berlin, Germany: Mouton de Gruyter.

García, O., Kleifgen, J. and Falchi, L. (2008) From English language learners to emergent bilinguals. *Equity Matters: Research Review No. 1.* New York: A Research Initiative of the Campaign for Educational Equity. http://www.tc. columbia.edu/i/a/document/6468_Ofelia_ELL__Final.pdf. Accessed 15.09.09.

Genesee, F. and Upshur, J.A. (1996) *Classroom-based Evaluation in Second Language Education.* Cambridge: Cambridge University Press.

Goldenberg, C. (2008, Summer) Teaching English language learners: What the research does – and does not – say. *American Educator* 32 (2), 8–23, 42–44. http:// www.aft.org/pubs-reports/american_educator/issues/summer08/ goldenberg.pdf. Accessed 18.07.08.

Hornberger, N. and Johnson, D. (2007) Slicing the onion ethnographically: Layers and spaces in multilingual language education policy and practice. *TESOL Quarterly* 41, 509–532.

Krashen, S. and McField, G. (2005) What works? Reviewing the latest evidence on bilingual education. *Language Learner* 1 (2), 7–10, 34.

Menken, K. (2008) *English Learners Left Behind: Standardized Testing as Language Policy*. Clevedon: Multilingual Matters.

Menken, K. and García, O. (eds) (2010) *Negotiating Language Education Policies: Educators as Policymakers*. New York: Routledge.

Menken, K. and Kleyn, T. (2009). The difficult road for long-term English learners. *Educational Leadership* 66. http://www.ascd.org/publications/educational_ leadership/apr09/vol66/num07/The_Difficult_Road_for_Long-Term_ English_Learners.aspx. Accessed 12.10.09.

Menken, K. and Kleyn, T. (2010) The long-term impact of subtractive schooling in the educational experiences of secondary English learners. *International Journal of Bilingual Education and Bilingualism* 13, 399–417.

Menken, K., Kleyn, T., Ascenzi-Moreno, L., Chae, N., Flores, N. and Funk, A. (2009) Meeting the needs of long-term English language learners in high school, Phase II. Unpublished report for the Office of English Language Learners of the New York City Department of Education.

Miles, M. and Huberman, A. (1994) *Qualitative Data Analysis: An Expanded Sourcebook* (2nd edn). Thousand Oaks, CA: Sage Publications.

National Clearinghouse for English Language Acquisition (2007) The growing number of limited English proficient students 1995/96–2005/06. Poster. Washington, DC: Author. http://www.ncela.gwu.edu/policy/states/reports/ statedata/2005LEP/GrowingLEP_0506.pdf. Accessed 12.06.08.

National Council of Teachers of English (2008) English language learners. NCTE webpage. Urbana, IL: Author. http://www.ncte.org/edpolicy/ell. Accessed 03.08.08.

New York City Department of Education, Office of English Language Learners (2008) *New York City's English Language Learners: Demographics and Performance*. New York: Author.

New York City Department of Education, Office of English Language Learners (2009) *New York City Dual Language Programs*. New York: Author. http://schools. nyc.gov/NR/rdonlyres/90EC9B10-88FF-4A06-98BC-23CC495032C9/53260/ NYCDualLanguage2009FINAL.pdf. Accessed 12.10.09.

Ramirez, R., Freeman, Y. and Freeman, D. (2008) *Diverse Learners in the Mainstream Classroom: Strategies for Supporting ALL Students across Content Areas*. Portsmouth, NH: Heinemann.

Shin, H. and Bruno, R. (2003) *Language Use and English-Speaking Ability, 2000: Census 2000 Brief*. Summary report of the U.S. Census Bureau. Washington, DC: U.S. Census Bureau. http://www.census.gov/prod/2003pubs/c2kbr-29.pdf. Accessed 30.07.08.

Short, D. and Fitzsimmons, S. (2007) *Double the Work: Challenges and Solutions to Acquiring Language and Academic Literacy for Adolescent English Language Learners*. New York: Carnegie Corporation and Alliance for Excellent Education.

Thomas, W. and Collier, V. (2002) A national study of school effectiveness for language minority students' long term academic achievement: Final report: Project 1.1. CREDE. http://crede.berkeley.edu/research/crede/research/llaa/ 1.1_final.html. Accessed 17.01.11.

Wiley, T. and Wright, W. (2004) Against the undertow: Language-minority education policy and politics in the "age of accountability." *Educational Policy* 18, 142–168.

Yang, H., Urrabazo, T. and Murray, W. (2001) *How Did Multiple Years (7+) in a BE/ ESL Program Affect the English Acquisition and Academic Achievement of Secondary LEP Students? Results from a Large Urban School District.* Dallas, TX: Dallas Independent School District.

Zehler, A., Fleishman, H., Hopstock, P., Stephenson, T., Pendzik, M. and Sapru, S. (2003) *Descriptive Study of Services to LEP Students and to LEP Students with Disabilities; Policy Report: Summary of Findings Related to LEP and SpEd-LEP Students.* Arlington, VA: Development Associates.

Chapter 6

Negotiating Multilingualism in an Irish Primary School Context[1]

B. O' ROURKE

Introduction

In today's globalised world of mobilities and flows, multilingualism has become a phenomenon that people encounter and have to manage in their everyday lives. Given the multilingual reality of contemporary societies, it comes as little surprise that schools can be identified as sites of linguistic diversity and questions about education and linguistic difference exercise policymakers and educators more so than ever before. However, despite the multilingual realities of schools in many parts of the world, the linguistic needs of bilingual and multilingual children have not been sufficiently addressed by education systems whose linguistic *habitus* (Bourdieu, 1991) has remained on the whole monolingual.

The monolingual *habitus* of Western education systems largely reflects the ideologies of linguistic uniformity engrained in the formation of European nation states. Heller (2002: 2) reminds us that, to the extent that these states tried to construct culturally and linguistically homogenous spaces, schools were seen as a means of constructing culturally and linguistically homogenous citizens. Indeed, the minorisation of many of Europe's lesser used or minority languages such as Breton, Irish, Welsh, Basque and Catalan reflects the monolingual ideologies of the homogenising nation states within which these languages were marginalised and excluded from the so-called 'high' functional domains (Ferguson, 1959; Fishman, 1967, 1980), including education. Over the 20th century, however, more favourable language policies within individual European nation states and at European Union level have shown increased support, or, at the very least, tolerance for Europe's autochthonous languages.

Nevertheless, despite institutional attempts to protect the linguistic rights of speakers of autochthonous languages (e.g. European Charter for

Lesser Used Languages), the linguistic rights of allochtonous migrant languages seem to be less clearly defined. Hélot and Young (2005) and Young and Hélot (2003), highlight that in a European context, with the exception of several local projects, which support the maintenance of community languages, the linguistic needs of bilingual (and multilingual) children are not sufficiently addressed by education systems whose focus tends to be on the teaching of the language of the host country. Thus, the monolingual *habitus* of linguistically diverse schools leads to an implicit rejection of an important part of children's identity whose family languages are often ignored.

This chapter explores these issues and looks specifically at the ways in which multilingualism is being managed and negotiated in a contemporary Irish educational context. It presents an example of a primary school context in Dublin, Ireland's capital city, characterised by the fact that a high percentage of the student population are speakers of an allochthonous language. The discussion presented here is based on observations of an ongoing multilingual action research project involving teachers, pupils and parents of pupils at *Lane Street Primary School*,[2] located in Dublin's inner city. Through the incorporation of a range of multilingual and language-awareness activities into classroom practice, the aim of the project has been to create a school environment which explicitly values and recognises the languages that children bring to the school. The chapter reflects on the way in which multilingualism has been negotiated and mediated at various stages of the project. Before discussing this particular case study, it will be useful to look more closely at linguistic diversity in an Irish context more generally and more specifically, to examine the ways in which multilingualism is being managed in primary school settings in Ireland.

Multilingualism in Ireland

Ireland has a long history of linguistic diversity. The Republic of Ireland has two official languages, Irish and English and the island of Ireland is also home to a number of other native languages, including Ulster Scots, Irish Sign language and Gammon or Cant (a language historically known to and used by Irish Travellers). Although English is the dominant language of everyday communication, for more than two-thirds of the population living in the Republic of Ireland, the Irish language has a strong ethnocultural value as a symbol of their Irish identity (Ó Riagáin, 1997). Since the foundation of the Irish State in 1922, language policy and planning initiatives have been in place, giving a privileged position to the Irish language in a number of domains, including educational domains, in particular within the primary school sector. However, questions about the need to re-address the bilingual focus of language policy in Ireland have arisen in light of increased in-migration to the country over recent decades and with it an increase in linguistic diversity. Socio-economic changes, specifically over the past 20 years, have meant that Ireland and particularly its capital city Dublin have become important points of entry for economic migrants, refugees and asylum seekers. Essentially, Ireland has gone from being a country traditionally characterised by an extraordinarily high rate of emigration to a country which now shows one of the highest rates of net immigration in the European Union.

Although there is so far no comprehensive set of statistics on the language abilities of the present Irish population, an idea of the scale of the linguistic complexity in the country can be gleaned based on figures collected from public body reports in the educational and health sectors and from census of population (Cronin, 2004). Figures from Ireland's Eastern Regional Health Authority from 2001 showed a total of 78 nationalities in the region. In a survey carried out on a representative sample of the group, it was found that there were 63 different mother tongues among the respondents. The most important minority was Romanian, with 28% of respondents speaking it as a first language. Bantu languages from Africa's main linguistic family, Niger Congo, accounted for 13% of respondents, and of these approximately 11% were Yoruba speakers, while 2% spoke Ibo/Igbo. Other languages spoken included Russian (8%), Arabic (7%), French (5%), English (4%), Polish (3%) and Albanian (2%). Fifty-three other languages accounted for 26% of the respondents. The scale of the change in the linguistic make-up of Irish society can also be gauged from the claim by the Eastern Regional Health Authority that it is dealing with over 130 languages. Similarly, the commitment by the Court Service in Ireland to provide translation and interpreting services in 210 languages gives further evidence of the country's new linguistic reality. While the latter figure may be somewhat inflated by private translation and interpreting companies with vested interest in exaggerating the number of languages they can offer, the figure of 167 reported in a recent EU report (see McPake & Tinsley, 2007) may offer a somewhat more accurate estimation. Insights can also be gleaned for the latest census of population figures in Ireland which indicate that, approximately one in 10 persons living in the Republic of Ireland are foreign born and speak a language other than English.

Managing Linguistic Diversity in Educational Contexts in Ireland

Given the changes in Ireland's linguistic landscape, it comes as a little surprise that Irish schools, particularly urban schools, can be identified as sites of linguistic diversity and thus concerns about the quality of education for children of minority heritage language now face Irish schools on a much more widespread level than have ever been experienced before. The focus of the Irish education system, very similar to others like it in Europe, has tended to be on the teaching of the dominant language of the host country (in this case, English) and much of the discussion and public debate concerning language-related issues to date has centred on the teaching of English as an additional language (EAL). At a national level, there is no explicit endorsement on the part of the Irish state of immigrants' linguistic rights and the maintenance or development of their own languages, and so allochtonous migrant languages do not have a legitimate status in Irish society. One of the strategies adopted by the Irish Department of Education and Science (DES) involved the establishment of a language-support service in 1999, making provision for pupils in the education system to study EAL. In the current system, EAL pupils participate in mainstream schooling and are withdrawn for periods during the school week to participate in language-support classes with a specialist language-support teacher. According to Lazenby Simpson (2002), the system which has been used in the Irish context falls into the category described by Tabors (1997: 5) as the *English-language classroom* where English is the sole language of instruction and the non-native English-speaking child is unlikely to have support in his/her mother-tongue unless there is another child in the class who also speaks that language.

The largely monolingual approach to the teaching of multilingual students is even more apparent in the fact that, despite bilingual policies within the Irish education system, which encourage the teaching of both Irish and English, a monolingual English language policy tends to be adopted for immigrant children, whose parents can apply for an exemption to Irish at school if the child arrives in Ireland after a certain age or does not speak English. As Wallen and Kelly-Holmes (2006: 144) argue, although this exemption may be perceived favourably by those struggling to learn English in a new educational and cultural context, they suggest that the policy is perhaps short sighted as it potentially restricts immigrants' understanding of many cultural and official aspects of everyday life in Ireland (e.g. much of the nomenclature). Moreover, access to the primary school teaching profession in Ireland requires a formal qualification in the Irish language and therefore, as Wallen and Kelly-Holmes (2006: 144) highlight, exemption from Irish instruction at school also effectively excludes immigrant children from access to this profession in later life. Therefore, the seemingly liberal ideology of 'allowing' immigrants to opt for exemption from Irish may in fact contribute to the reproduction of social differentiation, legitimising the exclusion of certain groups from civic and symbolic domains of the Irish nation state. And one could argue that adding another language to their existing linguistic repertoire is unlikely to cause them great difficulty.

There is anecdotal evidence to show that minority language students do still learn Irish and often outperform some of their Irish-born peers. It may be that these students have internalised the link between the Irish language and a sense of Irish identity and are thus motivated to learn the language despite the odds against them. It may also be the case that the existing bilingual (and often multilingual) repertoire of these students is unwittingly facilitating the learning of Irish as an additional language. According to Ó Laoire (2008: 259), the absence of support classes offered in Irish ignores the fact that the vast majority of immigrants are already bilingual, trilingual or multilingual. However, in adopting a monolingual policy for these students, both through their exemption from Irish and the lack of support for their own mother tongue, it could be argued that the largely monolingual *habitus* of the Irish education system with regard to multilingual students is ignoring immigrant students' ethnocultural motivation to learn the Irish language as well as their existing bilingual (and often multilingual) repertoire which potentially facilitates the learning of Irish and additional languages.

It must be noted, however, that the Department of Education and Science (DES) in Ireland is not unaware of the new multilingual reality of Irish schools. Some recognition is given to children who speak languages other than English by the National Council for Curriculum and Assessment in Ireland which provides schools with a set of written guidelines outlining how to manage and support linguistic and cultural diversity in Irish schools. Formal initiatives in place since the early 1990s, set forth by the Irish Department of Education related to teaching EAL children, led to the creation of Integrate Ireland Language and Training (IILT),[3] an agency charged with developing courses for adult refugees as well as benchmarks for primary and post-primary EAL students. Based on these benchmarks, one of the initiatives adopted by IILT was to create a version of the European Language Portfolio for primary schools (IILT, 2001), which can be used for non-English-speaking students. The Portfolio contains a language-awareness element which encourages students to reflect on linguistic and cultural diversity and on their own linguistic repertoires. More recently, a toolkit was designed to assist primary school teachers in the creation of more inclusive linguistic and cultural classrooms and there were plans for it to be rolled out to all primary schools in Ireland (David Little, 2007, personal communication).

While these initiatives represent important steps towards recognising the multilingual reality of Irish society and acknowledging and valuing migrant languages in the education system, if they are to move into commonplace classroom practice, more concrete steps need to be taken to facilitate their uptake by the principal actors within primary school education. The remainder of the chapter focuses on the Lane Street project which provides an example of a multilingual primary school context where an environment has been created which explicitly promotes and values the linguistically diverse student population in the school. The discussion presented here is based on observations of and reflections on the way in which multilingualism has been negotiated during the different stages of the project. It examines classroom practice, attitudes, behaviours and school language policy and looks at the effect of top-down initiatives on the behaviour and attitudes of teachers, pupils and parents at this school. Through an ethnographic approach, the project aimed to better understand the social and linguistic processes involved in a multilingual educational context and to draw attention to the complex and situated nature of the grassroot processes involved in the management of linguistic diversity at Lane Street Primary. This approach involved a range of methods including observation of classroom practices during my weekly visits to the school, in-depth interviews and discussion groups with teachers and parents as well as an analysis of the school's policy documents.

Negotiating Multilingualism at Lane Street Primary School

Similar to many of Dublin's inner-city schools, Lane Street Primary School is characterised by the fact that a high percentage of the student cohort are second-language speakers of English. The major groups in the school include students from Eastern Europe (mainly Poland and Romania but also from Albania and Bulgaria), Africa (including Nigeria and Ghana), Asia (principally Vietnam, Mongolia, India and the Philippines) and in a smaller number of cases from South America (mainly Venezuela). In some of the classes, especially the junior classes, the number of non-native English speakers is in an overwhelming majority in the classroom.

Prior to the commencement of the project a letter was sent to the acting principal at the school in January 2007 explaining the aims and objectives of the multilingual-awareness project and inviting the school's participation. While the principal's response to the project was on the whole favourable, it became clear from the outset that a certain amount of negotiation would be required in getting the different facets of the project approved and in convincing him of its long-term benefits. It also became clear that the multilingual project was just one in a long list of other potential projects about which the school had been approached, ranging from topics as diverse as dental health to anti-racism awareness. Nonetheless, the principal was sufficiently interested in agreeing to a meeting along with a number of other teachers at the school to participate in a group discussion on the topic of multilingualism and its role in educational practice. What emerged from this discussion was that teachers at the school were in general positively disposed to the idea of multilingualism and linguistic diversity. The acting principal, for example, lamented the fact that by the time children reached the end of primary school many had forgotten their home languages. He was supportive of the idea that pupils should be able to acquire the school language without abandoning their own languages and cultures. While many of the teachers shared this view, there were also some conflicting views. Some teachers, while supporting the idea of creating multilingual classrooms, were unsure about how this could be achieved in practical terms. They felt ill equipped to deal with situations in which several languages were present in the classroom, both in terms of resources available to teachers and the methodologies they should be using. As was already highlighted above, the National Council for Curriculum and Assessment (NCCA)[4] in Ireland does provide schools with a set of written guidelines, outlining the importance of linguistic and cultural diversity in schools. Nevertheless, despite the availability of such guidelines, the teachers at this particular school seemed vague about how these guidelines could be put into practice and how linguistic resources at their school could be acknowledged and amplified in view of the fact that English appeared to be the only possible language of instruction for a student body representing 10 or more different languages.

Another teacher, whose role was to provide additional resources to pupils of English as a second language was particularly concerned that if enough emphasis was not placed on English the children might fall behind or feel isolated from the rest of the group. He also pointed out that:

> One of the difficulties that we have is when a child comes to the school and has no English at all, and the parents don't have English either. The parents will speak their own language at home rather than practicing English and trying to incorporate it as part of their home

language. In the interests of the child, parents should make an effort to speak the language that the children are learning at school.

The demands of the English Language Support (ELS) teacher on parents to 'make an effort to speak the language that the children are learning at school' are somewhat contradictory given his initial comments that the parents do not in fact 'have English either'. Moreover, the somewhat seemingly *reprimanding* tone of his comments that 'parents should make an effort to speak the language that the children are learning at school', points to a subtle link often made in the minds of teachers and administrators between deficiency in the majority language and poor parenting.

While on the surface, the comments of the ELS teacher seemed negative, observation of his classroom practices and approach to teaching students who were second-language speakers of English provided a very different picture. Over the year-and-half period during which the project has been in place at the school, I was able to observe the teacher's explicit support for linguistic diversity through his continuous encouragement of students to share their linguistic experiences with others in the class and his use of multilingual-awareness activities as a learning tool in the classroom. He went far beyond the language-awareness tasks proposed in the European Language Portfolio and created a genuinely multilingual space in which the students lived out the linguistic diversity of the classroom on a daily basis during their ELS sessions with him. He also brought his own language experience to the class and to the broader school context through his use of the Irish language with students and teachers at the school. He used his knowledge of Italian to facilitate communication with Spanish-speaking and Romanian-speaking students, drawing on Latin-based commonalities across these three languages. He established links with a Romanian parent and with her help, compiled bilingual glossaries containing basic phrases in English and Romanian which he then used as a resource for Romanian new-comers to the school. He also showed me a Mongolian-English dictionary and phrase book which he had secured (with great difficulty) so as to enhance his communication with two Mongolian boys who had recently arrived at the school. The language-support teacher had also ensured that the school library was resourced with a wide range of story books and dictionaries in the different languages spoken in the school.

While the majority of teachers at the school were supportive of the idea of multilingualism, from comments made in discussions during the initial stages of the project, it was clear that they were interested in moving beyond abstract guidelines about how to manage linguistic diversity and towards the more concrete and practical ways in which the ideal of multi-lingualism could be converted into classroom practice. In line with these interests, one of the key aims of the project came to involve the exploration, with the teachers, of some of the practical and cost-effective ways to assist them in the development of multilingual strategies which promote linguistic diversity in their classrooms. To do this I drew on examples of innovative multilingual action research initiatives used by Chow and Cummins (2003) as well as language-awareness strategies and activities developed by Armand and Dagenais (2005). Working in a Canadian educational context, Armand and Dagenais (2005) developed and tested language-awareness activities for primary school children. Their work is based on European research and draws on the Language Awareness approach developed by Hawkins (1984) and his team as a means of fostering the development of positive representations and attitudes towards openness to linguistic and cultural diversity, metalinguistic abilities to facilitate the transition to second languages, and language-related knowledge, including language status. Their work is also influenced by further developments in language-awareness activities in the 1990s by French researchers who renamed the approach *Éveil au langage* (literally, 'Awakening to language'), then *Éveil aux langues* (literally, 'Awakening to languages'). These approaches were subsequently adopted under the *Evlang* (Candelier, 2003) and *Eole* (Perregaux *et al.*, 2003) EU programmes. Chow and Cummins (2003), also working in a Canadian educational context, have developed innovative multilingual action research initiatives in which they explore multilingual and multicultural approaches to learning and developed projects involving the use of dual-language books and multilingual stories and activities.

Car and Kemmis define action research as 'a form of self-reflective enquiry in social situations in order to improve the rationality and justice of their own practices, their understanding of these practices, and the situations in which the practices are carried out' (Car & Kemmis, 1986: 162). So action research is firmly located in the realm of the practitioner and is tied to self-reflection. In this project the principal practitioners were the teachers at this Dublin school and one of the aims of the project was to guide them in a self-reflective enquiry of their teaching practices and the inclusion of multilingual awareness in these practices. Through action research, the project adopted an end-user-focused approach (Cameron, 1992) to explore activities which would further enhance teachers', pupils' and parents' awareness of linguistic diversity. As the researcher in the project I worked in partnership with the teachers and together we formed the action research group.

Although the initial aim of the project was to introduce language awareness and multilingual activities across a range of age groups and classrooms at Lane Street Primary, the principal at the school recommended that such activities be restricted to the junior infants' (4–5 year olds) class. The principal's decision to confine the activities to the youngest cohort of pupils in the school was based on the rationale that for this age group such activities would be least disruptive in terms of complying with standard curriculum and in terms of acquiring the 'real' literacy skills (understood as English-language reading and writing skills) which would be required of older age groups. The junior infants' class consisted of 13 children, three of whom were Irish-born nationals and the remaining 10 children were of Bulgarian, Polish, Indian, Philippine, Vietnamese and Albanian origin. From a research perspective, the restricted focus on the junior infants' class did, of course, limit the scope of the project in terms of analysis across age groups. Nevertheless, from an action-research perspective, by placing a special focus on the youngest cohort of pupils at the school, children were being actively encouraged to develop their metalinguistic abilities from the initial stages of their educational journey. Through such intervention, the hope was to instil in children a sense of pride in their own linguistic identities and an appreciation for the diversity of languages spoken in their classroom.

Once access to the junior infants' classroom had been obtained, a certain amount of negotiation also took place relating to the extent to which multilingual- and language-awareness activities were to be incorporated into the regular class time. Initially, the activities were included as stand-alone, language-type activities that took place on Friday mornings during my weekly visit to the school and were independent of the regular curriculum. An example of this was an activity adapted from Armand's and Dagenais' (2005) set of language-awareness modules taken from the ELODIL [language awareness and openness to linguistic diversity] website and involved pupils sharing different ways of saying 'hello' in their respective home languages. As a follow-up activity each child created a 'Language Flower' with the word in his home language in the centre of the flower (see Figure 6.1). Each child decorated or coloured their 'Language Flower' and when completed it was posted on the wall alongside the other flowers. As well as raising awareness about linguistic diversity amongst teachers and pupils in the classroom, the exercise also created dialogue with parents, who, on their morning visits to the classroom with their children assisted us in the pronunciation of the new words. They were also able to provide us with the most colloquial way of saying 'hello' in their respective languages and often made adjustments to the sometimes

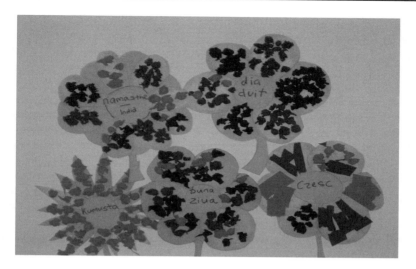

Figure 6.1 Language Flowers with 'hello' in the different languages of the classroom

incorrect versions of the word we had found on the internet. Parental input in the activity also alerted us to the fact that one of the pupils registered as being of Albanian origin had in fact Turkish as his mother tongue. This discovery also signalled the need for a more rigorous method of collecting language-specific data on the incoming students than was currently in place. Fact-finding exercise such as this constitutes the beginning of language policy planning at the school level. One of the questions which Corson (1999) suggests should be included in the development of a school policy relates to whether or not records of the home languages of children are kept and made available to all school staff. Although the school registration form, which parents of immigrant children are required to fill out on arrival to the school, contained a variety of questions including religious affiliation, country of origin, no explicit questions relating to the languages spoken in the home were included. The utility of such a question was highlighted to the principal and these recommendations were fed into the development of a broader school language policy.

As the weeks progressed, in collaboration with the teachers in the class we looked at ways in which to integrate multilingual awareness, not as a stand-alone activity but as an integral part of other school subjects such as nature studies, science, geography and art. In this way, language-awareness and multilingual activities were gradually interwoven into the fabric of classroom interactions, through the multilingual activities. 'The Life Cycle of the Butterfly' is an example of an activity which although designed as a nature study or science activity, also incorporated an explicit multilingual dimension (see Figure 6.2). As part of the activity, the pupils, with the help of teachers made a poster in which the phrase 'Watch me grow' (see below) appeared in the children's home languages. Again, as in the 'Language Flower' activity, dialogue was established with parents who had been sent a note by the teacher asking them to translate the phrase into their respective languages and to teach the child how to pronounce it.

These and other such activities were put on display for parents who were invited to attend an intercultural morning at the end of the school year. This event further strengthened links with parents and was seen as another way of reinforcing the message that their languages and cultures were valued. One of the parents of Indian origin brought children's books written in his mother tongue and taught teachers, pupils and the other parents how to pronounce different words. He told us that he was pleasantly surprised at the fact that we were interested in his language and culture as most people, he said, were simply not interested. The event

Figure 6.2 Multilingual poster created by children at Lane Street Primary

brought language issues centre stage and prompted interesting discussions with parents about the languages they use at home and questions on their part about how they should be managing their children's bilingualism. A Romanian mother expressed her concern that her child may be falling behind because of her own perceived lack of fluency in English and because of the fact that she and her family had continued to use Romanian at home. She blamed herself for not making a bigger effort to improve her own English language skills which would have given her the possibility of shifting to English with her son. She told me that an Irish nurse had in fact advised her to abandon Romanian altogether and to use only English with her child, claiming that maintenance of the home language would be a 'handicap' in the acquisition of English. Here we find an example of the powerful sentiments and discourses often used to devalue students' and parents' multilingual abilities. This incident was a reminder that parents, teachers and students were on a daily basis faced with the opinion held by certain sectors of society that immigrants should abandon their languages of origin in order to integrate successfully into the host society. The nurse's comments to the Romanian mother also implicitly linked deficiency in the majority language with negligent parenthood, echoing the previous comments of the ELS teacher discussed above.

Effects of Multilingual Activities on Language Attitudes and Behaviours

Despite much negotiation and mediation at various stages of the project, multilingual activities were put in place in the junior infants' class over two consecutive academic school years and the project had a number of specific outcomes. In the first instance, it sensitised teachers and pupils in the junior infants' class to linguistic diversity and made the teachers involved in the project more consciously aware of the range of languages spoken in the classroom and how to deal more positively with the linguistic diversity of their pupils. These teachers created a learning environment where students' prior knowledge of their home languages was explicitly recognised. Pupils' prior knowledge of their L1 languages and their respective cultures were explored and became a key part of students' learning. The children in the classroom created a positive image of their linguistic and cultural identities through their writings and illustrations. In other words, similar to the findings of Chow and Cummins (2003: 52) in their analysis of multilingual approaches to learning in a Canadian context, teachers in the junior infants' class at Lane Street Primary created an interpersonal space that encouraged students to invest their identities in learning. Student's knowledge of additional languages came to be seen as a resource rather than an impediment to overcome and the multilingual abilities of the students were no longer perceived as a burden or a 'problem' but as a positive resource that could be shared by all.

Second, through the development and testing of different multilingual- and language-awareness activities, teachers were exposed to some of the practical ways in which they could incorporate linguistic diversity into their classroom. At the end of the project they felt more confident and better equipped to deal with situations in which several languages were present in the classroom both in terms of resources available to them and the types of methodologies they could use. The third outcome which can be identified is that the project created a dialogue with parents who became key players in the development and creation of the multilingual activities. Through this dialogue a clear message was sent to parents that their languages and cultures were being recognised and valued. The fourth important outcome of the project was the extended effect that it had on other teachers and classes within the school. Although the main focus of the project was on developing multilingual activities in the junior infants' class, the project also had a positive effect on teachers from other classes. The first-class teacher, for instance, adapted the 'Language Flower' activity and used the different ways of saying 'hello' to create a poster representing linguistic diversity in her own classroom. The topic of linguistic diversity also began to emerge in the staffroom and teachers shared ideas and views about multilingualism. The project also opened the way for further dialogue with the teachers and administrators at the school and moves towards the development of an overall school language policy. The teachers in this inner-city Dublin school had of course through their interventions already begun to initiate their own school-based language policy. As Chow and Cummins (2003: 53) point out, language policy is a process rather than a product and is always dynamic and evolving, based on previous experience and collaborative discussion at the school level. This process became evident in discussions on the ways in which the school and its staff intended to take the multilingual project forward to its next stage. These included such initiatives as the posting of multilingual signs around the school, the enhancement of communication with parents through the translation of important notices, the initiation of multilingual storytelling involving parents and children and the identification of skills within the migrant population; skills which could be drawn on to enhance the multilingual and multicultural learning experience of pupils at the school.

Discussion and Concluding Remarks

Bruner (1996: 26) reminds us that schools are always shaped by the 'external' culture of society as a whole, and in turn contribute to wider societal cultures. Thus, what happens within schools is always a mediation of the local and the global contexts which they inhabit and a reflection of the patterns of power and inequality in these wider contexts. I will therefore conclude by trying to position the micro-levels of negotiation and mediation, which were observed at Lane Street Primary within this broader macro-level.

As highlighted in the discussion above, in general, teachers and administrators at Lane Street Primary were favourably disposed to the idea of multilingualism. Nevertheless, there were conflicting views about the way in which multilingualism should be managed. There were also mismatches between discourses and actual behaviour, leading to an interesting process of negotiation and mediation at various stages during which the current multilingual-awareness project has been in place. One of the most striking mismatches was between what initially appeared to be negative attitudes towards multilingualism on the parts of the ELS teacher and what later turned out to be overwhelming support for linguistic diversity as shown in his classroom practices. His explicit criticism of what he perceived to be a lack of effort on the part of non-English-speaking parents to switch to the dominant language of the school pointed to his apparent lack of support not only for a multilingual classroom, but also for language maintenance in the home. The subtle link between deficiency in the majority language and poor parenting by the ELS teacher was also echoed in an Irish nurse's recommendations to a Romanian mother to switch to English for the 'good' of the child. Milani (2008: 40) identifies similar discourses in his analysis of the public debate that took place in Sweden in 2002 in relation to the Swedish Liberal Party's proposal to introduce a language test for naturalisation. He also draws parallels between such discourses and the well-known 1995 court case in the US town of Amarillo in Texas, in which a judge ordered a mother not to speak Spanish to her child as a condition for keeping the child's custody, claiming, 'If she starts [school] with the other children and cannot even speak the language that the teachers and others speak, and she's a full-blooded American citizen, you are abusing the child' (cited in May, 2003: 103). The subtle implication in the arguments about linguistic diversity identified in Milani's (2008) study and those found in the Lane Street project is that a lack of the majority language and, by implication proficiency only in the minority language, is linked to the incapacity to act as a 'proper' parent.

Nevertheless, despite initially negative comments on the part of the ELS teacher, as was discussed above, such comments did not reflect his classroom practices and his generally supportive attitudes towards linguistic diversity. The mismatch between his attitudes and his behaviour can be explained in a number of ways. What seemed to have happened is that in his initial discussions involving a researcher, an outsider to the group, this teacher, wishing to be perceived in his role as the ELS teacher adopted a monolingual façade, which hid his multilingual *habitus* and only displayed the legitimate discourse associated with his official ESL role. At various stages during the project, arguments emerged which reflected official discourse about linguistic diversity, highlighting the ongoing struggle in which teachers and administrators were involved to accommodate pervasive policies set down by the Department of Education regarding curricular expectations and standards. This struggle was all too apparent in negotiating language-awareness and multilingual activities as part of the classroom activities. While administrators were supportive of the idea of multilingualism in the school, they were concerned that time spent on language-awareness and multilingual activities may distract from the 'real' curriculum, and specifically from advancing English-language literacy skills. Research on the role of language in education is very clear about the importance of mother-tongue maintenance in children's overall personal and educational development (Baker, 2000; Cummins, 2000; Skutnabb-Kangas, 2000) and maintenance and awareness of children's first language is regarded as crucial to their learning of additional languages and to academic progress and literacy skills in a new language. Cummins' (2001) model of bilingual development suggests that becoming literate in one's first language enables children to derive the intellectual benefits of additive bilingualism and to perform at a higher level than monolinguals. Although the intended aim of the multilingual activities was in fact to develop English-language literacy skills through mother-tongue literacy and multilingual awareness more generally, to the principal (and teachers) at the school this link was not immediately obvious. Their strong emphasis on English-language literacy skills was further evidence that they were struggling to accommodate to the monolingual habitus, which has long been characteristic of Western educational systems. However, in focusing on English-language literacy, it could be argued that Lane Street Primary is constructing very specific literacy practices, which, according to Carrington and Luke, 'may not yield the only significant discourses and practices which are required by individuals' (Carrington & Luke, 1997: 105). As we know, the model which restricts literacy to reading and writing in the dominant language of schooling, has been called into question by the growing body of research on 'literacies' in social practice (Conteh *et al.*, 2007: 14). Social education theorists such as Gee (2004), Kalantzis (2006), Kalantzis and Cope and the Learning by Design Group (2005) and Luke and Carrington (2002) advocate multiliteracies, which take into account the multiplicity of communication channels and media and an increasing salience of cultural and linguistic diversity (Kalantzis & Cope, 2000). Nevertheless, while at the theoretical level the idea of multiliteracies has gained ground, in the everyday running of a classroom, as can be seen from Lane Street Primary, multiliteracies are not always the default practice.

It is also likely that the particularly strong emphasis on English-language literacy skills at Lane Street Primary School reflects the fact that the school is one of 311 primary schools in Ireland to be labelled 'disadvantaged' and is subsequently part of the Disadvantaged Areas Scheme. Lane Street Primary School is located in a socioeconomically deprived part of Dublin's inner-city and a high percentage of the autochthonous population living in the area is characterised by high levels of unemployment, poor housing conditions and low levels of formal education, thus qualifying the school for the scheme. Being part of the Disadvantaged Areas Scheme means that the school receives a greater level of support in terms of pupil–teacher ratios, special grants and extra support for pupils to enhance literacy skills. Even prior to the arrival of the immigrant population to the school, literacy levels (understood as reading and writing skills in English) have tended to be low amongst the native English-speaking population in the area in which the school is located. Therefore, the school sees itself as being 'doubly disadvantaged', both in terms of the low literacy skills of the autochthonous population as well as in terms of the poor literacy skills of the more recently arrived 'new Irish' immigrant population whose first language is not English. The emphasis on English-language literacy skills by the principal and teachers at Lane Street Primary School reflects the ongoing struggle in which teachers and administrators are involved to meet targets in attaining literacy levels and to accommodate to policies set down by the Department of Education regarding curricular expectations and standards. Thus, the principal's consistent concern with meeting literacy targets in the school goes some way in explaining why the multilingual-awareness activities proposed in the project were restricted to the junior infants' class.

Coupled with these institutional pressures, teachers and school administrators are of course also faced with the powerful societal structures, which often support the belief that the home language constitutes a handicap or a 'problem' for the acquisition of the school language. The 'solve the problem' orientation to multilingualism in education is clearly voiced in the following excerpt taken from a 2007 radio interview with a well-known Irish journalist who was of the opinion that:

> there has to be a massive reform of the [Irish] educational system. The State sector has to be expanded and we have to have a doctrine for coping with foreigners speaking foreign languages in our schools. For example, there is good reason to outlaw foreign languages being spoken in the playground because the playground is the primary area for them to learn about the culture of the school and the society they are in. It is good to have foreigners in Ireland but it is not good to have them create a separate culture in their schools ...

The phrase 'coping with foreigners' immediately frames the issue of linguistic diversity in a negative light and of course more explicitly negative are the dictatorially framed references to the need to 'outlaw foreign languages being spoken in the playground', raising the whole question of language rights as a basic human right (Skutnabb-Kangas, 2000). Cummins (2001) highlights the disastrous consequences such an orientation can have for children (and their families) as it violates their right to an appropriate education and undermines communication between them and their parents. Dismissal of children's first language can of course also result in diminished self-esteem with a corresponding reduction in the motivation to learn. Wray and Medwell (1991: 39) make the point that by expecting children to abandon their language we are also expecting them to abandon self-definitions of who they are. The comments made by the Irish journalist highlight the monolingual habitus of many Western education systems, reinforcing, as Heller (2002: 2) points out, the societal belief that schools are seen as homogenous spaces used as a means of constructing culturally and linguistically homogenous citizens. The multilingual- and language-awareness activities introduced to teachers and pupils at Lane Street Primary have gone some way in intervening in that process and in constructing a more culturally and linguistically heterogeneous space for teachers and pupils at the school. However, the extent to which such activities can succeed in breaking the deeply rooted monolingual mindset of educational systems and in encouraging teachers, administrators, pupils and parents to resist monolingual societal and institutional pressures is questionable. The more explicit incorporation of multilingualism as part of a whole-school language policy on the part of Lane Street's school principal has moved the awareness of linguistic diversity beyond the junior infants' classroom. The document contains several explicit references to the promotion of linguistic diversity and positive steps towards acknowledging the multilingual reality of its student cohort. Nevertheless, its title, 'School Policy for English Language Support', would seem to suggest that support for diversity at Lane Street Primary continues to be hidden behind a monolingual façade. Here again we are reminded that, policies and practices proposed by teachers and administrators at Lane Street, and other schools like it, are being shaped by the 'external' culture of society as a whole (Bruner, 1996: 26). Although Lane Street is embracing, albeit sometimes in an implicit way, the linguistic diversity of its school and classrooms, it continues to struggle to comply with an official discourse of monolingualism.

Notes

1. The pilot stage of this project formed part of the larger research initiative, *Bridging the Research Policy Divide: Evidence-Based Practice in Irish Integration Policy* (coordinated by Dr Alice Feldman, University College Dublin) that was funded by the Irish Research Council in the Humanities and Social Sciences. The follow-up stage of the project was funded by the Carnegie Trust for the Universities of Scotland.
2. To protect the identity of the school a fictional name has been used.
3. Since the writing of this chapter, a decision was taken by the Department of Education to redirect funding allocated to IILT to other providers. This led to the closure of IILT in July 2008.
4. The NCCA was established in 1987 to advice Ireland's Minister for Education and Science on matters relating to the school curriculum.

References

Armand, F. and Dagenais, D. (2005) Langues en contexte d'immigration: éveiller au langage et à la diversité linguistique en milieu scolaire. *Thèmes canadiens. Revue de l'Association des études canadiennes,* numéro spécial printemps (Immigration and the intersections of diversity) 46–49.

Baker, C. (2000) *A Parents' and Teachers' Guide to Bilingualism* (2nd edn). Clevedon: Multilingual Matters.

Bourdieu, P. (1991) *Language and Symbolic Power* (J.B. Thompson, ed. and introduced). Cambridge: Polity Press.

Bruner, J.S. (1996) *The Culture of Education.* Cambridge, MA: Harvard University Press.

Cameron, D. (1992) *Researching Language: Issues of Power and Method.* London: Routledge.

Candelier, M. (ed.) (2003) *L'Éveil aux langues à l'école primaire – Evlang. Bilan d'une innovation européenne.* Brussels: De Boeck.

Car, W. and Kemmis, S. (1986) *Becoming Critical: Education, Knowledge and Action Research.* London: Falmer.

Carrington, V. and Luke, A. (1997) Literacy and Bourdieu's sociological theory: A reframing. *Language and Education* 11, 96–112.

Chow, P. and Cummins, J. (2003) Valuing multilingual and multicultural approaches to learning. In S. Schecter and J. Cummins (eds) *Multilingual Education in Practice. Using Diversity as a Resource* (pp. 32–61). Portsmouth, NH: Heinemann.

Conteh, J., Martin, P. and Helavaara Robertson, L. (2007) *Multilingual Learning: Stories from Schools and Communities in Britain.* Stoke on Trent: Trentham Books.

Corson, D. (1999) *Language Policy in Schools: A Resource for Teachers and Administrators.* Mahwah, NJ: Lawrence Erlbaum Associates.

Cronin, M. (2004) Babel Átha Cliath: The languages of Dublin. *New Hiberina Review* 8, 9–22.

Cummins, J. (2000) *Language, Power, and Pedagogy. Bilingual Children in the Crossfire.* Clevedon: Multilingual Matters.

Cummins, J. (2001) *Negotiating Identities: Education for Empowerment in a Diverse Society* (2nd edn). Los Angeles, CA: California Association for Bilingual Education.

Ferguson, C.A. (1959) Diglossia. *Word* 15, 325–340.

Fishman, J.A. (1967) Bilingualism with and without diglossia, diglossia with and without bilingualism. *Journal of Social Issues* 32, 29–38.

Fishman, J.A. (1980) Bilingualism and biculturalism as individual and as societal phenomena. *Journal of Multilingual and Multicultural Development* 1, 3–15.

Gee, J.P. (2004) *Situated Language and Learning: A Critique of Traditional Schooling.* New York: Routledge.

Hawkins, E.W. (1984) *Awareness of Language: An Introduction.* Cambridge: Cambridge University Press.

Hélot, C. and Young, A.S. (2005) The notion of diversity in language education: Policy and practice at primary level in France. *Journal of Language, Culture and Curriculum* 18, 242–257.

Heller, M. (2002) Language, education and citizenship in the post-national era: Notes from the front. LPI Working Paper n° 11, Toronto. On WWW at http://bank.ugent.be/lpi/workingpapers.htm. Accessed August 2009.

Integrate Ireland Language and Training (2001) *English Language Proficiency Benchmarks for Non-English-Speaking Pupils in Primary School.* Dublin: IILT.

Kalantzis, M. (2006) Changing subjectivities, new learning. *Pedagogies: An International Journal* 1, 7–9.

Kalantzis, M. and Cope, B. (2000) A multiliteracies pedagogy: A pedagogical supplement. In B. Cope and M. Kalantzis (eds) *Multiliteracies: Literacy Learning and the Design of Social Futures* (pp. 239–248). London: Routledge.

Kalantzis, M. and Cope, B. and the Learning by Design Group (2005) *Learning by Design.* Altona, VIC: Victorian Schools Innovation Commission, Melbourne, and Common Ground Publishing.

Lazenby Simpson, B. (2002) Meeting the needs of second language children: Language and literacy in primary education. Paper presented at the Conference of the Reading Association of Ireland, Dublin 3–5 October 2002.

Luke, A. and Carrington, V. (2002) Globalisation, literacy, curriculum practice. In R. Fischer, M. Lewis and G. Books (eds) *Raising Standards in Literacy* (pp. 231–250). London: Routledge Falmer.

May, S. (2003) Rearticulating the case for minority language rights. *Current Issues in Language Planning* 4, 95–125.

McPake, J. and Tinsley, T. (eds) (2007) *Valuing All Languages in Europe. ECML Research and Development Reports Series.* Graz: European Centre for Modern Languages.

Milani, T.M. (2008) Language testing and citizenship: A language ideological debate in Sweden. *Language in Society 37*, 27–59.

Ó Laoire, M. (2008) Educating for participation in a bilingual or multilingual society? Challenging the power balance between English and Irish (Gaelic) and other minority languages in Ireland. In C. Hélot and A.M. de Mejía (eds) *Foregoing Multilingual Spaces* (pp. 256–264). Clevedon: Multilingual Matters.

Ó Riagáin, P. (1997) *Language Policy and Social Reproduction in Ireland 1893–1993*. Oxford: Clarendon Press.

Perregaux, C., De Goumoëns, C., Jeannot, D. and de Pietro, J. (eds) (2003) *Education et Ouverture aux langues à l'école*. Neuchâtel: CIIP.

Skutnabb-Kangas, T. (2000) *Linguistic Genocide in Education – or Worldwide Diversity and Human Rights?* Mahwah, NJ: Lawrence Erlbaum Associates.

Tabors, P.O. (1997) *One Child, Two Languages*. Baltimore, MD: Paul Brookes Publishing.

The National Council for Curriculum and Assessment (2005) *Intercultural Education in the Primary School*. Dublin: NCCA.

Wallen, M. and Kelly-Holmes, H. (2006) 'I think they just think it's going to go away at some stage': Policy and practice in teaching English as an additional language in Irish primary schools. *Language and Education 20*, 141–161.

Wray, D. and Medwell, M.J. (1991) *Literacy and Language in the Primary Years*. London: Routledge.

Young, A. and Hélot, C. (2003) Language awareness and/or language learning in French primary schools today. *Language Awareness 12*, 234–246.

Chapter 7

Exploring New Pedagogical Approaches in the Context of Multilingual Cameroon

P. NGOMO

Introduction

Proudly presented by its people and leaders as 'Africa in miniature', Cameroon is an outstanding example of the multilingual countries that can be found in sub-Saharan Africa. The country is home to more than 250 national languages which represent three of the four major phyla that are found in Africa. It has inherited two languages from its colonial past, namely French and English, which places it in the arena of nations with official bilingual status. But the linguistic situation is far more complex because other languages play a considerable role during daily encounters not only locally, but at the regional or supra-regional level. The most prominent languages among these languages of wider communication (LWC) are the following: Cameroon Pidgin English or Camfranglais and 10 national languages, namely Beti-fang, Duala, Fe'fe, Fufuldé, Ghomala, Hausa, Kanuri, Mungaka, Wandala and Arab Shoa (Biloa, 2007: 81).

The aim of this chapter is to elucidate the multilingual situation in Cameroon and to try to tackle the following questions:

(1) Whether the policy of official bilingualism, as it has been implemented so far, has contributed to the development of the majority of the population of Cameroon.
(2) Whether national languages are sufficiently promoted to serve as opportunities for communication in multilingual contact situations.
(3) How national languages could play a role in education and in the holistic upbringing of individuals right from the beginning of primary school.

A brief review of the historical and sociocultural aspects of the sociolinguitics of Cameroon will highlight the different language policies that have been put in place since the country's independence. Drawing on ideas from research studies carried out elsewhere on the notions of 'Multilingual classroom ecology', 'Affordances' and 'Autonomy', the aim of this chapter is to illustrate how national languages could be exploited to play an active role in Cameroon's education system, while emphasising the initiatives teachers could take to change the situation on the ground.

Cameroon: Historical and Political Background

Cameroon is home to approximately 18,467,692 inhabitants and covers a total area of 475,440 km^2.[1] The country is often regarded by its people and authorities as 'Africa in miniature' because of its variety of geographical and sociolinguistic features: three out of the four major linguistic families (or phyla) are found on its soil (the only exception being the Khoisan phylum). Linguistically, Cameroon gives the impression of a 'labyrinth of languages' with its two official languages (French and English), a *lingua franca* (Cameroon Pidgin English), a new argot largely spoken by youths (Camfranglais) and at least 247 indigenous languages among which 11 (see above) count as LWC. Linguists' estimates differ regarding the number of national languages. Breton and Fohtung (1991), for example report 248 languages in use; but this number differs from Grimes (1996) whose report on *Ethnologue* accounts for 279 indigenous languages. The latter number is in turn outbid by Bitja'a Kody (2003) who puts the estimate as high as 285 languages in the *Annuaire Linguistique du Cameroon* (Biloa, 2007: 75).

Foreign languages are also present in French Cameroun: comprising Latin (taught in Catholic schools and used in Catholic liturgies), German and Spanish (taught in secondary schools mostly in French-speaking regions of Cameroon), Arabic (which is the language of Islam with 20% of the population as followers and which is taught in Koranic schools and introduced recently at the University of Yaoundé) and more recently Italian, Portuguese and Chinese which are taught in some language institutes across the country. The teaching of Chinese is boosted by the growing presence of Chinese businessmen in major cities in Cameroon and also some development projects initiated and financed by the People's Republic of China in Cameroon.

The first contact between Cameroon and Europeans lies many centuries ago when the Portuguese explorer Fernando Pô reached the coast of Cameroon in the year 1471 (Kody, 2004: 19). What then followed were scores of contacts with traders from Europe who usually exchanged low-value goods and liquors for local spices and slaves. The wave of scientific discoveries in Europe and the need for raw materials for industries ushered in a new era in relationships with Europe which resulted in the colonisation of the African continent. The corollary of that colonisation was the introduction of European languages to the daily realities of indigenous people. In the case of Cameroon, the Germans, for example, as colonial masters, implemented their language as a means of communication, although they always exchanged with local chiefs in Pidgin English. Kody (2004: 20) drawing on Tabi Manga (2000: 17) corroborates that the discussions that took place during the signing of the agreements between King Akwa and Dr Nachtigal in 1868 were made in Pidgin English. However, that situation did not last long and the Germans introduced a new language (Swahili in this case!) to counteract the confusion stemming from the rapid expansion of Pidgin English at the expense of German. Wolf (2001: 62) reports that a conference was held in Berlin in 1914 to decide upon the territorial language for Cameroon. Governor Ebermaier complained about the *'Sprachen-wirrwarr'* (Language confusion) and the *'seuchenartige Fortpflanzung des Neger-Englisch'* (epidemic spreading of nigger-English) and suggested that Swahili should become the *lingua franca* in Cameroon to close the gap between the country and German East Africa. But after having lost the First World War, the Germans left the country that was then taken over by France and England.

The situation did not change following the departure of the Germans since the new masters also wanted above all to impose their own language as a medium of communication. As Echu and Grundstrom explain, French colonial masters took drastic measures to impose their language promising incentives to those schools where French language and manuals were selected for instruction at the expense of manuals in autochthonous languages. The French authorities went even further and forbade the use of autochthonous languages at school:

> Dans un texte signé en Août 1917, elle (l'administration coloniale française) promet une subvention annuelle à toutes les écoles privées enseignant en langues locales qui se convertiraient à l'enseignement du français .... Ainsi, par un arrêté du Gouverneur Général de l'A.E.F. signé le 28 décembre 1920, l'enseignement en langues locales est formellement interdit : Aucune école ne sera autorisée si l'enseignement n'y est donné en français. L'enseignement de toute autre langue est interdit. Cet arrêté est suivi par une loi du 25 juillet 1921 émanant du chef de l'administration coloniale au Cameroun, et insistant sur l'emploi exclusif du français à l'école.[2] (Echu & Grundstrom, 1999: 5)

The country gained its independence in 1960 and first opted for mono-lingualism in both parts of the country (the French-speaking eastern part and the English-speaking part in the west). After reunification of the country, bilingualism was introduced on 26th October 1961 (Kody, 2004). From 1972 to 1982 promotion of official bilingualism followed. From 1983 to 1995 the focus slightly shifted to bolstering national languages in what is called 'state multilingualism'. This law was passed (law n° 98/004) on 14th April 1998 and laid emphasis on bilingualism *and* national languages. A further law (n° 2002/004) introduced in 4th January 2002 provided for the creation of a provincial inspectorate of pedagogy charged with monitoring the teaching of national languages (Kody, 2004).

The question that remains is the extent to which these laws are being implemented in the daily life of the people of Cameroon and to determine whether the national languages in particular have now ceased to be marginalised in the educational system.

The Sociocultural Reality in Sub-Saharan Africa

The late 1950s and early 1960s brought about the accession of independence to most countries in sub-Saharan Africa. On the sociocultural level, the newly independent countries were characterised by their ethnic, linguistic and cultural diversity with scores of ethnic groups coexisting together and sharing a common political fate stemming from colonisation. Many countries were faced with the option of, either imposing one of the multiple autochthonous languages to serve as medium of administration and government, or adopting the language of the colonial masters to ensure administrative continuity and efficiency. In most cases, the choice of ex-colonial languages as a means of official communication did not come as a surprise, since the local elites who took over were trained by the colonial administrations to serve their interests. This meant that too many people lacked the necessary education to influence the course of events in favour of the autochthonous population.

The most damaging corollary of the language policies of the post-colonial era was the cultural and linguistic alienation suffered by the majority of the population. This situation was worsened by new African leaders themselves who wanted above all to consolidate their grip on the state affairs and who enforced the colonial languages to achieve more power. The cultural and linguistic alienation of considerable masses of the population in sub-Saharan Africa could be seen as a possible explanation for many conflicts which are partly language related. The imposition of colonial languages as communication media and means of instruction kept the vast majority of the African population from education and development. After the departure of colonial authorities, the new administration made up of indigenous people tried to consolidate and keep the newly acquired power. This means that language was used as a weapon to settle the new administration by dominating (and possibly manipulating) the majority of the poorly educated population. Another problem is the political exploitation based on linguistic and ethnic grounds. Favouritism and nepotism are a breeding ground for most armed conflicts in that part of the world. In fact, local authorities usually surround themselves with collaborators from their ethnic origins and this mostly creates a feeling of exclusion for other ethnic groups. In some other cases, certain languages are favoured and others are excluded from public life.

The Sociocultural Reality in Cameroon after Independence

The sociocultural reality of Cameroon at independence in 1960 followed the pattern depicted above. The country first emerged as two different entities due to the historical situation which led to the Eastern part being ruled by France and the Western part by the British. The logical consequence was that after independence each part first adopted the language of the former colonial power, that is, French and English for administrative matters. After the reunification in 1961 the country opted for bilingualism (French and English). The reasons for the official choice of English and French was that Cameroonians did not want what happened at the departure of Germans to happen again, that is, a highly technical and philosophical language like German, the vehicle for modern progress and culture, to be swept away overnight. French and English furthermore play a role none of the indigenous languages fulfil, namely, they are the languages of sciences and modern technology, which are absolutely indispensable for our modern development (Chumbow, 1997). We can infer from this that no measures were undertaken to promote autochthonous languages which were deemed inferior and incapable of conveying philosophical ideas. It is a pity to find out that Africans were the first to exclude their own languages from public affairs. But as mentioned above, there were other considerations at stake. This resolve to adopt foreign languages for administration is seen to serve the interest of the minority elite. The corollary of that decision was the exclusion of the languages of the majority who was less educated and consequently less proficient in colonial languages (Webb, 1994).

After passing laws, suitable conditions for their implementation must be put in place. This means, for example, that there needs to be an adequate allocation of financial and material resources to tackle existing problems or to deal with new problems that surface on the ground. A viable development can come to happen, if and only if, the majority of the population (excluded to date from the development process because of illiteracy due to language policy) is given access to a sort of generalised education. In a nutshell, initiatives to promote access to education such as the LETAC – project aiming at elaborating principles of translation in the languages retained as pilot languages, that is, Basaa, Duala, Ewondo, Fufulde and translating the terms organised according to a variety of themes already determined by the LETAC project for the whole of Central Africa. It also aims at extending the elaboration and translation of specialised terminology to other languages beyond the pilot languages such as Fe'efe'e, Ghomala', Medumba and so on (Chumbow, 1997). This should gain momentum and benefit from government support and consequently ensure the participation of the majority of the population in human, social and economic development. At the same time, the national languages ought to be promoted. This was at least one of the goals of the National Forum on Education held in Yaoundé in 1995 aiming at promoting official bilingualism. The General Report on the National Forum on Education (1995: 17–18) makes it clear that the school should be a place, par excellence, for education and the exercise of national bilingualism. In short, from these objectives assigned to the school, it follows that the type of person educated shall be a patriotic, enlightened and bilingual (in French/ English) citizen, literate in at least one national language, steeped in his culture yet open to the world; an enterprising, creative, tolerant, responsible and honest citizen who is proud of his identity and imbued with ideals of peace, solidarity and justice and endowed with knowledge, know-how and good behaviour.

However, apart from mentioning the objective of bilingualism in the General Report, no concrete steps have been taken to ensure its implementation in the schools. What needs to be pointed out here is the lack of engagement on the part of the government to make sure that the situation changes in schools. Indeed, some laws were passed in favour of the teaching of national languages but there is no follow-up measure that guarantees the implementation on the ground (it is all about funding such resolutions = because such resolutions needs funding to be implemented on the ground). Hitherto, other attempts to ensure the teaching of national languages, for instance, the PROPELCA[3] project have not received sufficient attention, although many books have been introduced for instruction in national languages at secondary education level (cf. Amougou & Etogo Mbezele, 1976; Nseme *et al.*, 1990; Nyacka & Mben, 1976). At the higher-education level, we need to emphasise that immediately after the creation of the first university some national languages were taught. But they were quickly removed from the curriculum due to the unfounded fear that students whose mother tongues did not figure in the curriculum could trigger some sort of unrest and jeopardise national unity (see Echu, 2003: 37).

In the remainder of the chapter, attention is focused on interactions in the multilingual classroom with the aim of finding out the extent to which national languages are given the attention they deserve and secondly of describing the pedagogical opportunities (pedagogy of the possible) that unfold from interactions in the classroom.

Analysing the Situation on the Ground: Insights from Research

The issue of teaching and learning in a multilingual context, like that of Cameroon, poses a serious challenge to those involved in the educational process, bearing in mind that they are faced with numerous problems that stem both from the complex linguistic situation on the ground and from constraining economic and socio-cultural factors. This situation impinges on the daily micro-interactions among teachers and learners in the multilingual classroom.

Certain areas of research emerging in applied linguistics and applied sociolinguistics in recent years have developed helpful insights and perspectives when approaching the complexities of the multilingual classroom. Even though this research has been advanced outside the African educational context, it nonetheless provides helpful insights into how pedagogy for the multilingual classroom might be developed. Some of these insights are discussed here: for example, multilingual classroom ecology (MCE), autonomy and affordances.

Multilingual Classroom Ecology

This perspective draws on Haugen's (1972) term *'language ecology'* which he conceived as 'the study of interactions between any given language and its environment' (Haugen, 1972: 325). Haugen's understanding of the term 'environment' is linked to the 'society' using a language as one of its codes. In general, the issues involved in the discussion on language ecology include many language research aspects such as cognitive development and human interaction (Bronfenbrenner, 1979, 1993), the maintenance and survival of languages (Mühlhäusler, 1992, 1996) the promotion of linguistic diversity (Fill & Mühlhäusler, 2001) and language policy and planning (Phillipson & Skutnabb-Kangas, 1996). Fill and Mühlhäusler

(2001: 3) suggest that the notion of language ecology addresses different issues including the diversity that naturally exists among speakers of different languages or within a language in a given area (ecology) and factors that sustain that diversity among speakers and the functional interrelationships between the inhabitants of the ecology.

Creese and Martin draw attention to the multilingual classroom ecology and argue that

> ... despite the increasing amount of literature on the ecology of language, and the link with language policy and planning, there are few studies which focus on the inter-relationships between languages and their speakers in the educational context, specially, the multilingual classroom. (Creese & Martin, 2003: 163)

Concerns about language policy (and planning), language ideological orientations at school level, interrelationships between participants of a multilingual classroom on the one hand and the speakers of the other national languages in the community need to be properly addressed. Two recent studies conducted in rural and urban areas of the Centre Province have begun to address these concerns. The studies aimed at finding out how inter-community exchanges are mastered and what role the different languages (official and autochthonous as well as *lingua franca*) play during such encounters. A further aim was to find out, which attitude prevails towards the national languages whether and in which situation one considers knowledge of other community languages to represent a personal enrichment (and the readiness to learn them).

The *Theory of Affordances* can be traced back to the work of the psychologist Gibson (1977, 1979). Singleton and Aronin, drawing on Gibson (1979), conceive *affordances* 'as the perceived opportunities for action provided for the observer by an environment' (Singleton & Aronin, 2007: 84). That is, affordances can be understood as the possibilities that an object or environment appears to offer (or not offer) for action or functioning. In sum, drawing on the opportunities granted by the theory of affordances and given the situation of societal multilingualism in Cameroon, we would like to explore ways in which one can better exploit the rich linguistic environment in the classroom in order to give every learner the chance to have access to knowledge. This means, we must find out what happens to the linguistic input and possibilities provided by the different encounters with interlocutors of the other national languages. We need to determine how the so-called 'other' languages in the multilingual classroom ecology are treated and valorised. The emphasis will thus be on the different strategies used by learners to cope with the new linguistic challenges within the multilingual classroom.

Research on autonomous language learning in the early 1980s was primarily in the area of adult education. Learner autonomy, according to Holec, is 'the ability to take charge of one's own learning' (Holec, 1981: 1). There are many conceptions of the term autonomy and a detailed overview is provided by Little (2007). Two of the various orientations in the notion of autonomy are worthy of further attention because they can be useful in the analysis of situations in the multilingual classroom in Cameroon.

The psychological aspect of autonomous language learning as emphasised by the American social psychologist Deci emphasises that individuals are autonomous when they are '… fully willing to do what we are doing and embrace the activity with a sense of interest and commitment' (Deci, 1996: 2). He differentiates the concept of autonomy from independence as follows: 'Independence means to do for yourself, to not rely on others for personal nourishment and support. Autonomy, in contrast, means to act freely, with a sense of volition and choice. It is thus possible for a person to be independent and autonomous …' (Deci, 1996: 89). As a result, we have to lay more emphasis on learners' freedom to choose and act according to their needs and consequently give them more opportunities to take initiatives and determine their learning process.

As to the constructivist aspect which has to do with the process of acquiring knowledge, Barnes (1976: 81) differentiates 'school knowledge' that is external knowledge (someone else's knowledge) from 'action knowledge' which is personalised by the subject acquiring it). Little, drawing on Barnes (1976), focuses on the fact that sometimes learners' experiences at school are cut off from their outside school life, states that

> pedagogical measures designed to counteract this effect must engage learners in exploratory, interpretative processes that allow them to bring their action knowledge to bear on the school knowledge they are presented with … it allows learners the freedom to take a number of discourse initiatives that traditional pedagogies often deny them. (Little, 2007: 19)

Autonomous language learning could bring about considerable change in the Cameroon educational system and could influence the outcome of the learning process decisively.

Problems of Linguistic Diversity and (Changing) Identity in the Multilingual Classroom

After having focused attention on the political, historical and sociocultural aspects in the previous section, we will now move on to the concrete situation of teaching and learning in the multilingual classroom in Cameroon. We recall that, although existing laws do not explicitly forbid the use of other languages in the educational system, the policy of exclusion of national languages has not yet been abandoned. There are numerous problems hindering the use of many languages in the classroom due to the following:

- The non-existence or non-availability of didactic materials in other languages to support teaching initiatives.
- The insufficient qualification of teachers who have not been trained to promote autonomous language learning recommended in the curriculum.
- Considerable fear of loss of identity and consequent risk of alienation among learner-speakers of the national languages. (Tengan, 1994: 129–131)

Furthermore, the fact that in Cameroonian society there are four different varieties of French (Ebongue, 2007: 62) also complicates the situation. Moreover, it is not rare to come across linguistic varieties that are the product of the creativity of people mixing different codes (Camfranglais is one of such codes made up of a mixing between European languages and national languages (Biloa, 1999, 2003)).

We have to tackle the question of how to deal with the many different languages present in the multilingual classroom environment without causing frustration or dissatisfaction among participants. Let us assume that one national language is used as a means of instruction: on which ground should such a language be selected and why? What function should the other languages play?

Considering the huge number of languages in the Cameroon environment as depicted above, one would guess that participants in a multilingual classroom are always confronted with a constellation of at least five languages. Wolf found, for example

> that multilingualism of the Anglophone speech community, then, is generally reflected in the following combination of languages: Cameroonian L1, CPE, possibly another indigenous language, Cameroon-English and French. (Wolf, 2001: 219)

This kind of linguistic variety poses a serious challenge to the teachers since the didactic materials in languages other than the official languages are not available and the promotion of national languages is not high on the agenda. One would add to it the fact that traditionally, the teachers are perceived to be the only source of knowledge and give almost no room to their learners to contribute in the learning process (studies show that teachers speak at least two-thirds of the course time; cf. N'Gomo, 2004). Drawing on the theories outlined briefly in this chapter it is implied that multilingual learners in Cameroon could benefit more from the advantages and opportunities offered by the multilingual language environment. In addition, the difficulty that has to be bridged in order to institutionalise multilingual learning is the decision as to which language(s) must be taught, where and by whom. Considering the diversity of languages, it is suggested that certain guidelines could be adhered to:

(1) The rule of standardisation (which implies that the language(s) to be learnt should be available in literature and publications).
(2) The rule of territoriality (which stipulates that a language spoken in a precise area should be promoted in that area to facilitate community life and exchanges).
(3) The rule of demography and representation (whereby in a given area with many community languages the language with statistically large numbers should have the edge on other languages and be taught on a regular basis. This would give LWC the edge on local languages and contribute to huge gains in intercommunity exchanges and comprehension).
(4) The rule of integration and anti-discrimination (whereby even some less representative languages should be taught even irregularly to facilitate integration or intercommunity exchanges with their L1-speakers). But this foregoing reflection bears also some difficulties because the teachers, like in Europe and elsewhere, cannot possibly master all the languages of their multilingual classroom. That is the reason why one should seriously think of empowering learners to take learning initiatives where they become a resource for the teacher and their peers.

The problem of changing learners changing their identity in ways like this should also be addressed when focusing on the multilingual classroom. The concept of identity is very vast and multifaceted. As can be seen, learner and teacher identity can be considered to be the subject of construction and negotiation. This means that identity may result from the influence exercised by external (social, political and cultural) conditions dictated by the environment on the self. That is why it is considered to be dynamic since it may be subject to change to overcome or grapple with those external constraints. In the case of the multilingual classroom context, both learner and teacher identity can and would probably end up being influenced and altered as a result of contacts with other languages (see Cummins, 2006).

We will now address two ongoing ethnographic studies in rural and urban areas of Cameroon to illustrate what is possible to achieve in dynamic, multiple and conflictual classroom situations.

Study 1: Attitudes to Languages in the Local Community

Although this is still an ongoing investigation, we would like to give an account of some preliminary findings of the study. In the process of a post-doctoral research on multilingualism in Cameroon, an inquiry was launched (from December 2005 to March 2006 and from September to December 2007) in schools around the town of Ayos, Nyong and Mfoumou division, aimed at finding out attitudes towards languages (other than the L1) spoken in the local community and determining in which language(s) intercommunity activities and exchanges are made. This brief account is focused on the linguistic situation in a school (about a hundred learners) in the small village of Mbaka'a which is situated about 17 km from Ayos. The inhabitants mostly speak Omvang (about 85% of almost a thousand inhabitants), the other 15% speak and understand French (an official language) or Yebekolo (a neighbouring language which is the majority language in the town of Ayos).

We started an experiment with the teacher of the small school. Some learning material had to be presented in a national language (although a special authorisation from the local school authorities was needed to conduct such an experiment, we intentionally skipped it, the intent here was to show the teacher that he could take some initiatives and be autonomous). The teacher's L1 was Yebekolo, and he had the challenge to present the pedagogical material in a language that was not the students' L1. The objective of the study was to probe whether and how students would react to being taught in a language which was not the official language (French). The preliminary findings show that although the vast majority of students spoke Omvang as L1, the participants wished to learn the school subjects in the Yebekolo language and were very enthusiastic over the new changes and the considerable gains achieved by learners. This seems to be contradictory to the expectations of the teachers due to the fact that it is a minority language in the village; but a possible explanation may be that most of the students usually go to Ayos for shopping and exchanges and bargaining are made through the Yebekolo variety. That is why it was given the edge on other languages in the multilingual classroom ecology. The willingness to learn other community language was present because of the sense of togetherness which is still widespread in rural areas. One should also mention the fact that the official language (French) does not play a prominent role in community activities, though it is the medium of instruction at school. After class, exchanges take place in a local language, and even teacher and learners outside the classroom communicate in a national language accessible to each other (Yebekolo in this case). The students' evaluation of their intake is almost equal to the input: to be clear, the students estimated that they understood and learnt the material better because it was conveyed through a language that they were familiar with.

Study 2: Inquiry into Linguistic Habits in Towns

Launched in government schools of the 4th district of Yaoundé from December 2005 to March 2006 and from September to December 2007, the same inquiry was conducted to give an account of the multilingual situation in the classroom context and explore the ins and outs of learners' attitudes towards national languages. The situation in Cameroon towns is very different because of the huge diversity of languages stemming from the massive rural exodus of people who came to town in search of work. Chia (1992) gives an account of market languages which sheds light on that huge linguistic diversity.

Adding to the complexity of the linguistic situation in towns, Essono (1993) observes that in Cameroonian cities, French and English have, respectively, become the first language (L1) of an increasingly younger population. Thus, nowadays, it is not difficult to find a Cameroonian whose mother tongue is either English or French. In fact, many parents have opted to speak either French or English to their children because of the gains the foreign language would guarantee for their school achievements: it is the language of instruction at school and also a warrant for success in professional life since it serves also as means of communication for administration.

It goes without saying that neglect of national languages also poses the threat of loss of identity. This is mostly what is observed in families where children do not speak their mother tongue and this results in generation conflicts because grandparents do not speak the official languages. This part of the population is estimated at 20% of the inhabitants of urban zones. We tried to conduct the same experiment at a school in Yaoundé as we did in the rural school of Mbaka'a. Instead of choosing a national language as medium of instruction, we tried to teach through the medium of Camfranglais which is widely spoken in schools and popular among youths. Most teachers who were involved in our experiment are proficient in Camfranglais and it was not an obstacle using it to teach the curriculum. It is fair to mention that the class was bilingual, in the sense that what the teacher could not convey in Camfranglais was then said in French.

The preliminary findings that can be reported to date are as follows:

- Due to the situation described by Onguene Essono (1993), French (and to a smaller extent English) take a prominent place in the exchanges observed and consequently is the major medium of instruction in urban schools.
- The dominance of the official languages (French and English) is challenged by the emergence of the Camfranglais (Biloa, 1999, 2003), which is being widely spoken by the younger generations. The students estimated that they better understood the curriculum being conveyed through Camfranglais than through French. A possible explanation here could be that Camfranglais is more popular with them and that is why they would prefer to be taught in that language.
- The readiness to learn other national languages is reduced to the minimum because they probably play no significant role in the daily life of the participants (an undeniable fact in urban centres). Some reports show that the children are even intentionally exposed to French at home (whereas other languages are purely and simply neglected) because parents deem it to be a sign of better school achievement.
- The vulgarisation project of national languages have little chance to succeed in towns because of the lack of interest from the authorities, the shortage of funding, but it should not be abandoned. Most initiatives in this field have earned very little attention and funding (cf. PROPELCA-project and others). The cosmopolitan character of towns and the rich linguistic varieties should be better exploited.

Conclusion

These studies (in rural and urban schools) allow us to make the following observations. First, we recommend that primary instruction should actively encourage the use at school of learners' L1. We would imagine that during the first years of education the children's L1 should play a vital role alongside the official language (OL). Therefore, teaching should be made according to the formula OL + L1 in order to acquaint the children with the curriculum and promote their mental/psychological and societal development equally. In the Anglophone Regions of Cameroon, we recommend the use of Pidgin English (CPE), because it identifies the language that is common to all Anglophones. It also serves as an LWC in exchanges and interactions on a daily basis (see Biloa, 2007).

Languages such as major national languages with supra-regional character (like Ewondo, Basaa, Mungaka, Fuldé, etc.) should be introduced gradually at the beginning of secondary education. We would like to emphasise the work done by some scholars like Tadadjeu's and his notion of 'extensive trilingualism' (Tadadjeu, 1975), which calls for the promotion of the official languages, the indigenous languages and the foreign languages, or Tabi Manga (2000) who suggests 'quadrilingualism' through emphasis on the teaching of the OLs, mother tongues, the LWC and the foreign languages.

The use of national languages can be promoted through the media. There are some programs on radio mostly dealing with religion (Bitja'a Kody, 2004). It would be also better to diversify those programs and try to address other needs and interests of the population. We would recommend advertising even in national languages in order to reach everybody. Latest information shows that the teaching of national languages at Cameroonian schools takes effect as from September when school resumes for the academic year 2009–2010. But without a clear-cut language policy one has to raise the question to know on which basis which language will be taught when, for how long and to whom. The teaching of national languages leaves many questions unanswered. But all in all, it is a necessary start for a brighter future for new generations. Research in this field also needs to be encouraged and well funded because there is a need to probe and explore new ways of harmonisation and coexistence between official languages on the one hand, and national languages and Camfranglais or CPE on the other. Another concept that could play a vital role here is that of 'receptive multilingualism' as depicted by ten Thije and Zeevaert as the 'language constellation in which interlocutors use their respective mother tongue while speaking to each other' (Thije and Zeevaert, 2007: 1). The research in this domain could be useful in the Cameroonian context since would it suits the reality of everyday communication where many languages are used.

Notes

1. https://www.cia.gov/library/publications/the-world-factbook/geos/cm.html. Accessed 24.02.09.
2. 'In a text signed in August 1917, the French colonial administration promises an annual subsidy to all private schools providing education in local languages

which would exclusively switch their teaching to French … Thus, by a decree signed by the General Governor of French Equatorial Africa (A.E.F) on December 28, 1920, the teaching of indigenous languages is strictly prohibited: No school would be authorized to open if education is not given through the teaching of French. The teaching of any other language than French is strictly forbidden. This decree is followed by a law from the Chief of colonial administration in Cameroon emphasizing the exclusive use of French as sole means of instruction at school'.

3. PROPELCA (Operational Research Program for Language Teaching in Cameroon), in collaboration with the University of Yaounde and the Institute of Social Sciences, has been active since 1977 in the area of the unification and harmonisation of language teaching in Cameroon, be it in connection with official languages, national languages or foreign languages. The PROPELCA project centres around what Tadadjeu (1975) refers to as 'extensive trilingualism', a language model which dwells on the development of all major languages (more than 100,000 speakers), medium languages (between 50,000 and 99,000 speakers) and peripheral languages (less than 10,000 speakers) (see Gfeller, 2000: 134). Thanks to the work of PROPELCA, the writing system of Cameroonian languages was harmonised in March 1979, a factor that has contributed immensely to the standardisation of some indigenous languages.

References

Amougou, C. and Etogo Mbezele, L. (1976) *M'akad nâ*. Douala: College Libermann.

Barnes, D. (1976) *From Communication to Curriculum*. Harmondsworth: Penguin.

Biloa, E. (1999) Structure phrasique du Camfranglais: État de la question. In G. Echu and A.W. Grundstrom (eds) *Official Bilingualism and Linguistic Communication in Cameroon/Bilinguisme officiel et communication linguistique au Cameroun* (pp. 147–174). New York: Peter Lang.

Biloa, E. (2003) *La langue Française au Cameroun*. Bern: Peter Lang.

Biloa, E. (2007) Le Partenariat Anglais – Français ou le Problème Anglophone au Cameroun. In Agence Universitaire de la Francophonie (AUF) *Partenariat entre les Langues: perspectives descriptives et perspectives didactiques* (pp. 74–82). Journées Scientifiques Inter-réseaux organisées par le réseau DLF de l'Agence Universitaire de la Francophonie, Nouakchott, 5–7 Novembre 2007.

Bitjaa Kody, Z.D. (2004) *La Dynamique des langues Camerounaises en Contact avec le Français: Approche Macrosociolinguistique*. Université de Yaoundé I.

Chumbow, B.S. (1997) Thematic glossaries and language development. In B. Smieja and M. Tasch (eds) *Human Contact through Language and Linguistics* (pp. 271–290). Frankfurt am Main: Peter Lang.

Creese, A. and Martin, P. (eds) (2003) Multilingual classroom ecologies: Interrelationships, interactions and ideologies. *International Journal of Bilingual Education and Bilingualism* 6, 161–167.

Cummins, J. (2006) Identity texts: The imaginative construction of self through multiliteracies pedagogy. In O. García, T. Skutnabb-Kangas, and M.E. Torres Guzman (eds) *Imagining Multilingual Schools: Languages in Education and Glocalization* (pp. 51–68). Clevedon: Multilingual Matters.

Deci, E.L. (1996) *Why We Do What We Do: Understanding Self Motivation.* Harmondsworth: Penguin.

Ebongue, E.A. (2007) Partenariat français/langues locales dans la presse écrite camerounaise: entre continuum et hybridation. In Agence Universitaire de la Francophonie (AUF). *Partenariat entre les Langues: perspectives descriptives et perspectives didactiques* (pp. 62–73). Journées Scientifiques Inter-réseaux organisées par le réseau DLF de l'Agence Universitaire de la Francophonie, Nouakchott, 5–7 Novembre 2007.

Echu, G. (2003) Coping with multilingualism: Trends in the evolution of language policy in Cameroon. *PhiN. Philologie im Netz* 25, 31–46. On WWW at http://www.fu-berlin.de/phin/phin25/p25i.htm. Accessed 01.07.03.

Echu, G. and Grundstrom, A.W. (1999) *Official Bilingualism and Linguistic Communication in Cameroon/Bilinguisme officiel et communication linguistique au Cameroun.* New York: Peter Lang.

Gibson, J.J. (1977) The theory of affordances. In R.E. Shaw and J. Brandsford (eds) *Perceiving, Acting, and Knowing* (pp. 67–82). Hillsdale, NJ: Lawrence Erlbaum Associates.

Gibson, J.J. (1979) *The Ecological Approach to Visual Perception.* Boston: Houghton Mifflin.

Haugen, E. (1953) *The Norwegian Language in America* (Vol. 1). Philadelphia: University of Pennsylvania Press.

Haugen (1972) *The Ecology of Language.* Stanford, CA: Stanford University Press.

Heft, H. (2001) *Ecological Psychology in Context: James Gibson, Roger Baker, and the Legacy of William James's Radical Empirism.* Mahwah, NJ: Lawrence Erlbaum Associates.

Holec, H. (1979 & 1981) *Autonomy and Foreign Language Learning.* Oxford: Pergamon.

Little, D. (2007) Language learner autonomy. Some fundamental considerations revisited. *Innovation in Language Learning and Teaching* 1, 14–29.

Mühlhäusler, P. (1996) Linguistic ecology. *Language Change and Linguistic Imperialism in the Pacific Region.* London: Routledge.

Ngomo, E.P. (2004) *Wortschatzarbeit mit dem Regionallehrwerk, 'Ihr und Wir': Überlegungen zum Deutschunterricht in Kamerun.* Norderstedt: Books on Demand.

Nseme, C., Bitja'a Kody, Z.D., Sadembouo, E., Mbakong, A. and Ngueffo, N. (1990) *Textes de lecture en langues nationales.* Classes de 4e et 3e. Yaoundé: PROPELCA.

Nyacka, D. and Mben, J. (1976) *Basógól Bá nkal lé… Textes basaa pour l'enseignement.* Douala: Collège Libermann.

Phillipson, R. and Skutnabb-Kangas, T. (1996) English only worldwide or language ecology. *TESOL Quarterly* 30, 429–452.

Singleton, D. and Aronin, L. (2007) Multiple language learning in the light of the theory of affordances. *Innovation in Language Learning and Teaching* 1, 83–96.

Tabi Manga, J. (2000) *Les politiques linguistiques du Cameroun: Essai d'aménagement linguistique.* Paris: Editions Karthala.

Tengan, A.B. (1994) European languages in African society and culture: A view on cultural authenticity. In M. Pütz (ed.) *Language Contact and Language Conflict* (pp. 125–138). Amsterdam: John Benjamins.

Ten Thije, J.D. and Zeevaert, L. (2007) *Receptive Multilingualism*. Amsterdam/ Philadelphia: John Benjamins.

Webb, V. (1994) Revalorizing the autochthonous languages of Africa. In M. Pütz (ed.) *Language Contact and Language Conflict* (pp. 181–203). Amsterdam: John Benjamins.

Wolf, H.G. (2001) *English in Cameroon*. Berlin: Mouton de Gruyter.

Part 2

Deconstructing the Myth of Monolingualism

Perspectives on Identities, Ideologies and Politics

Chapter 8

Linguistic Diversity as a Bridge to Adjustment: Making the Case for Bi/Multilingualism as a Settlement Outcome in New Zealand

U. WALKER

Introduction

Like other immigrant nations, New Zealand stands to gain from the social, cultural or economic contributions new citizens can make to society. Whether it will also benefit from the rich linguistic diversity immigrants bring, depends on the extent to which bi/multilingual migrants can maintain their individual linguistic repertoires in a functional way. However, the socioeconomic conditions tend to work in favour of the dominant language English (Holmes, 2001), and the discourse of the economically dominant culture promotes the belief that migrants' native languages have little relevance in an English-speaking society. The inevitable shift to English further perpetuates a linguistic ecology with limited affordances for linguistic diversity. Despite an increasing recognition of the socioeconomic implications of societal monolingualism, the consequences of losing bi/multilingualism as a personal characteristic (Aronin & Ó Laoire, 2004) tend to be overlooked, not least with regard to the role migrants' languages can play in the social–emotional adjustment to the host society.

> New Zealand needs to shake off its monolingual complacency and recognise the value of language diversity for the nation's social, economic and cultural development.

With these words, spoken in the opening address at the 2007 national conference for language teachers (NZALT) in Auckland, Race Relations Commissioner Joris de Bres summed up a key challenge facing New

Zealand and its future social, cultural and economic advancement. He referred to the ability to secure a multilingual future (Human Rights Commission, 2007) in a country where a large English-speaking majority, official English/Māori bilingualism and an increasingly diverse migrant population constitute a complex mix. For migrants, mastering the host language is the key mechanism for successful social and economic participation in New Zealand (Department of Labour, 2007a). But more often than not, settlement and integration go hand in hand with sociolinguistic discontinuities. As migrants' linguistic repertoires undergo functional and symbolic changes, new ways of being seen and seeing oneself emerge, whereas familiar ways to interact and affirm identities may become less relevant or cease to be used altogether. What are the implications of these changes in terms of the affective functioning of migrants? In an increasingly diverse society it is important to gain a better understanding of the psychological dimension of integration and settlement and how bi/multilingual migrants deal with cultural and linguistic discontinuities, particularly in relation to identity and sense of self.

New Zealand: A Multilingual Ecology with a Monolingual Mindset?

New Zealand's linguistic diversity is reflected in the most recent Census (2006) figures, according to which there are more than 150 languages spoken. English speakers account for 95.9% and 4.1% speak New Zealand's indigenous language, te reo Māori (Statistics New Zealand, 2007a). In all, 74% of the population are monolingual English speakers (Statistics New Zealand, 2007a), which makes New Zealand a predominantly monolingual country. However, in the decade between 1996 and 2006, the number of multilingual people increased by 43.3%, as shown in Table 8.1 (Statistics New Zealand, 2007a). This increase is largely the result of a growing presence of overseas-born residents; at 23% New Zealand has in fact the fourth highest rate in the OECD of people born overseas (Ministry of Social

Table 8.1 Percentage of speakers with one, two or more languages 1996–2006

Number of languages oral	1996 Census	2001 Census	2006 Census
One	83.8	82.1	80.5
Two or more	13.6	15.8	17.5

Source: Statistics New Zealand (2007a, 2007b)

Table 8.2 Languages with large increases in speaker numbers 1996–2006

	1996 Census	*2006 Census*
Hindi	22,749	44,589
Mandarin	26,514	41,391
Korean	15,873	26,967
Afrikaans	12,783	21,123

Development, n.d.). Nearly half of the overseas-born adults (48.5%) and over a third (35%) of children up to the age of 14 are multilingual. This compares to 10% and 11.5% respectively among the New Zealand-born population (Statistics New Zealand, 2007a).

A comparison of Census figures for the same 10-year period reflects the country's increasing ethno-linguistic diversity, with some language groups showing dramatic increases in speaker numbers (Table 8.2).

For New Zealand's linguistic diversity to be sustainable there needs to be a social context with opportunities for language in use via access to domains, communities of practice and social networks (Milroy, 1987; Walker, 1996). Bi/multilingual practices do not exist in isolation; they are situated in the macro and micro conditions which determine the contextual affordances (Norton, 2000; Norton Peirce, 1995) available to migrants to develop and adopt linguistic practices through which they construct, transform and express their view of the world, and a sense of self within it.

Against this background the chapter aims to explore the role of migrants' bi/multilingual repertoires as a linguistic resource for identity and self-construction in the process of adaptation to the New Zealand sociolinguistic environment. Only in the last decade has this process become more circumscribed strategically and via policy, as a response to increasing diversity and with the aim to facilitate the integration of new migrants to promote positive social, cultural, linguistic and economic outcomes. New Zealand's settlement strategy aims directly at migration-related outcomes, including linguistic ones. How these outcomes facilitate or constrain the languages of migrants (ML) will be examined, with a particular focus on the affective aspects associated with these languages, drawing on empirical data from Walker (2004).

Language(s) in Policy

Unlike other English-dominant contexts, perhaps with the exception of Canada, New Zealand has a strong bicultural heritage. While English is the de facto official language, the indigenous te reo Māori, was made an official language in 1987. New Zealand Sign Language was declared an official language in 2007, reflecting a growing recognition of linguistic diversity at the official level. But in the absence of an overarching national languages policy (Peddie, 2003), strategic goals relating to all languages in New Zealand have been scattered across different, albeit linked policy areas, which are also directly relevant to migrants: these are the *Strategy for Adult Esol* (Ministry of Education, 2003), *Our Future Together: New Zealand Settlement Strategy* (Department of Labour, 2007a), the 2007 *Curriculum Framework for Schools* (Ministry of Education, 2007) and the *Diversity Action Programme* (Human Rights Commission, n.d.).

Despite diverging orientations across these different policy areas, there is overt recognition of cultural and linguistic diversity in all of them. For example, the *Strategy for Adult Esol* states that:

> Migrants and refugees bring to New Zealand a diversity of skills, cultural practices and understandings, which enrich us as a multicultural society. (Ministry of Education, 2003)

ESOL provision is also clearly identified as 'intrinsically linked to, and an essential part of, the settlement and resettlement process' (Ministry of Education, 2003: 11). The strategy is regarded as 'one of the most fundamental tools in assisting migrants and refugees to more actively participate in society, the economy and their communities' (Ministry of Education, 2003: 11). It makes an explicit link between improved English skills and successful settlement outcomes and aims to halve the number of people with no English language skills by 2012. To this end, the New Zealand government allocated NZ$63,390 million of settlement funds over four years, two-thirds of which are ESOL-related (Department of Labour, 2004: 13). 'When the English language barrier is removed, it significantly increases a person's ability to participate in New Zealand's economy and society' (Ministry of Education, 2003: 7). The strategy's focus is thus clearly on promoting proficiency in English, but it is also acknowledged that 'a lack of bilingual instruction and support can impede progress, and learners are sometimes unable to understand' (Ministry of Education, 2003: 14). Based on this basic recognition of the multilinguality of ESOL learners, bi/multilingual approaches are recommended to address three key areas (15):

- Information: for improvement of access
- Implementation: to promote flexibility of programmes and inclusion of bilingual community-based provision
- Professional development: to assist bilingual tutors

Migrants' L1 is seen as having functional value in order to improve information uptake at a crucial time, when new migrants need to have a fundamental understanding of schooling, employment, housing, health and so on. Its instructional use with learners who have little English proficiency also seems to aim at maximising understanding, which suggests that the recommended bilingual practices are transitional and not aimed at bilingual outcomes as such. It is nonetheless encouraging that a major ESOL provider such as the 'Esol Home Tutors' are committed to 'reframing the future through diversity', as their 2009 conference theme indicates.

A more explicit thrust towards creating a positive climate for multilingualism and greater investment in languages has come from the Human Rights Commission, in particular through its Diversity Action Programme (Human Rights Commission, n.d.), which provides a framework for developing strategies integrating English for speakers of other languages, Te Reo Māori, New Zealand Sign Language, Pacific languages, community as well as heritage languages and foreign languages. The Action Programme is very much at the forefront of promoting discourse and public debate about linguistic diversity, particularly through the 'Language Forum' at the biannual 'Diversity Forum'. In August 2008, the forum dealt with the topic of 'Languages in Schools, Schools in Communities', a clear signal that issues of linguistic diversity in society are, by extension, issues affecting schools. While the diversity debate continues, a key policy framework tasked to address wider issues of settlement, including language, is in fact in place: the New Zealand settlement strategy.

Settlement Strategy in New Zealand

New Zealand prides itself as a society that embraces diversity. As a nation with a long history of migration it is also 'committed to ensuring that migrants settle well in New Zealand' according to David Cunliffe, former Minister of Immigration (Department of Labour, 2007a). As an open-ended process settlement takes time and 'can involve change in all aspects of life – economic, social, cultural, political and environmental' (Department of Labour, 2007a: 12). More specifically, settlement has been defined as a complex process where:

> new settlers move from dealing with immediate issues of finding somewhere to live, getting a job and adapting to unfamiliar systems and customs, to becoming active participants in social, civic, economic, cultural and spiritual affairs of the new homeland. Settlement is a two

way process, requiring learning, adaptation, tolerance and respect by both new settler and host communities. (Woolford, 2005: 9)

It was not until 2004, that a strategic approach to the settlement of new migrants in New Zealand was articulated to address the needs of migrant employment, access and participation. It recognises that '... those from diverse cultural and language backgrounds may require additional assistance, especially in the early stages of settlement' (Department of Labour, 2007a: 12). An initial settlement strategy outline, *A Future Together* (Department of Labour, 2004) prepared the ground for the settlement strategy document proper, *Our Future Together*, which was launched in 2007 (Department of Labour, 2007a). The strategy operates at three levels, all of which make specific reference to diversity (Department of Labour, 2007a: 9–11):

(1) The vision statement emphasises three cornerstones of New Zealand's prosperity: inclusivity, integration and shared respect for diversity.
(2) The higher-level goals express the notion that host and origin culture complement each other:

Migrants, refugees and their families have a sense of place and belonging in New Zealand, while maintaining their cultural identities that contribute to New Zealand's social and cultural vibrancy.

(3) The intermediate-level goals represent a list of specific outcomes:

Migrants, refugees and their families:

(a) are accepted and respected by host communities for their diverse cultural backgrounds and their community interactions are positive;
(b) obtain employment appropriate to their qualifications and skills and are valued for their contribution to economic transformation and innovation;
(c) become confident using English in a New Zealand setting or are able to access appropriate language support;
(d) access appropriate information and responsive services that are available in the wider community;
(e) form supportive social networks and establish a sustainable community identity;
(f) feel safe within the wider community in which they live;
(g) accept and respect the New Zealand way of life and contribute to civic, community and social activities.

One goal (c) relates to a specific linguistic outcome, albeit one limited to English. Other outcomes are arguably facilitated by English, particularly goal (b). The strategy's associated implementation plan does refer to 'heritage language preservation', but this is aimed to protect Pacific languages at risk of extinction.[1] The strategy's overall orientation towards English contrasts with the expression of respect for migrant's diverse cultural backgrounds and the expectation that migrants maintain their cultural identities in order 'contribute to New Zealand's social and cultural vibrancy'. Thus, what on the surface appears as a conceptualisation of settlement as a two-way process is pervaded by a monolingual mindset. It is of course undisputed that knowledge of English is essential when dealing with the demands of adapting to the New Zealand environment. Nonetheless, while cultural diversity is overtly desired as an enrichment to New Zealand society, it appears to be taken as a given and remains without an explicit goal articulated in its support.

New Zealand's commitment to settling migrants, to all intents and purposes then, is linked to outcomes associated with or facilitated through English. The contribution migrants are expected to make in order to help bring about economic transformation is contingent on English. The overt celebration of diversity appears to be a bonus outcome and, as a consequence, the strategy is unlikely to actively foster cultural diversity as an outcome, let alone linguistic diversity. However, to ignore migrants' linguistic capital or to reduce it to a transitional communicative tool is to marginalise its affective dimension and the role migrants' languages play for identity.

Settlement Matters are Identity Matters

Commitment to a new society and the willingness to become an active participant in it is promoted by a sense of belonging and identification with the new environment. The outline version of the settlement strategy recognises the sense of connection and identities which migrants bring:

> Cultural identity matters to us all and this is no less the case for migrants and refugees. It is important that we celebrate and value the ethnic and cultural diversity migrants and refugees bring to our society. (Department of Labour, 2004: 10)

Such official recognition of cultural diversity helps validate different cultural identities, but to what extent the contextual conditions exist to express these through linguistic means is another matter (Norton, 2000; Norton Peirce, 1995). *Our Future Together* (Department of Labour, 2007a) aims for migrants to 'feel safe within the wider community in which they live' and 'establish a sustainable community identity', moving away from the earlier goal of 'expressing ethnic identity' in the 2004 outline. The notion of 'community identity' in goal (e) may be vague, but has potential to accommodate both host and ethnic community. Community identity refers to group identity, and membership in social and cultural entities clearly represents an important outcome in the process of adapting to a new society. However, it is individuals who forge new alliances, develop networks and seek affordances to facilitate social interaction and economic participation. Receiving societies focus on settlement in terms of the desired socioeconomic outcomes for the whole of society; the individual, in contrast, is at the centre of the process of being and becoming. The effects of this process are felt at the individual level and may have psychological implications.

The psychological adaptation of immigrants and refugees has been studied across a wide range of contexts, particularly in studies of mental or psychological stress (Al-Issa & Tousignant, 1997; Pernice & Brook, 1996; Roer-Strier, 2000). Other studies examine the emotional resonance first languages have for their speakers and the 'emotional possibilities that a given language has for a bilingual, the sense of self that language makes possible' (Besemeres, 2004: 154), affording migrants a bilingual self-concept which promotes continuity in the process of change (Walker, 2004). Reduced exposure to or loss of functional opportunities, as in the case of Afrikaans in New Zealand, may be felt as 'linguistic longing' (Barkhuizen & Knoch, 2005).

In this chapter the focus is on the individual. It explores issues of identity and self through a theoretical framework which aims to conceptualise the complexities of the process of settlement from a social constructivist view. From this perspective, identity formation and self-construction are understood as social processes and therefore dynamic and contingent on interaction facilitated through language. The poststructural approach to language and identity (Lantolf & Pavlenko, 2000; Norton, 2000) as well as the social–psychological perspective (Fivush & Buckner, 1997) emphasise on a socially situated view of the self, articulated through linguistic means in social interaction. Thus, when people interact through language 'they are not only exchanging information with target language speakers, but they are constantly organizing and reorganizing a sense of who they are and how they relate to the social world' (Norton, 2001: 166). This verbal enactment of a sense of self is based on an understanding of identities as partially 'discursive products' (Stevens, 1996: 228) which facilitate social positioning (Davies & Harré, 1990). Bi/multilinguals have a range of sociolinguistic resources to draw on, affording them 'contrasting experiences and positional identities' (Koven, 1998: 410). From this perspective, self-conceptualisation does not only involve an outward expression of cultural identity, but also the projection of a deeper sense of subjectivity, as is related by this migrant:

> It speaks not of the identity which I project in public now, but rather of my personality and sense of self since birth. When I speak in Spanish, I feel I speak from my soul. (Korzenny, 1999: 4)

Given the dynamic and complex relationship between language(s) and identity it is crucial to gain a better understanding of the process of self-construal in situations of language contact, fluctuating proficiencies and changing sociocultural practices. In contact situations such as migration, linguistic behaviour '... is both an expression of multiple identity and a response to multiple identity' (Clyne, 2003: 2). More specifically then, the question arises, what implications linguistic discontinuities have in the process of settlement. Language is, after all, regarded as a key factor in settlement and integration, but more often than not it is seen in terms of migrants' language problems and a lack of host language proficiency. Such a monolingual perspective fails to recognise bi/multilinguals as complete people and typecasts them as inadequate monolinguals. The sole focus on English may also be in stark contrast with migrants' own self-perception as bi/multilinguals. It ignores their existing linguistic repertoires, which form part of the dynamics of the overall sociolinguistic ecology and the wider sociocultural conditions.

As a repository of personal histories ML have the potential to connect people's past with their future *being and becoming* (Fishman, 2001) in a new sociocultural context. (Re)constructing one's sense of self as a migrant thus is not just a matter of picking up where one left off before migrating. Bi/multilingual proficiencies equip individuals with the ability to balance the dual needs of maintaining cultural roots and acculturation. In the Vygotskian sense, the self-concept comes into being via a dynamic relationship between an individual's social and psychological functioning (Vygotsky, 1978), where language acts as the crucial medium through which individuals both construct and present a sense of self. As part of a person's mental/cognitive makeup, the self-concept also functions as a cognitive structure which helps make sense of new experiences in unfamiliar context by '... linking new experiences to old ones and thereby provides for stability rather than change' (Hormuth, 1990: 167).

Migrants' languages can thus provide a mechanism for self-construal and help to promote stability in situations of change. By the same token, linguistic discontinuities can act as potential destabilising force, affecting the very mechanism that might help migrants cope with the challenges they face, while trying to maintain or reconstruct a bi/multilingual sense of being. This is a tall order in a linguistic environment that favours English, where a monolingual English majority reinforces monolingual perspectives and practices and where languages other than English (LOTES) have limited cultural and linguistic capital. The shift towards English may appear inevitable from a monolingual perspective and even be a desirable outcome that facilitates participation. But it is also a precursor of becoming monolingual, with diminishing linguistic means for a language-generated sense of self (Figure 8.1) and increasing reliance on non-linguistic ways where identities used to be constructed and presented through ML.

In this context, Fishman's (2001) notion of *continuity of being* suggests an important linkage between language and self-identity, one that is borne out at three levels: knowing, doing and being. *Knowing* arises from culture-specific representations (e.g. kinship); *doing* is enacting culture-specific practices and *being* refers to passing on the essence of what is perceived to represent an ethnocultural collectivity. Language is crucial at all three levels, and losing this link, for example, due to language shift, can mean relinquishing the past and abandoning of one's ancestral connections, which are not necessarily translatable (Fishman, 2001: 5). *Continuity of being* thus suggests a continuity of self via ethnolinguistic membership,

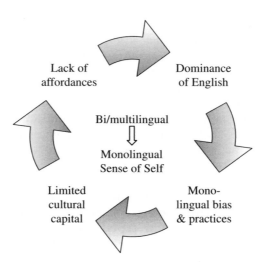

Figure 8.1 Shift to monolingual self

which in turn is facilitated by ML. In this complex process, multiple proficiencies and practices can act as a mechanism to connect with the past and a common cultural heritage through shared linguistic practices, which help to strengthen ties with family and community and facilitate a more positive self-concept (Gibbons & Ramirez, 2004).

Identity in New Zealand: A New Zealand Identity?

In New Zealand, the expectation to adopt a new identity is popularly tied to the idea of becoming a 'Kiwi'.[2] But despite their potential inclusiveness, single identity labels such as 'Kiwi', 'Pakeha' or 'New Zealander' have been shown to be among the least preferred options for many migrants (Jancovic-Kramaric, 2001; Walker, 2004). Identification with a group or label does not necessarily correspond to the emotional involvement or sense of belonging to that group as Raza (1997) found. The complex process of being and becoming may, in their experience, not be effectively captured through an idealised single host membership. Instead, individuals find new ways to express multiple affinities through creative combinations, as this person's example illustrates: 'I am Maria Márquez from Chile, but I've lived here in New Zealand since I was two, so I'm a Chiwi' (Office of Ethnic Affairs, n.d.: 3).

Duality can be complementary and enriching or it can create a sense of being 'neither here nor there', an experience resulting in dislocation and isolation and a challenge particularly felt by young migrants. One of the major challenges young migrants identified is a sense of being pulled in different directions and not fitting into their own communities because they do not speak their language (Ethnic Voice New Zealand, 2005), as a result of growing up in New Zealand. They also articulated the need to 'create a new identity for the youth' by integrating both traditional and new cultural identities (Ethnic Voice New Zealand, 2005: 19). This suggests that for youth too, ML affords a sense of connection and a 'sense of place and belonging'; it functions as the connective tissue between different generations, without interfering with the process of navigating between cultures.

Deriving a continued sense of identity via the heritage language does not necessarily come at the expense of acculturation. Phinney *et al.* (2006) examined adolescent acculturation patterns in a wide range of contact settings and found that bilinguals preferred integration as an acculturation strategy. Furthermore, a positive orientation towards both ethnic identity and identification with the host society was found to correlate with a preference for integration, rather than separation or marginalisation as acculturation strategies. This evidence suggests that bilingualism promotes integration, in line with a two-way concept of settlement.

In the New Zealand context, a longitudinal study of social integration and settlement (New Zealand Immigration Service, 2004) found that practices associated with the origin culture were not only valued by participants in the study but that they became '... increasingly important to carry on the values and traditions of their ethnic group the longer they had spent in New Zealand' (New Zealand Immigration Service, 2004: 7). Cultural continuity was perceived to be more important after 18 months of residence than after six months (Department of Labour, 2004: 10), reflecting the desire to ensure intergenerational transmission of both culture and language:

> Most refugees said it was important to maintain their own culture in New Zealand in order to preserve a cultural identity for future generations, to share with others, and because they were proud of it. The most common ways to maintain their culture were through eating traditional food, practising religion, and speaking their language. (Department of Labour, 2004: 10)

Assuming adaptation to the host society to be tied almost exclusively to English, at least by those who come from non-English-speaking backgrounds, perpetuates a one-way view of acculturation. It is too simplistic to account for the affective complexities of the identification process and ignores the role of bi/multilingual repertoires in (re)constructing a sense of self in changing sociolinguistic contexts, as data from the New Zealand illustrates.

A Linguistic Sense of Continuity and Being: Migrants in New Zealand

The results of the study reported here illustrate how linguistic discontinuities are felt not only in terms of identifications with changing externalities such as national identity, but also at a deeper level of self. The study involved a highly multilingual[3] group of migrants ($N = 370$) from diverse ethnolinguistic backgrounds representing 81 birthplaces and 68 languages. Data were collected through focus groups and a postal survey,[4] which generated responses from regional and urban centres in both the North and South Islands.

Figure 8.2 provides a sense of how respondents prefer to identify themselves through common descriptors as an outward expression of ethnolinguistic, cultural or national identification. The majority opted for open-ended labels of their own choice, containing a single (e.g. Filipino, Cosmoplitan, Person) or a combined descriptor (e.g. Chinese-New Zealander) with the open or self-defined category in first position. These

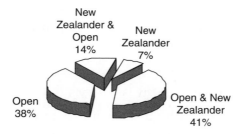

Figure 8.2 Frequency of self-identification labels $N = 340$

choices suggest an underlying desire to signal ongoing cultural affinity with their origins. The fact that the single 'New Zealander' label was the least popular is perhaps an indication of the respondents' sense of fluidity, duality and emergence, rather than lack of commitment to being a New Zealand citizen.

The differences between choices became even more defined over time, as shown in Figure 8.3. Even after 15 years of residence, preference for the single 'New Zealander' label declined over time. Among these long-term residents 93% still preferred a label that allowed them to refer to their cultural origins, either exclusively or in combination with the 'New Zealander' tag. The minor significance of the latter at a time when migrants are expected to have well and truly settled in does not necessarily indicate a failure to identify with the host society. But it does show the manifestation of a dual or multiple sense of identity and an ongoing need to express ethno-cultural and possibly linguistic origins.

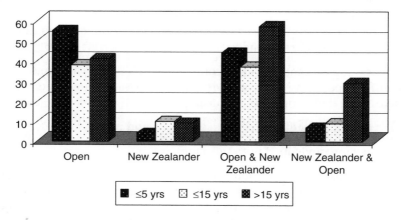

Figure 8.3 Preferred self-identification by length of stay

More specific evidence as to the role of migrants' languages in the process of self-construction was found in responses which expressed a fundamental belief that ML afforded a sense of self:

It identifies me with myself.

I can be myself when I use my language.

Migrants who speak or acquire English as a second language often share a lived reality of immersing themselves into an English-dominant environment, to learn to function and settle in it successfully, as described in the official settlement definition (Woolford, 2005). For some, however, there comes a point of realisation when they lose, and possibly rediscover, the deep emotional attachment to their ML and through that, they may lose and possibly rediscover part of themselves. This experience was described by one respondent as follows:

> When I came to NZ first [ML] wasn't as important as it is now. The first sort of few years, because I was married to a New Zealander I was very keen to get taught lessons in English and submerge into the culture. I didn't even seek any contacts with other German people because I wanted to learn English. I wanted to be part, I wanted to belong here. But once I got over that hurdle, I'd say 5 years down the track, and we started having children it became suddenly – I realized [...] part of me wasn't there and I wanted to make it alive again. And also it was something I wanted to pass on to my children, so it became very important then and I went into rescue mission, suddenly speaking German to my children, and all their German books and German videos and so on. Something happened, initially I denied I was here by myself and then I realized – me. I think it was a coping mechanism to learn a new language and culture. But really I couldn't, I could not exist without my language, my German language – I'd die. (Walker, 2004: 303)

This example points to a self-confirming function of ML and a deep sense of subjectivity. Many other respondents referred to this emotional dimension of their languages, for example:

It's part of my culture, feelings, emotions and me.

My feeling developed with this language.

It's not just communication it's part of you being you, isn't it, keeping your own language for yourself and your children eventually. Even if I never spoke [ML] again I'd still feel it is mine, I can read it and whenever I talk it I'm pleased to talk it – because it's part of me.

ML appear to be connected with a sense of inner subjectivity, or a sense of being which may not be translatable as Fishman (2001) suggests; therefore, the absence of ML brings about a deep sense of loss:

It is important for my soul.

If you take that language away I don't think I'll be like the way I am now.

Without it I should be denying the essence of my being.

I call it my window, my road, it's my door, it's my life. Without it I have no identity. It's how I see the world, you know, I cannot be in this world unless I have that.

Thus, to the extent that ML affords a person a sense of self, it helps to shape one's perception (window), gives future direction (road) and grants access (door) to one's sociocultural environment. Other statements referred to the multidimensional nature of an individual sense of self, which encompasses an 'other' element that connects a person with the group and promotes a sense of belonging through group identity and cultural membership.

My languages give one an identity and a sense of belonging. I am this person only in my language. All my internal being is being expressed through my mother language. At the same time this is the language of my people I share my identity with. It means: I am really me only in my language.

How much ML is associated with lived experience, past and present, is evident in this person's comment:

My language is part of who I was before and of who I am today. It forms part of my personality.

It is not surprising then that ML are also perceived as a source of happiness, for example, when enjoying a rare opportunity to speak the ML. The following example of a Telugu speaker illustrates this:

It takes me about 5 minutes because I'm rusty, my words get stuck in my mouth, I can't speak as fluently, but after 5 to 6 minutes I go on happily. I'm very pleased with that. It means I haven't forgotten. Probably, I haven't really since you now ask I never realized why I'm happy or why I'm doing it, there's probably an unconscious reason or an unconscious something that wants me to re-establish links.

The role of ML in self-conceptualisation was further examined through a measure of linguistic sense of self. As no self-concept measures were found that included a language dimension,[5] self-concept dimensions were derived from the literature (Byrne, 1996; Hattie, 1992; Williams & Burden, 1997) and pre-survey focus groups. The measure consisted of four variables which served as indicators of emotional states or cognitive processes facilitated through linguistic means:

- Confidence (aligned to self-esteem)
- Spontaneity
- Being 'oneself'
- Expression of feelings

The data in Figure 8.4 support the notion of a linguistic sense of self in relation to the four indicator variables. Only a small proportion of responses (7–13.5%) did not associate any of their languages with the variables. ML accounted for 40–47% of the preferred choices across all four variables, which reflects the importance of ML for facilitating a linguistic self-concept. Other key points highlighted in the data were:

- ML was the preferred code for *expressing feelings* and *being oneself*, with 47% and 46%, respectively.
- English was the preferred choice for 32% of the respondents when it came to *expressing feelings* but only 13% associated *being oneself* with English.
- Communication of one's inner feelings is more likely in the language one is more proficient in, whereas the sensation of *being oneself* may be more connected with an emotional bond with ML and its associated ethnocultural representations, making it less dependent on proficiency.[6]

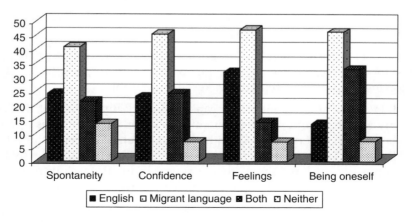

Figure 8.4 Linguistic manifestation of self-concept variables ($N = 370$)

- The most explicit self-concept measure *be oneself* is also strongly associated with 'both' languages (33%), suggesting self-conceptualisation through bilingual means and the possibility of an emerging 'bilingual self'.

Not surprisingly, the perceived role of ML for linguistic self-conceptualisation was found to be mediated by length of stay in New Zealand. Significant differences were found across all four variables (be spontaneous $p = 0.011$, express feelings $p = 0.000$, feel confident $p = 0.000$ and be oneself $p = 0.001$, 2df). Respondents who had been in New Zealand less than five years showed the strongest preference for ML as self-concept conduit. In contrast, long-term residents increasingly favoured English, particularly for *expressing feelings* (42% compared with ML 30%). This might be the consequence of improved English proficiency, which facilitates communication of feelings, but does not necessarily afford the emotional 'force' associated with ML, as suggested by the finding for the *be-oneself* variable. Here ML remains the preferred choice for 37% even in the long-term group, but down from 65% among recent migrants. In all, 40% of the long-term residents said they achieved *confidence* and a feeling of *being oneself* through bilingual means.

The Next Generation

If migrants' languages can be understood as a mechanism to promote a sense of balance, belonging and continuity, they are of critical intergenerational importance. The parents in the study were indeed very conscious of the challenges their children faced while navigating between cultures. 'They are Kiwis, but knowing their background gives them a sense of stability' (Walker, 2004: 315). They believed that being monolingual in English would reduce the linguistic resources available for their children; 93% ($N = 353$) thought ML was important for the next generation and, not surprisingly, expressed strong support for their children to remain bilingual. Cultural connection was given as a key reason, which was perceived to provide an ongoing link with the parents or relatives as well as the origin cultures:

The greater [the children's] knowledge, the greater is their appreciation of their cultural background. It also leads to greater 'closeness' with parents and relatives, especially when they visit their ancestral homeland or relatives visit them. (Walker, 2004: 313)

So that they feel that they are not strangers in the home country, although they grew up here in New Zealand.

Migrant languages can keep families connected; but beyond that they equip children with the ability to cross between different cultures. They 'gain a broader outlook on life with the usage of more languages', an ability clearly tied to the command of more than one language in the view of this parent. But in a linguistic ecology marked by all-encompassing dominance of English and a lack of functional relevance or formal support for migrants' languages, the odds are stacked against families in their desire to retain a niche for ML, even as the language of the home.

> We're surviving in a place that's in a way quite hostile to other lan-
> guages. We're doing the best we can. It's a matter of how much do you
> try to bash your head against a wall. (Walker, 2004: 368)

Parents are not alone in their concerns over the future of their children's bi/multilingual competencies. Not only is there a lack of recognition in wider society but a distinct disadvantage in the educational context, where the medium of instruction is often different from the home language. According to international literacy surveys such as PISA, New Zealand has reportedly the largest 'home language gap' in terms of literacy achievement (Wilkinson, 1998, cited in May, 2005: 374). For example, students from the Pacific Islands (e.g. Samoa, Tonga, Niue, etc.) who use languages in the home which are different to the medium of instruction 'are consistently and disproportionately represented in the lowest levels of English literacy proficiency' (May, 2005: 274). Continued reliance on a monolingual approach in these children's education is to deny them the opportunity to draw on their home languages as bilingual resources (Martin-Jones & Saxena, 2003; Swain & Lapkin, 2000), which offer an affective and cognitive tool to support their learning, for example, as 'funds of knowledge' (Martin-Jones & Saxena, 2003: 267).

Beyond the Strategic: Investing in Bi/Multilingual Outcomes through Education

New Zealand's settlement strategy may well serve as an instrument to provide strategic direction and validation of diversity. However, it will not be sufficient to address the linguistic and affective needs of migrant language speakers in New Zealand. Achieving tangible bi/multilingual outcomes requires targeted policies dedicated to linguistic diversity as well as practices to model and develop these outcomes. Both of these exist, at least in principle, in the educational domain.

Educational policies and practices have a key role to play, as they determine not only the overall positioning of language and languages in curricular configurations, but also affect the pedagogical approaches to diversity in classrooms. In the absence of a national policy for languages the national school curriculum has come to represent a key tool for policy making (Starks & Barkhuizen, 2003). It provides greater recognition of and support for language learning in New Zealand's primary and secondary schools and has resulted in 'broader public awareness and understanding of the individual and collective benefits of being bilingual/ multilingual' (Spence, 2004: 389). The Curriculum Framework for New Zealand schools (Ministry of Education, 2007), recognises the significance of the Treaty of Waitangi[7] and reflects the multicultural nature of New Zealand society. Crucially, the document provides overt validation of second- or foreign-language learning; it also recognises the importance of first languages for identity and the cognitive benefits through increased language awareness.

> Language is a vital medium for transmitting values and culture. Confidence and proficiency in one's first language contribute to self-esteem, a sense of identity, and achievement throughout life. (Ministry of Education, 2007: 10)

The values which guide public education in New Zealand tie in directly with the wider goals of settlement including, amongst others, diversity, equity, community and participation (Ministry of Education, n.d.). These values underlie the 2007 New Zealand Curriculum for Schools, which aims to foster participation and community contributions as competencies that engender 'a sense of belonging and the confidence to participate within new contexts' (Ministry of Education, n.d.: 13). The New Zealand Curriculum represents an important shift and a renewed commitment to 'Language and Languages/*Te Korero me nga reo*', one of its seven 'Essential Learning Areas' (Ministry of Education, 2007). Languages are recognised for their social, cultural and cognitive benefits, and hence a key concern is to raise the profile and status of second-language learning. Schools are therefore expected to offer students the opportunity to learn another language in years 7–10, although it is not compulsory for students to do so.

Despite this important curricular shift, language-related policy and curriculum goals will be difficult to translate into tangible bi/multilingual outcomes without adequate teacher resourcing (East, 2007; Peddie, 1997) and teacher training (Spence, 2004). Adequate provision of language-learning opportunities will depend on the ability of schools to find linguistically proficient teachers. However, the expectation of schools to work closely with communities to design relevant learning programmes could open an avenue to tap into the linguistic resources of diverse migrant communities (Kim & Elder, 2002; Shameem, 2003; Watts & Trlin, 2000), opening up a niche to utilise bi/multilingual abilities and affording ML prestige and new functional opportunities. This would also provide a way of linking language classrooms to the broader sociocultural and linguistic context, at a time of growing recognition of diverse classroom ecologies (Creese & Martin, 2003). More inclusive pedagogies (Glynn, 2003) will provide a way forward, as will bilingual approaches to ESL (Walker, 2005), making learning English 'a process of enrichment rather than a remediation or replacement' (Coelho, 2003: 9). These steps will help create a place and legitimate role for ML in educational contexts, both in terms of instructional practice as well as learner identity.

Discussion and Conclusion

In English-dominant contexts such as New Zealand, sociocultural affordances are stacked in favour of English, predicting monolingual outcomes and diminished cultural capital of bi/multilingual repertoires, despite continued growth in ethno-cultural diversity. In view of the findings presented in this chapter, a better understanding of the emotional repercussions of linguistic discontinuities is needed because migrants' languages play a pivotal role in sustaining and enriching their social–psychological functioning and maintaining a sense of continuity in situations of change. There is, in fact, increased recognition of the emotional dimension of adapting to a new sociocultural environment (Barkhuizen & Knoch, 2005: 230; Walker, 2004). Feelings and emotional attachment cannot be dissociated from the pre-migration linguistic lives and experiences, which continue to be associated with or actualised via ML. Yet, discourses of the powerful position of English reinforce the sole emphasis on functional benefits of English and conceal the affective dimension of migrants' languages and their crucial role as means for identity expression and self-construction. The 'widespread failure to recognise new and mixed identities' (Rampton, 1995: 338) in diverse societies is indicative of a monolingual mindset which is out of touch with the reality of bi/multilingual migrants and ignores the complex relationship between language(s), the self and diverse societies.

Thus, we cannot with good conscience continue to look at monolingual solutions to the settlement and integration of bi/multilingual migrants. Effective English skills are necessary for integration and socio-economic participation (Department of Labour, 2004). But ML are far from irrelevant in the process of adaptation to a new sociocultural environment. They represent the linguistic means for self-construction and identity in a social–psychological process, which may promote cultural and linguistic continuity by reconciling individuals' pre-migration past with the present and future.

A strong bilingual sense of self helps individuals to position themselves in their diverse social environments and may thus enhance psychological well-being. It is this insight which has led agencies such as The Refugee & Migrant Service to realise that 'we may like to think of resettlement as a 'process' but belonging in a new country is a feeling' (Skyrme, 2008: 6). It is, therefore, paramount that socio-economic participation goes hand in hand with emotional settlement. ML provides a tool for translating oneself during the process of cultural crossing and can help turn the experience of linguistic and affective loss into one of recovery and enrichment (Pavlenko & Lantolf, 2000). A better understanding of the linguistic self-concept as adaptive mechanism may help harness its potential for more effective settlement and a greater awareness of the benefits of linguistic diversity.

Positive outcomes of linguistic diversity in society are, however, unlikely to happen through strategy alone. Creating the societal conditions where bi/multilingual repertoires are valued and actively supported requires resources and models of bi/multilingual practices. The educational context, itself faced by the challenges of increasingly diverse classrooms, is ideally placed to nurture bi/multilingual competences. Migration and settlement constitute a tool for nation building, as does education, and so both should share the same goals where language is concerned. Schools, after all, are tasked with 'equipping' all New Zealanders with the knowledge, skills and values to be successful citizens in the 21st century.

Sole emphasis on the dominant language English is short sighted at best and perpetuates a monolingual mindset at a time of increased globalisation, when societies cannot do without cultural and linguistic diversity. For New Zealand to become a 'truly multicultural nation', as envisioned by Hon David Cunliffe, former Minister of Immigration (Department of Labour, 2007a: 3), it needs to move beyond a celebratory approach as a society, towards one which actively promotes conditions that facilitate bi/multilingual practices and promote investment in New Zealand's multilingual capital. It seems that nothing short of bi/multilingualism as a settlement goal will help provide direction and promote psychological adaptation as part of a wider settlement outcome. All languages have a role to play in making New Zealand an inclusive and multilingual society. In the words of one recent migrant 'language adds to the diversity and richness of New Zealand. I dread the day when only English is spoken' (Walker, 2004: 420), a principle it seems, which both new migrants and indigenous people can aspire to:

He taonga nga reo katoa.

All languages are to be treasured.

Notes

1. These languages include Cook Islands Maori, Niuean and Tokelauan (Department of Labour, 2007b: 12). New Zealand has special responsibility for these languages alongside te reo Māori as they are indigenous to the New Zealand realm.
2. Kiwi is a popular label to describe New Zealanders, after the native Kiwi bird.
3. In all, 32% were at least bilingual; 68% reported to have three or more languages or dialects.
4. Access was gained through organisations such as ethnic councils, migrant networks or other agencies representing or supporting migrants.
5. Except where it represents part of the academic self-concept or is linked to academic success.
6. *Being oneself* accounted for 17% ($\eta^2 = 0.17$) of the mean proficiency variability suggesting an association between ML proficiency and preference of ML.
7. A treaty signed in 1840 by representatives of the British Crown and chiefs of New Zealand Maori, now regarded as New Zealand's founding document.

References

Al-Issa, I. and Tousignant, M. (eds) (1997) *Ethnicity Immigration and Psychopathology.* New York: Springer.

Aronin, L. and Ó Laoire, M. (2004) Exploring multilingualism in cultural contexts: Towards a notion of multilinguality. In C. Hoffmann and J. Ytsma (eds) *Trilingualism in Family, School and Community* (pp. 11–29). Clevedon: Multilingual Matters.

Barkhuizen, G.P. and Knoch, U. (2005) Missing Afrikaans: 'Linguistic longing' among Afrikaans-speaking immigrants in New Zealand. *Journal of Multilingual and Multicultural Development* 26, 216–232.

Besemeres, M. (2004) Translating one's self: Language and selfhood in cross-cultural autobiography. *Life Writing* 1, 219–222.

Byrne, B.M. (1996) *Measuring Self-Concept Across the Life Span. Issues and Instrumentation.* Washington: American Psychological Association.

Clyne, M. (2003) *Dynamics of Language Contact.* Cambridge: Cambridge University Press.

Creese, A. and Martin, P. (eds) (2003) *Multilingual Classroom Ecologies.* Clevedon: Multilingual Matters.

Coelho, E. (2003) *Adding English. A Guide to Teaching in Multilingual Classrooms.* Don Mills, ON: Pippin Publishing.

Davies, B. and Harré, R. (1990) Positioning: The discursive production of selves. *Journal for the Theory of Social Behaviour* 20, 43–63.

Department of Labour (2004) *A Future Together. The New Zealand Settlement Strategy in Outline.* http://www.immigration.govt.nz/NR/rdonlyres/7137ABC7-9569-4BAE-BB09-227914CECE50/0/NZImmigrationSettlementStrategyOutline.pdf. Accessed 3.3.09.

Department of Labour (2007a) *Our Future Together. New Zealand Settlement Strategy.* http://www.immigration.govt.nz/NR/rdonlyres/F2D460BA-8A84-4073-8A12-84C2BE0B1BB8/0/Strategy.pdf. Accessed 16.2.09.

Department of Labour (2007b) *Settlement National Action Plan.* http://www.immi gration.govt.nz/NR/rdonlyres/5A045541-0E5F-4B37-A2F4-0D0A80ABF2D6/ 0/ActionPlan.PDF. Accessed 22.1.09.

East, M. (2007) Commentary: Learning languages in New Zealand. How successful can it be? *The New Zealand Language Teacher* 33, 7–9.

Ethnic Voice New Zealand (2005) *Voice of the Ethnic Youth.* Ethnic Youth Congress, 15 October 2005, Orakei Marae, Auckland.

Fishman, J.A. (2001) Why is it so hard to save threatened languages? In J.A. Fishman (ed.) *Can Threatened Languages Be Saved* (pp. 1–22). Clevedon: Multilingual Matters.

Fivush, R. and Buckner, J. (1997) The self as socially constructed: A commentary. In U. Neisser and D.A. Jopling (eds) *The Conceptual Self in Context. Culture, Experience, Self-Understanding* (pp. 176–181). Cambridge: Cambridge University Press.

Gibbons, J. and Ramirez, E.G. (2004) *Maintaining a Minority Language. A Case Study of Hispanic Teenagers.* Clevedon: Multilingual Matters.

Glynn, T. (2003) Responding to language diversity: A way forward for New Zealand education. In R. Barnard and T. Glynn (eds) *Bilingual Children's Language and Literacy Development* (pp. 273–281). Clevedon: Multilingual Matters.

Hattie, J. (1992) *Self-Concept.* Hillsdale, NJ: Lawrence Erlbaum Associates.

Holmes, J. (2001) *Introduction to Sociolinguistics* (2nd edn). Harlow: Pearson Education.

Hormuth, S.E. (1990) *The Ecology of the Self. Relocation and Self-Concept Change.* Cambridge: Cambridge University Press.

Human Rights Commission (n.d.) *Te Ngira: The NZ Diversity Action Programme.* http://www.hrc.co.nz/home/hrc/introduction/tengirathenzdiversityaction- programme/tengirathenzdiversityactionprogramme.php. Accessed 7.12.08.

Human Rights Commission (2007) *New Zealand Needs to Go Multilingual.* http:// www.hrc.co.nz/home/hrc/newsandissues/racerelationscommissioner-newzea landneedstogomultilingu.php. Accessed 5.12.08.

Jancovic-Kramaric, J.F. (2001) *Ethnic identity among the Croatian community in Auckland.* Unpublished master's thesis, University of Auckland, New Zealand.

Kim, S.H. and Elder, C. (2002) When mother-tongue medium becomes foreign language object: The case of native-speaker teachers in New Zealand. *New Zealand Studies in Applied Linguistics* 8, 63–86.

Korzenny, F. (1999) *Acculturation vs. Assimilation among US Hispanics: e-mail Self-Reports.* Belmont, CA: Hispanic & Asian Marketing Communication Research. http://www.cheskin.com/assets/HispanicAcculturationAssimilation.pdf. Accessed 12.11.08.

Koven, M.E.J. (1998) Two languages in the self – The self in two languages: French-Portuguese bilinguals' verbal enactments and experiences of self in narrative discourse. *Ethos* 26, 410–442.

Martin-Jones, M. and Saxena, M. (2003) Bilingual resources and 'funds of knowledge' for teaching and learning in multi-ethnic classrooms in Britain. *International Journal of Bilingual Education and Bilingualism* 6 (Special Issue), 267–282.

May, S. (2005) Bilingual/immersion education in Aotearoa/New Zealand: Setting the context. *International Journal of Bilingual Education and Bilingualism* 8, 365–376.

Milroy, L. (1987) *Language and Social Networks* (2nd edn). London: Routledge and Kegan Paul.

Ministry of Education (n.d.) *The New Zealand Curriculum.* http://nzcurriculum.tki. org.nz/the_new_zealand_curriculum. Accessed 28.11.08.

Ministry of Education (2003) *Strategy for Adult Esol.* http://www.minedu.govt. nz/~/media/MinEdu/Files/EducationSectors/TertiaryEducation/ AdultESOLStrategyPDF.pdf. Accessed 10.12.08.

Ministry of Education (2007) *The New Zealand Curriculum Framework.* http://www. minedu.govt.nz/index.cfm?layout=document&documentid=3561&indexid= 1004&indexparentid=1072. Accessed 15.12.08.

Ministry of Social Development (n.d.) *Connecting Diverse Communities.* http:// www.msd.govt.nz/work-areas/cross-sectoral-work/connecting-diverse- communities/why.html. Accessed 28.1.09.

New Zealand Immigration Service (2004) Migrants' experiences of New Zealand – Pilot survey report. *Longitudinal Immigration Survey: New Zealand. Te Ara o Nga Manene.* Wellington: Department of Labour. http://www.immigration. govt.nz/NR/rdonlyres/257DBD3C-E649-4E31-9A4B-F8F61173CF44/0/ LisNZPilotSurveyReportMarch2004.pdf. Accessed 14.8.08.

Norton, B. (2000) Investment, acculturation and language loss. In S.L. McKay and S-L.C. Wong (eds) *New Immigrants in the United States* (pp. 443–461). Cambridge: Cambridge University Press.

Norton, B. (2001) Non-participation, imagined communities and the language classroom. In M. Breen (ed.) *Learner Contributions to Language Learning* (pp. 159– 171). Harlow: Pearson Education Ltd.

Norton Peirce, B. (1995) Social identity, investment and language learning. *TESOL Quarterly* 29, 9–31.

Peddie, R. (1997) Why are we waiting? Languages policy development in New Zealand. In W. Eggington and H. Wren (eds) *Language Policy: Dominant English, Pluralist Challenges* (pp. 121–146). Amsterdam: John Benjamins.

Peddie, R. (2003) Languages in New Zealand: Population, politics and policy. In R. Barnard and T. Glynn (eds) *Bilingual Children's Language and Literacy Development* (pp. 8–35). Clevedon: Multilingual Matters.

Pernice, R. and Brook, J. (1996) Refugees' and immigrants' mental health: Association of demographic and post-immigration factors. *Journal of Social Psychology* 136, 511–519.

Phinney, S.J., Berry, J.W., Sam, D.L. and Vedder, P. (2006) Understanding immi- grant youth: Conclusions and implications. In J.W. Berry, J.S. Phinney, D.L. Sam and P. Vedder (eds) *Immigrant Youth in Cultural Transition. Acculturation, Identity, and Adaptation across National Contexts* (pp. 211–234). Mahwah, NJ: Lawrence Erlbaum.

Rampton, B. (1995) *Crossing. Language and Ethnicity among Adolescents.* New York: Longman.

Raza, F. (1997) *Ethnic identity, acculturation, and intergenerational conflict among second-generation New Zealand Indians.* Unpublished master's thesis, University of Auckland, New Zealand.

Roer-Strier, D. (2000) Socializing immigrant children: Home and school coping with cultural differences. In E. Olshtein and G. Horenczyk (eds) *Language, Identity, and Immigration* (pp. 65–80). Jerusalem: The Hebrew University Magnes Press.

Shameem, N. (2003) Community language teacher education needs in New Zealand. In R. Barnard and T. Glynn (eds) *Bilingual Children's Language and Literacy Development* (pp. 225–245). Clevedon: Multilingual Matters.

Skyrme, G. (2008) *The Contribution of Non-Government Organisations to the Settlement of Refugees and Migrants in Aotearoa New Zealand*. National Association of ESOL Hometutors, Wellington, New Zealand. http://www.englishlanguage. org.nz/news/research/nr1213607229.pdf. Accessed 15.08.08.

Spence, G.P. (2004) The practice of policy in New Zealand. *Current Issues in Language Planning* 5 (4), 389–402.

Statistics New Zealand (2007a) *QuikStats about Culture and Identity. Languages Spoken*. http://www.stats.govt.nz/census/2006-census-data/quickstats-about-culture-identity/quickstats-about-culture-and-identity.htm?page= para011Master. Accessed 7.10.08.

Statistics New Zealand (2007b) *2006 Census Data: Languages Spoken*. http://www. stats.govt.nz/census/2006-census-data/quickstats-about-culture-identity/ quickstats-about-culture-and-identity.htm?page=para011Master. Accessed 10.10.08.

Starks, D. and Barkhuizen, G. (2003) Students as fact gatherers in language-in-education planning. In R. Barnard and T. Glynn (eds) *Bilingual Children's Language and Literacy Development* (pp. 247–272). Clevedon: Multilingual Matters.

Stevens, R. (1996) *Understanding the Self*. Milton Keynes: The Open University.

Swain, M. and Lapkin, S. (2000) Task-based second language learning: The uses of first language. *Language Teaching Research* 4, 251–274.

Vygotsky, L.S. (1978) *Mind in Society*. Cambridge, MA: Harvard University Press.

Walker, U. (1996) Social networks as code choice determinants in individual bilingualism: A case study of four German-background immigrant children. *New Zealand Studies in Applied Linguistics* 2, 33–47.

Walker, U. (2004) *Language, Migration and Continuity of Being: Notions of Migrant Language Proficiency and Self-Concept among Multilingual Migrants in Aotearoa-New Zealand*. PhD thesis, Palmerston North, Massey University, New Zealand.

Walker, U. (2005) L1 in ESL – Paradox or prospect? Community languages in ESOL classrooms. In J. Major and J. Howard (eds) *CLESOL 2004: Refereed Conference Proceedings of the 9th Community Languages and English for Speakers of Other Languages Conference* (pp. 1–14). Christchurch.

Watts, N. and Trlin, A. (2000) The use of NESB immigrant resources and service provision in New Zealand's public sector organisations. *NZ Studies in Applied Linguistics* 6, 1–22.

Wilkinson, I. (1998) Dealing with diversity: Achievement gaps in reading literacy among New Zealand students. *Reading Research Quarterly* 33, 144–167.

Williams, M. and Burden, R. (1997) *Psychology for Language Teachers. A Social Constructivist Approach*. Cambridge: Cambridge University Press.

Woolford, G. (2005) *Settlement Services Project and Framework for the Development of a Wellington Regional Settlement Strategy: Final Report to the Wellington Regional Mayoral Forum*, Wellington. http://www.wellington.govt.nz/haveyoursay/ meetings/committee/Strategy_and_Policy/2005/21Apr0915/pdf/Report_7_ Settlement_App_1.pdf. Accessed 13.1.09.

Chapter 9
Three is Too Many in Australia[1]

M. CLYNE

Introduction

Although Australia is a multilingual country, it is dominated by a monolingual mindset. This is reflected in an obsession with monolingual English literacy. Any breakthrough has been to support bilingualism rather than trilingualism. Even in Victoria, which has a relatively support-ive languages-in-education policy and where there are opportunities to take one language other than English within day school and another after hours, only 2% of Year 12 students take two languages other than English for the end of secondary school examination. Paradoxically, the reluctance of many primary schools in multilingual areas to teach the main commu-nity languages of the district enable students with bilingual backgrounds to learn a third language.

Some secondary schools prevent recently arrived students from taking a third language. This is because they think students should concentrate on English as second language (ESL). And yet local research based on qualitative data from learners has pointed to the advantages of bilinguals learning a third language at school over monolinguals learning the same language (Clyne *et al.*, 2004). Their metalinguistic awareness enables them to compare features of languages. Their learning of a third language stim-ulates an interest in languages in general and encourages the use of the home language.

This chapter attempts to discuss the barriers to multilingualism as the norm in the Australian classroom. It begins with some demographic data on language use and school language learning in Australia. Then follows a consideration of the residual positive policies promoting linguistic diver-sity and of the negative myths propagated through clichés discouraging multilingualism in education. The next section considers the possible impact of new developments on the learning of a third language, and the final section reviews some recent changes.

Some Statistical Information

The 2006 Australian Census records about 400 languages spoken in the homes of Australians. In all, 151 are indigenous languages; there are also sign languages and English-based creoles. Over 230 of the languages are immigrant languages, most of them the products of post-Second World War migration from all over the world. Australia can truly be described as a multilingual society. But alas, it is also afflicted with a monolingual mindset. Most decisions are based on the belief that monolingualism is the norm and multilingualism is exceptional or a problem. For instance, it is the monolingual mindset of decision makers that has created the myth of the 'crowded curriculum' that does not have room for a language other than English. This means that, while languages other than English (LOTEs) are a key learning area, they are not taken seriously. Language policy varies between states, from Victoria where students are 'expected' to take a LOTE for the 10 years of compulsory education although this is not enforced, to that of New South Wales, where students must take 100 hours of a LOTE in one of the first three years of secondary school, 7, 8 or 9. In Victoria, in 2006 73% of children in Year 1 of government schools took a LOTE at their mainstream school, 63.3% in Year 3, 88% in Year 6 and 94.6% in Year 7. By Year 9, the percentage is down to 50.7 and continues to decline (Yvette Slaughter, personal communication). Languages are dropped in favour of more 'important' or more 'interesting' distractors, such as photography, cooking or dancing, which are often alternative options in middle school. Even the goal that a quarter of all students taking a LOTE as a subject in the final year of secondary school by 2001 (Dawkins, 1991) has only been half achieved. Only 13.4 % were doing this in 2003. This too varied across Australia from 20.2% in Victoria to 5.8% in Queensland. The marginality of languages applies most especially to government schools, which are attended by the majority of students from bilingual backgrounds, and least in independent schools, which tend to charge high fees. However, in Victoria, for instance, the percentage taking two or more LOTEs in Year 12 is 2%.

Multicultural Developments

In the 1970s and 1980s, when Australia developed from an assimilationist to a multicultural society, many new initiatives were started in the languages' area. They included the establishment of government and community multilingual radio and television stations, the telephone interpreter service, the development of multilingual library facilities and the expansion of offerings of language subjects at school and university to reflect more the language demography of the nation. But the commitment of governments in this regard has waned, especially in the past decade.

Bi- and Trilingualism in the Census

The 1976 census was the first to elicit information on language use. The question was worded 'Does the person speak a language other than English speak a language other than English regularly now?' This was the first and last time that the Australian Bureau of Statistics processed more than one LOTE by person. All subsequent censuses elicited information on home use of languages other than English and the census officials selected one language, usually according to the order in which they were reported on the census form. More recently, respondents have been asked to select the most frequently used even if two or more LOTEs were used at home according to interlocutor or situation. It would appear that Australian authorities are afraid of 'too many languages'. The 1976 Census found that while 12.3% then used a language other than English regularly (in 2006 16.8% spoke a LOTE at home), there were 1.2% using three or more languages regularly. The most popular combinations were Macedonian and Greek, Polish and German, Spanish and Italian, and French, Italian and Greek. Now the combinations would include Mandarin and Hakka or Cantonese and Hindi and Punjabi.

The Situation of Languages in Australian Schools

Traditionally, French was taught in Australia as the main 'foreign language', with Latin or German offered as an option in some schools as an additional language. The language demography of the school was not taken into account in the choice of languages. Yet, learning two 'foreign languages' simultaneously was by no means impossible. The development of multiculturalism policy initially extended the number of languages taught in mainstream (day) schools and assessed for the final secondary school examination, at least in some states. As English is the national language of Australia, there is no one second language that has to be learned by all students, and Australia's language demography and regional environment can be factors in the offering and choice of languages. The main languages taught in Australian schools are French, Italian, German, Japanese, Indonesian and Chinese. Table 9.1, based on 2001 statistics, indicates that, except in the cases of Italian and Chinese this does not reflect the ethnolinguistic composition of the population or the

Table 9.1 The top 10 community languages in Australian schools, 2001

Ranking/Language	No. of students	Ranking in top 20 languages nationally	Ranking in top 20 0–14 age group nationally
1. Japanese	402,882	a	17
2. Italian	394,770	1	5
3. Indonesian	310,363	20	13
4. French	247,001	18	20
5. German	158,076	9	15
6. Chinese (Mandarin)	111,464	6	6
7. Arabic	31,844	4	1
8. Greek	28,188	2	4
9. Spanish	24,807	7	7
10. Vietnamese	22,428	5	2

[a]Not in top 20.
Source: From Clyne *et al.* (2004: 7).

school-age population. Since 2001, there has been a 58% increase in the number of Australian residents using Mandarin at home, while Arabic (16.4%) and Vietnamese (11.8%) have also experienced considerable increases in home use and Italian a decline of 10.4%. It is expected that by August 2011, Mandarin will be the number 1 community language and that there will be nine with more than 100,000 home users in Australia.

While secondary schools generally offer two (or even more) languages, students are usually only permitted to take one of them. The National Policy on Languages (Lo Bianco, 1987) promoted Australia's multilingualism on grounds of social equity, economic strategies and cultural enrichment and resulted in increased funding for a larger range of language programmes in schools. However, most students in at least government secondary schools were restricted to choosing one.

The 1970s saw the expansion of the teaching of the most widely used community languages, Italian and Modern Greek, and of German, which had already had a tradition as a 'foreign language' but was also a prominent community language. This term became popular in the mid-1970s to make the point that languages spoken by communities in Australia were not 'foreign'.

In addition to mainstream (day) schools, there are two other means by which schoolchildren can take a language. One is at a part-time ethnic community school. There are now 80,000 students learning a total of over 70 languages in 1050 such schools throughout Australia. The number in Victoria is 35,000 students in 191 schools learning a total of 44 languages. Ethnic community schools operate on Saturday or Sunday mornings and/ or on weekday afternoons after school, using the premises of government schools. They now receive Australian government subsidies provided that the teachers meet certain criteria of qualifications and assistance with in-service. Some of the schools are also subsidized by the country of origin. There is an umbrella organization of part-time ethnic community schools which also acts as a lobby group for language education.

The other multilingual framework for language education is government schools of languages, which operate in Victoria, New South Wales, South Australia and the Northern Territory, and there have been moves afoot to establish similar institutions in some other jurisdictions. They are part of the respective Department of Education and are open to students from any school, government or non-government to take a language not available in their own school at the required level. They too operate on Saturday mornings (or in some cases, on weekday afternoons after school) and give any students the opportunity to take languages not offered in their school. They may be languages taught in some day schools, such as French, German, Japanese or ones only confined to after hours programmes, such as Filipino, Khmer, Ukrainian. Each centre, housed in a government school, teaches a number of languages in local demand. There are currently 15,000 students learning a total of 44 languages at 40 centres and in addition 1300 students in distance education programmes. The number is open-ended, and the Victorian School of Languages has recently introduced Dinka (a Sudanese language), Karen (a Burmese language) and Somali. Dinka is also offered in the South Australian School of Languages. For many languages, ethnic schools cover primary and junior secondary schools and government schools of languages middle and higher secondary. Many day schools record the progress of students in Saturday schools in reports. While Saturday classes have to cope with the competition of sporting and recreational activities, the schools of languages have mainstreamed community languages. Very significantly, ethnic schools and schools of languages enable students to take two LOTEs. Often, but certainly not always, the language taken on Saturdays is one in which they have a home background and quite often one which they had taken at primary school. There are 47 languages accredited for the final secondary school examination in New South Wales, South

Table 9.2 Languages currently assessed in year 12: New South Wales, South Australia, Victoria and Western Australia

Amharic, Arabic, Armenian, Australian Sign Language, Bosnian, Classical Greek, Croatian, Dutch, Farsi, Filipino, French, German, Hebrew, Hindi, Hungarian, Australian indigenous languages, Indonesian, Italian, Japanese, Khmer, Korean, Latin, Macedonian, Maltese, Mandarin, Modern Greek, Persian, Polish, Portuguese, Punjabi, Romanian, Russian, Serbian, Sinhala, Spanish, Swedish, Tamil, Turkish, Ukrainian, Yiddish

Australia and Victoria, six of which (Albanian, Bengali, Czech, Latvian, Lithuanian, Slovenian) have been suspended (i.e. abolished) due to very low candidature. Hungarian and Maltese are at risk. The languages currently examined are shown in Table 9.2.

A number of states are collaborating in a national examination scheme by which one state offers the examination in a particular language for the whole of Australia.

Fear of Multilingualism

Not only are languages marginal among the key curriculum areas. There is a fear of 'too many languages' among many educational decision-makers. Most especially in the most multilingual areas of Melbourne, for instance, some primary school principals have argued that their school should not have to teach a LOTE because almost all the children already speak one; and many of them are attending classes in it on Saturdays. Some of them are teaching a cultural sensitization course instead. Slaughter and Hajek (2007) have shown that, in Brimbank, a multilingual Melbourne municipality, to the north-east of the metropolitan area, 16% of the schools are not offering a LOTE and 48% were teaching only Italian. Brimbank has a high concentration of Vietnamese speakers and 13 other languages with more than 1000 home users.

The schools of Greater Dandenong, Melbourne's most multilingual municipality, in the south-east, also with a high concentration of Vietnamese speakers and 14 other languages with over 1000 users, teach mainly French. By default this gives many students the opportunity to acquire a third language.

However, it is interesting to note that in the 1970s and 1980s, Italian was taught because it was an important community language. Now, like French, it is taught as a 'neutral' language. This means that language acquisition and teaching is not able to benefit from the community resources in and around the school. It also demonstrates the obsession with some misguided myths of equality.

The Myths of the Crowded Curriculum and Competing Literacies

One of the impediments to multilingualism is well-meaning but ill-informed positions encouraging English at the expense of other languages. This is embodied in the fallacy that spending time on another language, whether for maintenance or second-language acquisition purposes, is detrimental to the development of English literacy. In 2007, the Australian Primary Principals' Association developed a national charter for Australian schools with a core curriculum reduced to English literacy, numeracy, science and social education (history and geography of Australia and as an afterthought, 'other places and cultures'). The charter argues that 'substantial involvement in the other learning areas depends on the critical and prior importance of ensuring that all children make satisfactory progress in the core areas' (APPA, 2007: 2–3). Nowhere is there, as has been customary in Australia, any recognition of the cultural diversity of the Australian school let alone any acknowledgement of the relation between first- and second-language development. In fact, the assumption from the above quote is that those with a background in a LOTE can only develop skills formally in that language if they have a proven record of prowess in English, mathematics, science and social education. The charter of the APPA was in line with the core curriculum proposed by the then Howard Government – comprising English, mathematics, science and Australian history.

This is not the place to advance arguments for biliteracy, literacy transfer and the role of bilingualism and second-language acquisition in literacy development. Baker (2006: 223–248), Bialystok (2001), Jiminéz *et al.* (1995), Calero-Breckheimer and Goetz (1993), Yelland *et al.* (1993: 423–444), among others, have already done this. There are even Australian data that demonstrate literacy transfer across languages with different scripts (see Arefi, 1997; Burragh-Pugh & Rohl, 2001: 664–676). But it did not seem relevant to the Australian Primary Principals' Association. No doubt the implementation of their core curriculum would reduce the already inadequate allocation of time for languages even further and in most cases annihilate LOTEs from the primary school, make languages and LOTE methodology disappear from primary teacher training, and have a monolingual spin-off effect on the secondary level. To date there have been no developments in this direction.

Many schools shunt recently arrived immigrant students into ESL classes which are time-tabled against the LOTE. This is based on three false premises. One is that the brain has limited capacity for learning languages. The second premise is that children with a first language other than English have more difficulty in learning another language than monolingual English speakers, because they already know English. The third is that if you already know *two* languages, it is a waste of time learning another. When students compelled to take ESL instead of another language no longer require ESL classes, it is too late to catch up and they miss out on the opportunity to acquire a third language. Most of the students in a Year 7 ESL class of 14 in a secondary school in which we have been conducting research are not motivated to advance their skills in L1. This applies to speakers of Hindi, Sinhala, Persian and various Chinese varieties such as Cantonese and Hakka. Only one Greek, one Korean and two Mandarin speakers are going to Saturday classes in their LOTE and it is likely that at least the others will soon encounter language attrition under the pressure of English as medium of school and other non-home domains. In a remedial literacy class of 12 in another secondary school in which we have been conducting research, most of the students have very modest skills in their parents' language or have parents from two different language backgrounds who speak English at home. No attempt is made to encourage them to take up the study of their home language or their parents' L1 and as we will see, the National Curriculum being developed by the successor Labor government does include Languages Other than English.

The 'Unfair Advantage'

The Year 12 examination is the gatekeeper for highly competitive admission into coveted faculties at prestigious universities, and a complicated system of scaling has been devised to ensure that the 'wrong' people do not get into such faculties. The less desirable languages are especially affected by the global scaling system. Global scores attempt to rank subjects according to the overall performance in all subjects of all the students taking the subject. This detracts from their value in assessing the students' competence in any subject. Thus, a student's score will be scaled up from 40 to 49 in French and 48 in German but scaled down to 39 in Turkish and Persian because the mean score of all the students taking the respective language is deemed to be lower. This is one of the reasons why relatively high achievers with high aspirations who have taken their community language to Year 10 will not run risks by continuing to Year 12. But there is a specific concern expressed by educationists with a monolingual mind-set that some students who have a family background in a language, in particular in an Asian language such as Chinese, Indonesian, Japanese, Korean, have an 'unfair advantage' over other students taking that language. This has resulted in different examinations and/or assessment systems for those considered to have an advantage on the language as a result of interrogation usually on forms. Sometimes those affected in this way are mainly international students and recently arrived migrants; but it may also affect those who have had all or most of their schooling in Australia. As it is impossible to draw boundaries, students who have worked hard to maintain or learn their family's language are often demotivated from continuing to do so, or, at least, from studying it as a subject, which would give them more highly developed skills in it. Students with a family background in a language would otherwise generally not have had the opportunity to develop active skills in it to a high level. Some may be exposed to a non-standard or mixed variety at home. Others would not have developed formal registers in the language. In Western Australia it is second-generation Australians who are targeted because of the way in which an economist, who was charged with suggesting a policy on this, had interpreted the critical age hypothesis.

Languages are often thought to be a nuisance because otherwise incompetent students may on the basis of their scores in a language in which they have a background attain an entry score which enables them to enter the university faculty of their choice. The advantages that some students may have in theatre studies, music, art or information technology because of their home background are discounted in this discussion. In Victoria, the situation is complicated by a 10% bonus in a LOTE, introduced to promote language study, which is believed by some educationists also to give bilingual students an 'unfair advantage'. The effort that goes into language maintenance and the value to the nation of a reservoir of competent bi- or multilinguals is readily ignored. (For a more detailed discussion of issues in the two paragraphs above, see Clyne, 2005: 118–136.)

In addition, many community languages are now not taught at university. Due to neo-liberal policies in tertiary education, only 29 of 66 languages offered in Australian universities 10 years ago are still taught, and seven of those remaining are only available in one university (Go8, 2007). Yet, some years ago, as part of the Monash University language policy, it was found that a sample of students whose admission scores were enhanced by their excellent results in their community language obtained equally excellent results in other languages at the university, including totally unrelated ones (Clyne *et al.*, 1995).

The Impact of Bilingualism on the Acquisition of Additional Languages

A local study of English-speaking monolinguals and bilinguals from a range of backgrounds learning Modern Greek or Spanish at secondary school showed that the bilinguals approached the study in a different way, something that they were aware of and attributed to understanding better how language worked (Clyne *et al.*, 2004). The bilinguals were constantly comparing the target language with both their home language and English and, even though they were often surmising relationships that were not correct, the comparisons were helping their acquisition of the additional language. Also, the third language had motivated a more general interest in languages and had encouraged them to acquire lexical items from and information about languages spoken by their schoolmates (this concurs with a large body of European research, including Auer & Dirim, 2003; Kotsinas, 1998; Rampton, 1995), demonstrating the acquisition by children of migrants of one another's languages in informal social contexts. The acquisition of the third language in turn promoted a greater willingness to maintain their own community language and use it outside the home.

New Perspectives

In November 2007, the Howard Liberal-National Party Government was soundly defeated. It had worked hard to remove cultural and linguistic diversity from the Australian sociopolitical agenda (Clyne, 2005; Lo Bianco & Wickert, 2001). After coming to office, the Labor Party under Kevin Rudd committed $65 million over four years for a strategy for the teaching of Asian languages in schools throughout Australia. A National Curriculum Board was set up. Initially it considered English, mathematics, science and history. Languages (together with geography) are the next key learning area for which a national curriculum is currently being developed. One issue will be to decide whether LOTEs would be compulsory subjects. When promising the 'digitalization' of every classroom in the country, the then Prime Minister (now Foreign Minister) gave 'foreign languages' as one of the learning areas that would benefit. It is well known that Rudd speaks fluent Mandarin. During the 2007 election campaign he mentioned it in an interview with a Chinese television network. He has since demonstrated several times the value of being able to negotiate internationally in Mandarin. The 'Asian languages' which are being promoted are Chinese (Mandarin), Indonesian, Japanese and possibly Korean, the languages Rudd advanced in an earlier report *Asian*

Languages and Australia's Language Future (Rudd, 1994), which led to the National Asian Languages and Studies in Schools Strategy implemented from 1994 to 2003. There is a danger that the push for certain Asian languages might damage other languages, especially European ones or even all community languages, as occurred in the 1990s. The fact that Mandarin is Australia's fastest-growing community language is rarely mentioned as an argument for learning the language. The language is being promoted in the interests of regional and international understanding. On the other hand, any departure from the parochialism of the previous government's educational agenda is a symbolic expression of a return to an Australia where multilingualism is valued. Just before the 2010 election campaign, Rudd was replaced as Labor leader and therefore Prime Minister by Julia Gillard. On forming a minority government, she completed Howard's mission by abolishing the portfolio of Multicultural Affairs, which was continued in the Rudd Government by a parliamentary secretary. It is unlikely that she will have the same commitment to languages as Rudd.

Much of Australia's language potential will remain untapped until Australia discovers the value of encouraging and enabling bilinguals to become multilingual. There has been no discussion similar to that in Europe around EuroCom, where students are learning one language as a basis for a whole family of languages (see e.g. Duke *et al.*, 2004; Hufeisen & Marx, 2007) or about learning one language (in the European case English) as a basis for multilingual education (see Kwetz, 2004; Rück, 2004), building on Eric Hawkins's notion of language apprenticeship (Hawkins, 1981).

Given the prevalence and widespread acceptance of the 'overcrowded curriculum' cliché, the cognitive benefits of multilingualism, especially for metalinguistic awareness and literacy development, need to be further researched and discussed as widely as possible. It is important for languages to be taught at the primary school in a way that will maximize benefits for literacy and metalinguistic awareness. The 'overcrowded curriculum' cliché, which was largely a specialty of English-speaking countries, has started to infect the educational debate in countries such as Germany, Norway, Sweden and Italy. This has had the effect of establishing and strengthening English as the main, first or only foreign language taught and marginalizing other languages or even removing them from the curriculum. In turn, the notion of 'one global English is enough' has strengthened the widespread belief in Australia in the ideology which will, until proven wrong, continue to limit the development of Australia's language potential.

The multilingual classroom presents opportunities and challenges which are not frequently exploited. There are many innovative teachers who due to their own experience foster an interest in languages in their students. Generally, languages are taught as if monolingualism were the norm. That is, teachers tend to overlook the fact that bilingual or multilingual learners of any target language (TL) are not the same as monolingual learners. Confronted with the daily contingencies and challenges of administration, assessment and curriculum, educators may lose sight of what Creese and Martin refer to as '... a range of complex inter-relating issues around the promotion of multilingualism in educational settings' (Creese & Martin, 2003: 161). Attitudes and policies as well as imbalance in power relations influence the undervaluing of resources in the multilingual community and classroom. The monolingual mindset wishes to protect bilingual children from more languages, assuming that this will cause a deficit in English, instead of encouraging them to develop a general interest in languages. Now that languages are valued more, the dominant (monolingual) group also wishes to ensure that they will be the beneficiaries. It is thought to be unfair that students with a symbolic relationship to the language who have taken the trouble to develop a good proficiency in it can now benefit from it. But it is not until a considerable number of multilinguals are in decision-making positions within education systems that there will be sufficient understanding to revert to developing enlightened languages-in-education and multicultural policies akin to those of the 1970s and 1980s (Clyne, 2005). Only in this way will individuals and the nation fully benefit from their multilingualism.

Note

1.   I thank Muiris Ó Laoire and Christine Hélot for helpful suggestions.

References

APPA (2007) *The Charter on Primary Schooling*. Canberra: Australian Primary Principals' Association.

Arefi, M. (1997) The relationship between first and second language writing skills for Iranian students in Sydney: An application of the interdependence hypothesis. PhD thesis, University of Western Sydney.

Auer, P. and Dirim, I. (2003) Socio-cultural orientation, urban youth styles and the spontaneous acquisition of Turkish by non-Turkish adolescents in Germany. In J. Androutsopoulos and A. Georgakopulos (eds) *Discourse Constructions of Youth Identity* (pp. 223–246). Amsterdam: John Benjamins.

Baker, C.R. (2006) Foundations *of Bilingual Education and Bilingualism*. Clevedon: Multilingual Matters.

Bialystok, E. (2001) *Bilingualism in Development: Language Literacy and Cognition*. New York: Cambridge University Press.

Burragh-Pugh, C. and Rohl, M. (2001) Learning in two languages: A bilingual program in Western Australia. *The Reading Teacher* 2001, 664–676.

Calero-Breckheimer, A. and Goetz, E.T. (1993) Reading strategies of biliterate children for English and Spanish texts. *Reading Psychology* 14, 177–204.

Clyne, M. (2005) *Australia's Language Potential*. Sydney: University of New South Wales Press.

Clyne, M., Jenkins, C., Chen, I. and Summo-O'Connell, R. (1995) *Developing Second Language from Primary School*. Canberra: National Languages and Literacy Institute of Australia.

Clyne, M., Rossi Hunt, C. and Isaakidis, T. (2004) Learning a community language as a third language. *International Journal of Multilingualism* 1, 35–52.

Clyne, M., Fernandez, S. and Grey, F. (2004) Languages spoken in the community, languages taken at school – A comparative dimension. *Australian Review of Applied Linguistics* 27, 1–17.

Creese, A. and Martin, P. (2003) Multilingual classroom ecologies: Interrelationships, interaction and ideologies. *International Journal of Bilingual, Education and Bilingualism* 6, 161–167.

Dawkins, J. (1991) *Australia's Language: The Australian Language and Literacy Policy*. Canberra: Australian Government Publishing Policy.

Duke, J., Hufeisen, B. and Lutjeharms, M. (2004) Die sieben Siebe des EuroCom für den multilingualen Einstieg in die Welt der germanischen Sprachen. In H. Klein and D. Rutke (eds) *Neuere Forschungen zur europäischen Intercomprehension* (pp. 109–134). Aachen: Shaker.

Go8 (2007) *Languages in Crisis: A Rescue Plan for Australia*. Canberra: Group of Eight Universities.

Hawkins, E. (1981) *Modern Languages in the Curriculum*. Cambridge: Cambridge University Press.

Hufeisen, B. and Marx, N. (eds) (2007) EuroComGerm – Die Sieben Siebe: Germanische Sprachen Lessen Lernen. Aachen: Shaker.

Jiminéz, R.T., Garcia, G.E. and Pearson, P.D. (1995) Three children, two languages and strategic reading. *American Educational Reading Journal* 32, 67–97.

Kotsinas, U.-B. (1998) Language contact in Rinkeby, an immigrant suburb. In J. Androutsopoulos and A. Schulz (eds) *Jugendsprache* (pp. 125–148). Frankfurt: Peter Lang.

Kwetz, J. (2004) Polyglott oder Kauderwelsch? In K. Bausch, G.G. Königs and H-J. Krumm (eds) *Mehrsprachigkeit im Focus* (pp.181–190). Tübingen: Narr.

Lo Bianco, J. (1987) *National Policy on Languages*. Canberra: Australian Government Publishing Service.

Lo Bianco, J. and Wickert, R. (eds) (2001) *Australian Policy Activism in Language and Literacy*. Melbourne: National Languages and Literacy Institute of Australia.

Rampton, B. (1995) *Crossing: Language and Ethnicity among Adolescents*. London: Longman.

Rück, H. (2004) Neugier und Sprachen wecken und zwar früh! In K. Bausch, G.G. Königs and H-J. Krumm (eds) *Mehrsprachigkeit im Focus* (pp. 206–214). Tübingen: Narr.

Rudd, K. (1994) *Asian Languages and Australia's Economic Future*. Brisbane: Queensland Government Printer.

Slaughter, Y. and Hajek, J. (2007) Community languages and LOTE provision in Victorian primary schools: Mix or match? *Australian Review of Applied Linguistics* 30 (1), 7–22.

Yelland, G.W., Pollard, J. and Mercuri, A. (1993) The metalinguistic benefits of limited contact with a second language. *Applied Psycholinguistics* 14, 423–444.

Chapter 10

Integrated Bilingual Education: Ethnographic Case Studies from the Palestinian–Jewish 'Front'

Z. BEKERMAN

Introduction

My interest in bilingual education was raised by the opportunity I had for the last decade to study an integrated bilingual Palestinian–Jewish educational initiative in Israel. Issues surrounding bilingualism have always been present in the education system (i.e. Hebrew and Arabic), as efforts continue to integrate populations with a long history of conflict. Thus, the research question emerged concerning how an educational environment so committed to bilingualism and investing great efforts in its achievement could fail for one group (Jews) while being successful for Arabs.

Initial research explored the relationship between bilingual programs and sociopolitical contexts (Bekerman, 2005) the results of which showed how the integrated bilingual schools in spite of the investment of sustained efforts continued to suffer from somewhat contradictory practices, perspectives and expectations in relation to its goals. The chapter extends this research by focusing on the potential relationship between the wider socio-political context, educational practices and their outcomes.

I will first shortly review theoretical issues related to bilingual education and in particular to research carried out on dual-language programs; then I will analyze some of the ethnographic data gathered during the study and describe the sociopolitical context of the bilingual initiative. Finally, I will try and draw conclusions regarding the potential of bilingual initiatives to overcome contextual constrains.

Bilingual Education and Contextual Limitations

For the most part dual-language programs adhere to a variety of similar criteria for their development. Dual-language programs aspire to reach high standards of academic achievement; their students are expected to reach high literacy levels in both languages (Torres-Guzmán, 2002) and they seek to promote positive cross-cultural attitudes among their participants (Lindholm-Leary, 2001). Dual-language programs also vary in terms of the percentage of L1 and L2 instruction with models ranging from a 90/10 to 50/50 rate in the instruction of both languages. They also vary on the language distribution along the curriculum (Jong, 2002). Whatever their composition, the research conducted in them has consistently shown their potential for developing high levels of academic achievement and cross cultural awareness among participants (Gomez *et al.*, 2005; Howard & Christian, 2002; Thomas & Collier, 2002).

Research in this area has also raised some critical points regarding dual-language programs. Valdés (1997) has pointed out that the success of these programs is dependent on the will of the native-language majority population and their perceptions regarding the need of their children to become bilingual in a world going global. Tosi (1999) has shown the importance played by local conditions in individual communities as factors which contribute to language maintenance and revitalization. Close observations of dual-language practice has shown that contextual conditions seem to influence the use of the minority language by both ELL and native learners (Edelsky, 1996; McCollum, 1999). External social factors have been shown to influence social informal activities in dual-language programs exposing the students' preferences to interact with children of their in-group when choosing, for example, with whom to sit, or who to invite home (Lambert & Cazabon, 1994). Other studies point to the dominance of the L1 and the native speakers in the dual-language classroom product of the dominance of L1 in the larger context (Amrein & Peña, 2000) pointing at the possibility that these programs might tend to replicate existing social and political realities outside (Amrein & Peña, 2000; Freeman, 1998; Valdés, 1998).

In bilingual programs, intergroup power relations play an important role in either reproducing or overcoming conditions that subordinate language minority students and their communities (Paulston, 1994; Ricento & Hornberger, 1996). Martin-Jones and Heller (1996) review a wide range of literature on education in multilingual settings and argue that the language practices of educational institutions are caught-up in the legitimization of power relations among ethno-linguistic groups. Recent studies conducted by Papademeter and Routoulas (2001) emphasize the ambivalence reflected in the views and opinions of minority immigrant groups toward bilingual and bicultural education. Bissoonauth and Offord (2001) suggest that the association of language with high status and prestige influences language use in multilingual societies. Obeng (2000) shows how attitudes encompassing a wide spectrum of values, beliefs and emotions concerning language influence participants' perspectives toward languages in general and toward educational bilingual initiatives in particular.

As has been shown in recent ethnographic studies, there is no doubt that political and historical contexts affect people's judgments and opinions about languages and their use (Obeng, 2000; Smith-Hefner, 1990). Yet, for the most part, studies in language attitudes have paid little attention to these (Bourhis & Sachdev, 1984; Bradac, 1990).

Ricento (2000) pointing at how language planning has shifted from its traditional focus on problem solving to an emphasis on linguistic human rights suggests that what separates previous positivistic outlooks from present postmodern interests is the latter's serious consideration of the roles of individuals and collectives in language use, attitudes and policies. He challenges researchers to integrate micro and macro levels of investigation so as to provide better explanations for language behavior than those currently available, suggesting that the ecology of language paradigm might be in need of further conceptual development in order to better serve the needs of language education planning in the future. It is toward this challenge that the following description and analysis work.

The Educational Initiative

The Israeli–Palestinian conflict can be traced to the beginning of Zionist colonization of Palestine, claimed by Jews as the land of their birthright, toward the end of the 19th century. The seemingly intractable conflict resulted out of at least two dominant ideological discourses (one Jewish, one Palestinian) on the control of the land and recognition of group sovereignty. Historically, the region was never autonomously controlled, having had a long history of colonial and imperial rule (Khalidi, 1997). The dissolution of the Ottoman Empire, which controlled Palestine for four centuries and the raise of anti-Semitism and the holocaust of World War II serve to position the conflict in its wider international context. The 1948 war, called the War of Independence by the Israelis and the *Naqbe* (the Catastrophe) by the Palestinians, was the first open military clash between the Zionist and Palestinian nationalist movements.

Palestinians in Israel (20%) are an indigenous minority, who formed the majority in Palestine (two-thirds of the population) until 1947. Since then, and with the ongoing violent Israeli occupation of the Gaza Strip since 1967 peace has not been in sight in the area. The West Bank and the *Intifada* outbreaks in 1997 and 2000 shattered the optimism for a peaceful solution that emerged after the Oslo agreements between the Israeli Government and the PLO in 1993. It remains to be seen whether the recent disengagement from the Gaza strip holds any future promises; the 2006 second Lebanese war and the recent overtake by Hammas of the Gaza area of the Palestinian Authority leave little place for optimism.

Israel, since its inception, as is clearly stated in its Declaration of Independence, has been committed to full political and social equality for all its citizens, irrespective of their religion or ethnic affiliation. Yet, even the Israeli government agrees that it has not been fully successful in implementing this ideal and has, for the most part, implemented segregationist policies toward its non-Jewish minorities; policies which only recently are starting to be challenged in the courts of justice (Gavison, 2000). In general, the Palestinian–Israeli population is geographically segregated and institutionally and legally discriminated against (Al-Haj, 1995; Kretzmer, 1992).

In spite of Israel's declared goals of offering equal opportunity to all its citizens through the educational system, the gap between the Jewish and Palestinian sectors remains. In 1991, 45.4% Palestinian and 67.3% Jewish children earned a matriculation diploma, while in 2001, the percentage increased to 59.1% and 69.7%, respectively (Central Bureau of Statistics, 2002).

Not only are the school systems segregated, but so too are the curricula. While Jewish students are called to engage in the collective Jewish national enterprise, Palestinian students (PS) are called on to accept the definition of Israel as a Jewish Democratic state (Gordon, 2005; Majid Al-Haj, 2005). All in all, the Palestinian educational system in Israel lacks the preferential support given by the government to the Jewish educational system, thus creating an enormous gap and leaving the Palestinian educational system behind.

Five integrated bilingual schools are presently functioning in Israel. The first opened its doors in 1984. In 1998, two new schools were established and the fourth school was opened in 2004. The schools are recognized as nonreligious schools supported by the Israeli Ministry of Education. They use, for the most part, the standard curriculum of the state, that is, the nonreligious school system, the main difference being that both Hebrew *and* Arabic are used as languages of instruction. The schools employ a bilingual approach, which emphasizes symmetry between both languages in all aspects of instruction (Garcia, 1997) and two 'homeroom' teachers, a Palestinian and a Jew, jointly lead all classes.

The schools have to confront what Spolsky and Shohamy (1999) have characterized as being a Type 1 monolingual society: that is, one in which a sole language (Hebrew) is recognized as being associated with the national identity while other languages (i.e. Arabic), although officially recognized as a second language for education and public use (Koplewitz, 1992; Spolsky, 1994), have been marginalized.

Context and Method

The integrated bilingual schools in this study, as others of their type in the world are characterized by their structured approach to bilingual education. They attempt at systematically integrating minority language speakers (Palestinians whose mother tongue is Arabic) with majority language speakers (Jews speaking Hebrew) while teaching both groups their own and the other groups' language. What might be considered special about these schools is that they attempt to integrate groups which suffer from what has come to be known as an intractable conflict which involves states or other actors with a long sense of historical grievance, and a strong desire to redress or avenge things (Bar-Tal, 1998). In spite of the fact that ethnographic research has been ongoing in these schools for almost a decade now, the events presented here unfolded in one of the schools which initiated its activities in 1998 with first and second grade. The school is the largest integrated school in Israel today with an enrolment of 254 children in 2004–2005 and 306 students for the 2005–2006 academic year (the years from which the data is supplied), with a total of 10 and 12 classrooms, respectively. The classrooms ranged from kindergarten to sixth grade during the first year of our research and added the seventh grade (middle school) in the second year.

The following diagram (Figure 10.1) offers a representation of the ethnic/national composition of the totality of the school population for the year 2004–2005. For the first year our research focused on the first and third grades and continued into the second and fourth grades during the second year. The first-grade class had 32 children (15 Palestinians and 17 Jews) and the third grade had 29 children (13 Palestinians and 16 Jews). In all, 85% of the parents of the Jewish children hold academic degrees as well as 55% of Palestinian parents; others hold independent professions and only two parents report as being blue-collar workers.

All six homeroom teachers whom we observed hold degrees in education, three of them in special education. Three hold an MA degree and one was working toward it. Two of the Jewish teachers had an intermediate and high command of the Arabic language, which allowed them to feel rather at ease in the bilingual environment. Two had no command of the

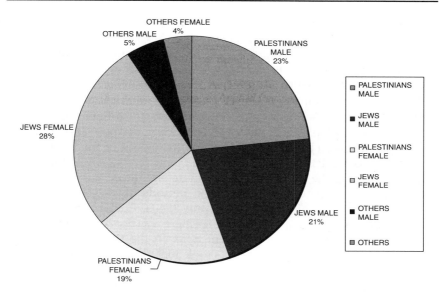

OTHERS FEMALE
4%
OTHERS MALE
5%
PALESTINIANS
MALE
23%
JEWS FEMALE
28%
JEWS MALE
21%
PALESTINIANS
FEMALE
19%

PALESTINIANS
MALE

JEWS
MALE

PALESTINIANS
FEMALE

JEWS
FEMALE

OTHERS
MALE

OTHERS

Figure 10.1 Ethnic/national composition of the school population for the year 2004–2005

Arabic language, in this sense being more representative of the school's Jewish body of teachers.

Findings

Language use

When discussing the field notes and our observations, we raised questions regarding the amount of talk done by the teachers and the students. We discussed our belief that the Jewish group seemed to dominate conversations particularly among the students, but also among the teachers. In our field notes, we used focused and detailed descriptions to substantiate these statements. Nevertheless, we wanted to go into more detail, hoping to understand better what was going on. We report here on the first results from our first detailed analysis. We found it useful to use certain quantitative measures as outlined below.

The transcripts we counted included six hours of classroom activity in the first grade and a similar amount in the third grade. These hours include both the Palestinian and Jewish teachers. In the second and the fourth grades we counted two hours of Palestinian–Jewish co-teaching. We also recorded the Palestinian and Jewish teachers working individually (alone) in class. In each case we counted three hours of activity. The recordings include a variety of subjects such as language, maths and memorial days (Rabin, Holocaust).

If we ask who dominates in terms of turns, the findings show the Jewish group as the one ahead. In the case of the teachers, the differences were not significant; when looking at the totals (including teachers and students) the Jewish Teacher (JT) took 2511 (28.25%) turns out of the 8889 (100%) counted while the Palestinian teacher (PT) took 2230 (25.09%) turns. The difference among the students is much more significant and justifies our impressions throughout the observation periods. Jewish students took 2608 (29.34%) turns while the PSs took only 1540 (17.32%) turns.

As we expected, the gap among the teachers was not consistent. Factors other than ethnicity might be present here. In the first and the fourth grades, the gap was inverted. The PTs took 30.90% and 39.95% turns talking while the Jewish teachers took only 28.33% and 13.67% of the turns talking. When considering that in first and the fourth grades, the PTs are experienced, have strong personalities, are much appreciated and are long-time participants in the system, personality and seniority seem to be more plausible explanations than ethnicity.

The gap among the students fluctuates very little and is never reversed. In the second grade, the smallest gap appeared where Jewish students only took 1.50% more turns than their Palestinian peers. The greatest gap was seen in the third grade where Jews took almost 20% more turns than the PSs. The differences reflect very well what Palestinian parents mentioned regularly in their interviews regarding their expectations that the bilingual school will encourage their children to be more open and participatory during social interactions (formal and informal). The Palestinian parents believe their children develop in environments that do not encourage open expression. Later, when we present findings regarding the classroom language of choice for communication, we will consider whether language choice (in this case, the preference for Hebrew) can also account for these discrepancies.

The gaps in turn taking seemed to be reduced when the PT taught alone in class. Our analysis shows that when the PT taught alone, PSs took 21.93% (out of total = 1327) of the turns; while when the Jewish teacher taught alone, they took 16.39% (out of total = 2050) of the turns. Since we are lacking analysis of more particular situations related to the presence of teachers teaching content subjects, it is difficult to draw valid conclusions. However, we can say that it seems that the presence of a teacher of similar background helped the PS to feel more comfortable participating. Deciding if this heightened a sense of comfort as the result of the language being used or the personality of the teacher needs further research.

Regarding the language of choice of the participating teachers and students (Hebrew or Arabic) our findings show that the balance expected to be achieved between the languages is not attained. Out of the 2511 utterances counted in the transcripts under analysis, Jewish teachers (JT) expressed themselves in Hebrew 2456 (97.81%) times, in Arabic 26 (1.04%) times and 29 (1.15%) times we counted events of code-switching or code-integration. In contrast, PTs used Arabic in 1563 (70.09%) out of 2230 utterances, Hebrew in 221 (9.91%) utterances and code integration or switching on 446 (20.0%) occasions.

The children's linguistic behavior mirrored the teachers' and accentuated it. Out of a total of 2608 utterances made by Jewish students, 2490 (95.48%) were made in Hebrew, 84 (3.22%) in Arabic and 34 (1.30%) using code-switching or code-integration. Out of the 1540 utterances made by PSs, 850 (55.19%) were made in Arabic, 672 (43.64%) were made in Hebrew and 18 (1.17%) involved code-switching or code-integration.

When we look further into different segments of the transcripts, we realize that the averages in language choice for the PTs changed throughout the years. For the PTs, the choice to speak in Arabic grew from first grade (55%) to the second grade (80%), stayed steady during third grade, but reduced to 60% in the fourth grade. When the PT taught alone, the average use of Arabic did not rise. Throughout, the Jewish teachers maintained their 95%+ use of Hebrew. Again, it is difficult to explain these findings and it would be irresponsible to posit any final conclusions. Although helpful, the analysis adopted is in need of more in-depth analysis, which we hope to conduct in future studies. Still, it could be assumed that the increased rate of Arabic use from the first to the third grade is a result of the fact that the Jewish children are starting to recognize the language which allows the PTs to use it more in their daily conversation. The decrease in the use of Arabic in fourth grade could be connected to a sense of despair by the PT and an acceptance that the Jewish children, given present circumstances, might not go much further in their language acquisition. The presence of the Palestinian cohort throughout does not change the situation because their goals (as described by their parents) do not support a bilingual endeavor for their Jewish peers, while their bilingualism is secured in any event through the classroom practices.

The fact that when the PT teaches alone and that the use of Arabic is not higher might be connected to the fact that (as on any other occasions) the use of Arabic by a PT is not dependant on her individual decision, but is strongly related to the social context in which the language evolves. In our specific case, it is worth considering that although she is alone, and does not have to attune herself to her monolingual Jewish co-teacher, all other elements have remained the same. Both the Palestinian and the Jewish children have not changed and stick to their language behavior and expectations.

Children's language choices remained rather stable. Palestinian children chose Arabic 55% of the time and Jewish children chose Hebrew 95% of the time. Palestinians decreased their choice for Arabic use as they grew older. In the first grade we recorded 70% Arabic use, in the second grade, 56% Arabic use and in the third grade, 63% Arabic use. There was one topic in which Arabic was used more frequently and this was mathematics. In the first grade, we recorded 80% use and in the third grade 68% use (we have similar findings for the teachers). One of the reasons for this difference might be related to the language skills needed for this class which use, in a sense, a much more restricted vocabulary that is repetitive and relatively easy to retrieve. Finally, when a PT was alone in class, the Palestinian children averaged 66% turns in Arabic and the Jewish children recorded a lower average use of Hebrew (87%). Possibly a good step toward increasing Jewish bilingualism would be longer periods where the PTs direct the class alone.

Language practice

In this section, we offer examples of events related to language use and how interactions/discourse were organized in order for Hebrew to be more prominent than Arabic. The excerpts are rendered in the original languages used in class (i.e. Arabic and Hebrew) followed by an English translation.

The first scene is presented to give a sense of a very basic classroom exchange when only one teacher, in this case the PT, is present. The scene takes place in the first-grade class almost two months into the school year. Nun, the PT, has been dealing with some administrative issues and has now informed the class that Yod, the Jewish co-teacher, will not be coming in to school today. In lines 3 and 6, Nun speaks in Arabic. The loud intervention of a Jewish student indicating she does not understand (line 6) as well as the Arabic being spoken requires attention by the teacher. She can respond in one of two ways. Either she will translate some of the words used in the last sentence into Hebrew or; because a PS has already hinted in Hebrew at the content of the conversation (see line 12) she will continue in Arabic. The preferred option will be difficult to predict but when dealing with what might be understood as not such important issues, the second option will be preferred (as in the case below). What usually will not happen is that the call by a Jewish student will be left unattended. It is also important to remember that though we have records of Palestinian children not understanding Hebrew, we do not have records of loud intervention by Palestinian children demanding a translation.

DVD No. 9–28/10/04-PT teaches alone 1st grade: Transcript lines 97–103

TP (Teacher Palestinian):   OK י ' مريضة اليوم مش هوم راح تيجي انا راح نكون معاكو
حالي

TP: ok Yod is sick today she will not come I will be with you alone

CLASS: יאי:: אל:: ((דלים מביעים קולות של שמש וא בצע))

TP: بليز، دير اورو الكافو علي ساعدوني ساعدوني عنجد اوكي،

TP: please ((in English)) pay attention to me, help me seriously ok?

SJG?:   אני לא מבינה, אני אל מבינה

SJG (Student Jewish Girl):   I DO NOT UNDERSTAND I DO NOT
                            UNDERSTAND

TP: افاي شي قريت مريضة , مع حام

TP: Y is sick, with fever

SPB: שי הל שארב חום

SPB (Student Palestinian Boy):   Does she have fever in her head

SJB: וירוס

SJB (Student Jewish Boy):   Virus

SJG: המ, עכשיו לכ התיכה הלוח?

SJG: What, every body is sick in class now!
              ((שער בכתה))
              ((noise in class))

TP: OK, لك واحد ( ) مين بالطاولة تبعتو الو الاد مش موجودين؟

TP: ok, each one ( ) who has in his table children who are not here?
              ((עמשנ שער))

Jewish students claim their language with ease.

In this next section, we see Nun initiating a turn in Hebrew (line 3), a Palestinian child taking a turn in Hebrew (line 5) and Nun changing back into Arabic, but integrating Hebrew into her utterances (underlined in English text) words (lines 8–9). The use of Hebrew by the PT seems to be preferred since otherwise, a somewhat important message regarding the need to contact absent students will not be understood by the Jewish children. Still, in line 17 the Jewish child complains about not understanding. This statement brings Nun to integrate more Hebrew into her next turn (lines 19–20).

DVD No. 9–28/10/04-PT teaches alone 1st grade: Transcript lines 166–182

TP: ((סנכנ 'ח ,תבשייתמ)) ( ) אל תשקבמ ינא ,בשא ינא

TP: I will sit, I ask not ( ) ((teacher sits H'comes in))

SPB (Student Palestinian Boy): דלי דוע .אב דלי דוע ((קחוצ)) ((

SPB: ((laughing)) one more child came in. one more child.

TP: دلو لك مويلا نم الحلصمة لأ .ةرداق شم انأو ةلمج يكحا يدب ونأ نيهبتنم وتنأ
بغي لك دلي انعدر مبتيח הספר ,ابدنا نيدلو انولصتي

Nadia: you can see that I want to say a sentence and I can't. I can't say the sentence. From today each child that is missing, every child who is missing from school, we want two children to call

SPB: [انا]

SPB: [me]

SPB: دحاو دلو مش نيدلو [شيل]

SPB: [why] two children and not one child
يسن دحاو اذا ناشع ,شيل فراع نيدلو انبد :ةيدان

TP: we want two children do you know why, so if one forgets

SJG?: הניבמ אל ינא

SJG: I DO NOT UNDERSTAND

TP: شاج ام شيل اولأساي اولصتي סידלי ינש ةرم لك انم הספר תיבל אב אל דלי םא
علي المدرسة المل אل אב. OK

TP: If a child does not come to school each time, from us, two children, will call ask why he didn't come to school why he did not come ok.

The next episode exemplifies how Arabic is managed when the two teachers are present in class. When together, the teachers complement each other. The PT still integrates a few Hebrew words but much less (line 5). The Jewish teacher does not necessarily translate her but, as in this case, adds by conceptualizing the activity as an argument among types of groceries (line 8).

DVD No. 5–21/10/04 Palestinian and Jewish teachers teach together 1st grade: Transcript lines 32–44

PT: ش شش, مث (علط) بيلحلا نم علط قيربالا ,ىلا بيلحلا نم قيربالا ىلا :لاقو
انا طعام الميفد, ومني العظم ينم مظعلا :يزيدو. תומצע הז מظعلا .تومצע هز مظعلا يزيدو: ومني يينم
اصدقاء, تكبرو وتصبحوا اوقياء.

PT: shsh, then the milk came out from the pitcher to the- the milk came out of the pitcher, and said: I am the helpful food, the bones grow from me, bones the bones. And he added: drink me friends, you will grow and become strong.

JT: שממ [מחלוקת ביו] לך ה[מאכלים]

JT (Teacher Jewish):   a true argument among all the foods

PT: [לאינד], [החילס].   לאינד.

PT: [Daniel ... sorry] Daniel

JT: בושה יכה אוהש בשוח דהא לכ.

JT: every one thinks it is the most important

PT: ( ) קطعة الجبن, من مع جبنة؟ من مع جبنة؟

PT: ( ) a piece of cheese, who has cheese with him? Who has cheese with him? ((מירמומ סידלי מימירמ סייי אומרדרים)): انا.

((children raise their hands)) me

كل منتوجات الالبان. ( ), عفرا بس. عفرا. وقالت: اذا ارادتم صحة   דינה: عفرا

من الاجبان, بيضاء كانت, ما صفراء. قفزت البيضة ((שוע תעונת גלימ)), من الاجبان

שפו ותفشاه البيضة؟ ( ), ((דייים))

PT: raise, only raise ((only raise your hands)). And said: (I am of the health). Eat cheese products. ((demonstrated with her hands)) of the cheeses, either white of yellow. The egg jumped ((waves her hands to demonstrate)), (   ) did you see this egg.

Our last example relating to language use shows conversational give and take among four children in the third grade. Three Palestinians (two girls and one boy) and a Jewish boy are working together on an assignment where they were asked to relate to some experiences from the vacation that they had gone to. The example clearly shows the pattern of language use that regularly developed among mixed groups. Even in this specific case, where three out of the four participants were Palestinian, the *lingua franca* used by the group is Hebrew. The Palestinians are the ones who sustain the floor (almost 85% of the turns of talk) and for the most part lead the conversation and activity. The two Palestinian girls lead the activity. Both are good students, one of them among the best in class and known for her strong political awareness. The Palestinian and the Jewish boys are average students, but the Jewish boy is outstanding in that he frequently declares his willingness to learn Arabic and has, on multiple occasions, expressed his interest in Palestinian culture.

National pride and commitment to recognizing otherness are much of what could be needed to secure Arabic use. But even under these extremely favorable circumstances, the Arabic language is displaced and the Palestinian children speak more Hebrew (their second language) than Arabic (their first) while the Jewish student speaks only in Hebrew. The Palestinian boy speaks the most Arabic (21 out of his 48 turns in the conversation). The Palestinian girls use Arabic less than a quarter of their turns (26 out of 100 and nine out of 104).

From our first analysis of this scene, we tried to identify the conditions under which Arabic might make its appearance. The following points became apparent:

(1) Arabic seems to be used when one of the Palestinians involved in the interaction does not understand the activity which has been assigned. Most of the strings of conversation in the segment are started by one of the Palestinian girls explaining to the Palestinian boy what needs to be done.
(2) When such a situation occurs and another PS joins the conversation, there is a good chance that he will join in speaking Arabic.
(3) When the Jewish child is involved in the conversation, all three Palestinians speak Hebrew.

These rules are not fixed. However, they represent fairly well many of the events we recorded during formal activities in class (for informal activities, i.e. breaks we have less information although when playing in mixed groups, Hebrew seems to dominate).

What children teachers and parents say

We report here on the interviews briefly, going into detail only when particular answers to particular questions offer insights we believe to be noteworthy. Jewish children in the first grade seemed to have a fairly realistic assessment of their knowledge of Arabic. Only two students said they knew the language and the rest stated their difficulties and limitations, always adding that Arabic is not an easy language to learn. These difficulties did not seem to interfere with their sense that learning Arabic is important. With the exception of two students, all others, for different reasons ('because there are Arabs around', 'because it is important to learn languages'), found learning Arabic important. Questions about Arabic at school allowed for some fascinating dialogues with the children. These dialogues revealed their deep understanding of the connection between politics and the school's curriculum ('it aims at allowing for co-existence and peace') and the connection between Arabic/Hebrew literacy and wider contexts ('Andi knows more Hebrew than I know Arabic because here in Jerusalem the majority speaks Hebrew').

Palestinian children in the same grade when asked about their perception of the Hebrew language were generally very positive about it. Some mentioned that Hebrew is a rather easy language to write ('the letters need not be connected'). Others mentioned the importance of knowing foreign languages or mentioned that Hebrew was helpful in order to get along with 'security people' and one, rather surprisingly, said, 'because if I learn a lot I will feel like a Jew later'. This appreciation for Hebrew did not stand in the way of their understanding that learning Arabic was also very important to them because 'it is our language'. The one student who was not so convinced that learning Arabic was important stated 'because I'm Arab and I need to know Hebrew'.

Jewish children in the third grade testified as to having *some* knowledge of Arabic. Only one student said she knew Arabic well and one other student said that he did not know it at all. From the students who stated that they knew some Arabic, some mentioned that they liked it but immediately added that it was difficult; while other students were even less enthusiastic. Still, they all believed it was important to learn Arabic. Their responses were more articulated and complex than the ones in first grade in that they emphasized the possibilities knowing Arabic afforded them in terms of communicating with Arab populations. Ein offered an answer that touched on problems of social justice and the need to offer recognition to the Palestinian minority. Dalet mentioned she 'loves the Arabic language she just does not like learning it'.

Palestinian children in the third grade agreed that the main characteristic that set the school apart was its bilingual and bi-national character. Learning Hebrew was important for them so that they could speak to Jews, have Jewish friends, understand the news, and because 'I have too, I'm Arab and I need to know Hebrew'. Learning Arabic was important for more sentimental reasons, 'it is our language'. Others seemingly voicing their parents emphasized the importance knowing Hebrew had for their future education when reaching the university and even further when joining the work force.

Teachers in both groups expressed strong beliefs in the bilingual agenda adopted by the school. Jewish teachers seemed to be much more ready to accept the reality which was known to them all, that Jewish students were lacking the expected competencies in Arabic. They sounded saddened by this fact but explained it as a natural outcome of a nonsupportive context. They also rested on the success they perceived the school was achieving in terms of guiding Jewish children in the path of recognition of Palestinian culture. PTs strongly agreed, but expressed great dissatisfaction with the achievements of the Jewish cohort in Arabic. From their perspective, being competent in Arabic for the Jewish children was the most important entry point to the creation of a true dialogue among the children of both groups. They also emphasized that there cannot be true cultural understanding if the language of the culture in case was not available to those interested in understanding it.

Jewish parents support bilingualism as long as it did not harm educational excellence. They seemed satisfied with an educational initiative that allows them to substantiate their liberal positions and to offer their children cultural understanding and sensitivity toward the 'other' 'We did want our children to learn Arabic, but given the context it is difficult and it will be enough [for them and us] to get to know Arabic culture and tradition'. If these goals were achieved, the lack of success in bilingual achievements could be forgiven.

Palestinian parents sending their children to the school were after the best education they could find for their children in the present Israeli sociopolitical context. Israel's present sociopolitical conditions made it almost impossible for parents to dream about a soon-to-arrive top-down multicultural multilingual policy. It is also not totally clear whether the parents would adopt such a policy if it were imposed. As members of the upper-middle socio-economic sector of society, they perceived education as a means to mobility in an increasingly global world. Thus, they preferred an English *lingua franca* and high Hebrew literacy in order to achieve the dreams for their children's future.

Discussion

All teachers and students seem to be doing their jobs. Jewish teachers do their job when using only Hebrew in an educational context where two teachers serve as homeroom teachers. Each is responsible for teaching her language according to the dictates of the existing models of bilingual education which stipulate that teachers should teach exclusively in one language. By speaking Hebrew, the Jewish teachers do their job for the Jewish students and ensure that these students maintain a high level of Hebrew, their first language. These teachers also do their job for the PSs, ensuring that they achieve a high level of Hebrew proficiency their second language, one of their main reasons (as expressed by their parents and themselves) for attending school.

The PTs might not be doing their job in terms of the declared bilingual goals of the school nor from a perspective of the acknowledged models of bilingualism; but do they have any other options? Or we should also ask; are they not indeed doing their job? Sticking solely to Arabic would put them in the difficult situation of being antagonistic to the Jewish children, who already complain loudly (at times) that they 'do not understand'. It would also make them antagonistic to the Jewish parents for similar reasons for the parents do not necessarily see the Arabic competency of their children as a must but easily see their ideological needs fulfilled by having their children gain some multicultural sensitivity. By not only speaking

Arabic the PTs might somewhat hurt the Arabic competency of the Palestinian children, however, this is not much of a concern in a context where Palestinians live mostly in segregated areas where their language is rather safe. Moreover, we need to remember that the main reason for the Palestinian cohort participation in the bilingual school rests with the parents' desire to secure a high level of Hebrew literacy and the PTs' use of Hebrew, in some ways, supports this need.

Last but not least, using only Arabic would make it almost impossible for the PTs to present to the Jewish cohort the national, religious and cultural topics perceived by the teachers as essential in their struggle for recognition and equality. We should also remember that for Jewish parents these educational 'multicultural' aspects would be considered enough of an achievement and their lack (and not the lack of Arabic competency) would be considered a failure.

The children are also doing their job. Jews participate patiently in a context which offers recognition to the Arabic language without ever needing to learn it as a functional tongue and Palestinians learn Hebrew, the key to their future mobility. Moreover they can easily feel supported by their parents' perspectives when adopting their positions.

As is the case in many bilingual programs, the bilingual school studied suffers from somewhat contradictory practices, perspectives and expectations in relation to its goals. The current Israeli socio-political context seems to discourage the teaching and learning of Arabic as L2. Even when the monetary resources are available to create a nearly perfect bilingual environment with declared, across the board, ideological support, bilingualism seems not able to take root.

The ethnographic data exposed multiple practices which could be judged as contradictory of bilingual principles but also as being well attuned to the macro contextual levels within which bilingual education is embedded. We could easily find fault with the teachers and parents involved in our program. We could blame them for consciously or unconsciously conveying negative messages about the minority language in spite of their overt efforts to create a school environment and a curriculum that represents a balanced bilingual effort. But this would be clutching at straws. If placed anywhere, the 'blame' should more accurately be placed on an adaptive, wider, sociopolitical system in which Arabic carries little symbolic power. In Bourdieu's (1991) terms, it can be said in general that in Israel, speakers of Hebrew have more cultural capital in the linguistic market place than those who speak Arabic.

It is not clear that the parents participating in the initiative are interested in changing the existing power relations in Israel (Bekerman & Tatar, 2009). The Jewish parents, as the majority hopeful in creating more humane and respectful environments for the Palestinian–Israeli minority, do not necessarily see the need for radical change. The Palestinian parents, who belong to an aspiring middle class, understand the advantages of linguistically empowering their children's entrance into the reigning bureaucracy and the need to adapt to the rules of the game, specifically in a school context which, at least declaratively, stands behind an emancipating option.

We cannot assume that solutions to parents' perspectives, which seemingly work against bilingual achievements, can be found in the narrow limits of the school and their surrounding communities. It could even be considered immoral to complain about Palestinian parents who seem to disregard the importance of their own language at the school level; no one has the right to accuse minority parents of searching for a way to better their children's lot. What undoubtedly needs to be addressed are the deeply entrenched paradigmatic perspectives which support the nation state ideology and its traditional monoculturalism and monolingualism. The nation state's monologic stance is the product of an epistemology which posits the individual as imprisoned in reified understandings of identity and culture (Bauman, 1999; Billig, 1995; Gellner, 1983) much embedded in language perspectives and policies. If a dialogue about the epistemological bases which substantiate this attitude is not initiated, I doubt whether bilingual educational initiatives, even the best intentioned of them, will achieve the dream of an equality that allows for and acknowledges socio-cultural differences as affirmed in multicultural, bilingual discourse. But even if this dialogue does take place, we should be careful not to be blinded by our own theoretical/ideological constructs. Language is not necessarily the only way through which we organize the world, or the only path to a socially just and multicultural society. Moreover, educational institutions need not be the first (nor the only as they usually are) places in which to achieve linguistic rights and even when chosen for that purpose, they should be viewed in the wider national/political and communal/cultural contexts in which they come to function, paying special attention not to fall back into the reification of unitary groups (ethnic/national/religious or other).

All in all, we should remember that the poststructuralist/postmodern revolution benefited research by calling upon us all to overcome 'universals' and sweeping generalizations. Working in this direction might help pave the way to new, more generous imaginings in sociopolitical organization. More importantly in our case, working in this direction, might free the imagination for more productive multicultural, multilingual, educational work. Dealing in the particular may be complex but seems to be the only, albeit difficult, way to consider bilingual policy. Paying careful attention to a variety of particular settings and populations, we will be encouraged to develop flexible categories, policies and strategies.

Acknowledgments

This study is part of a longstanding research project, supported by the Bernard Van Leer Foundation. I want to thank Julia Schlam for her critical insights and assistance when editing the manuscript.

References

Al-Haj, M. (1995) *Education, Empowerment, and Control: The Case of the Arabs in Israel.* Albany, NY: SUNY Press.

Al-Haj, M. (2005) National ethos, multicultural education, and the new history textbooks in Israel. *Curriculum Inquiry* 35, 48–71.

Amrein, A. and Peña, R. (2000) Asymmetry in dual language practice: Assessing imbalance in a program promoting equity [Electronic Version]. *Education Policy Analysis Archives* 8 (8). http://epaa.asu.edu/epaa/v8n8.html. Accessed 11.11.08.

Bar-Tal, D. (1998) Societal beliefs in times of intractable conflict: The Israeli case. *International Journal of Conflict Management* 9, 22–50.

Bauman, Z. (1999) *Culture as Praxis.* London: Sage.

Bekerman, Z. (2005) Complex contexts and ideologies: Bilingual education in conflict-ridden areas. *Journal of Language Identity and Education* 4, 1–20.

Bekerman, Z. and Tatar, M. (2009) Parents' perceptions of multiculturalism, bilingualism, and peace education: The case of the Israeli Palestinian–Jewish bilingual primary schools. *European Early Childhood Education Research Journal* 17 (2), 171–185.

Billig, M. (1995) *Banal Nationalism.* London: Sage.

Bissoonauth, A. and Offord, M. (2001) Language use in Mauritian adolescents. *Journal of Multilingual and Multicultural Development* 25, 381–400.

Bourdieu, P. (1991) *Language and Symbolic Power.* Cambridge: Harvard University Press.

Bourhis, R.Y. and Sachdev, I. (1984) Vitality perception and language attitudes. *Journal of Language and Social Psychology* 3, 97–126.

Bradac, J. (1990) Language attitude and impression formation. In H. Giles and W.P. Robinson (eds) *Handbook of Language and Social Psychology* (pp. 387–412). New York: Wiley.

Central Bureau of Statistics (2002) *Statistical Abstract of Israel.* Jerusalem: Central Bureau of Statistics. http://www.cbs.gov.il/engindex.html. Accessed 11.11.08.

Edelsky, C. (1996) *With Literacy and Justice for All: Rethinking the Social in Language and Education.* London: Taylor & Francis.

Freeman, R.D. (1998) *Bilingual Education and Social Change.* Clevedon: Multilingual Matters.

García, O. (1997) Bilingual education. In F. Coulmas (ed.) *The Handbook of Sociolinguistics* (pp. 405–420). Oxford: Blackwell.

Gavison, R. (2000) Does equality require integration. *Democratic Culture* 3, 37–87.

Gellner, E. (1983) *Nations and Nationality*. Oxford: Basic Blackwell.

Gomez, L., Freeman, D. and Freeman, Y. (2005) Dual language education: A promising 50–50 model. *Bilingual Research Journal* 29, 145–164.

Gordon, D. (2005) History textbooks, narratives, and democracy: A response to Majid Al-Haj. *Curriculum Inquiry* 35, 367–376.

Howard, E.R. and Christian, D. (2002) *Two-way Immersion 101: Designing and Implementing a Two-way Immersion Education Program at the Elementary Level*. Santa Cruz, CA: Santa Cruz: Center for Research on Education, Diversity and Excellence, University of California.

Jong, E.J.D. (2002) Effective bilingual education: From theory to academic achievement in a two-way bilingual program. *Bilingual Research Journal* 26, 65–86.

Khalidi, R. (1997) *Palestinian Identity: The Construction of Modern National Consciousness*. New York: Columbia University Press.

Koplewitz, I. (1992) Arabic in Israel: The sociolinguistic situation of Israel's linguistic minority. *International Journal of the Sociology of Language* 98, 29–66.

Kretzmer, D. (1992) The new basic laws on human rights: A mini-revolution in Israeli constitutional law? *Israel Law Review* 26, 238–249.

Lambert, W.E. and Cazabon, M.T. (1994) *Students' Views of the Amigos Program* (Research Report No. 11). Santa Cruz, CA and Washington, DC: National Center for Research on Cultural Diversity and Second Language Learning.

Lindholm-Leary, K. (2001) *Dual Language Education*. Clevedon: Multilingual Matters.

Martin-Jones, M. and Heller, M. (1996) Introduction to the special issues on education in multilingual settings. *Linguistics and Education* 8, 3–16.

McCollum, P. (1999) Learning to value English: Cultural capital is a two-way bilingual program. *Bilingual Research Journal* 23, 113–134.

Obeng, S.G. (2000) Speaking the unspeakable: Discursive strategies to express language attitudes in Legon (Ghana) Graffiti. *Research on Language and Social Interaction* 33, 291–319.

Papademeter, L. and Routoulas, S. (2001) Social, political, educational, linguistic and cultural (dis-)incentives for languages education in Australia. *Journal of Multilingual and Multicultural Development* 22, 134–151.

Paulston, C. (1994) *Linguistic Minorities in Multilingual Settings*. Amsterdam: John Benjamins.

Ricento, T. (2000) Historical and theoretical perspectives in language policy and planning. *Journal of Sociolinguistics* 4, 196–213.

Ricento, T. and Hornberger, N. (1996) Unpeeling the onion: Language planning and policy and the ELT professional. *TESOL Quarterly* 30, 401–428.

Smith-Hefner, N.J. (1990) Language and identity in the education of Boston-area Khmer. *Anthropology and Education Quarterly* 21, 250–268.

Spolsky, B. (1994) The situation of Arabic in Israel. In Y. Suleiman (ed.) *Arabic Sociolinguistics: Issues and Perspectives* (pp. 227–236). Richmond: Curzon Press.

Spolsky, B. and Shohamy, E. (1999) Language in Israel society and education. *International Journal of the Sociology of Language* 137, 93–114.

Thomas, W.P. and Collier, V.P. (2002) A national study of school effectiveness for language minority students' long-term academic achievement. http://crede.berkeley.edu/research/crede/pdf/rb10.pdf. Accessed 11.11.08.

Torres-Guzmán, M.E. (2002) *Dual Language Programs*. Washington, DC: National Clearinghouse for Bilingual Education (NCBE).

Tosi, A. (1999) The notion of 'community' in language maintenance. In G. Extra and L. Verhoeven (eds) *Bilingualism and Migration* (pp. 325–343). Berlin: Mouton de Gruyter.

Valdés, G. (1997) Dual-language immersion programs: A cautionary note concerning the education of language minority students. *Harvard Educational Review* 67, 391–429.

Valdés, G. (1998) The world outside and inside schools: Language and immigrant children. *Education Researcher* 27, 4–18.

Index